Endurance and Competitive Trail Riding

Endurance and Competitive Trail Riding

By Wentworth Tellington
and Linda Tellington-Jones

Foreword by Alexander Mackay-Smith

DOUBLEDAY & COMPANY, INC.
GARDEN CITY, NEW YORK
1979

Library of Congress Cataloging in Publication Data

Tellington, Wentworth Jordan.
Endurance and competitive trail riding.

Includes index.
1. Endurance riding (Horsemanship) 2. Trail
riding—Competitions. I. Tellington-Jones, Linda.
II. Title.
SF296.E5T44   798'.23

ISBN: 0-385-14277-3
Library of Congress Catalog Card Number 78-18568

We wish to dedicate this effort to the person we regard as the "dean of the endurance riders," the one person to whom we all owe a debt of gratitude for organizing and defending the idea of this sport and encouraging the use of technical data collected by professional enquirers from universities and other testing agencies to the everlasting benefit of horses whether they are representing us in the Olympic Games or carrying a child across a soft green meadow in Vermont . . .

to

WENDELL T. ROBIE

1.

Contents

Illustrations

Foreword

During the past 25 years there has been an enormous increase in the number of horses and riders participating in competitive long-distance trail rides. There are two types. The first, known as the Competitive Ride, was pioneered in the 1930s by the Green Mountain Horse Association of South Woodstock, Vermont. The 100-mile Competitive Ride takes place over a period of 3 days—40 miles per day on the first 2 days, 20 miles on the third. Competitors are required to ride at the same speed. They may not lead their horses but may advance only when mounted. No assistance is allowed, either on the trail or at any other time. Awards are based on the judges' opinion as to condition, soundness, manners, way of going, and horsemanship, which includes the care of horse and equipment both under saddle and at all other times.

The second type, the Endurance Ride, dates from the institution, by Wendell Robie in 1955, of the Western States 100 Miles in 24 hours Ride, from Lake Tahoe to Auburn, California. This is a race for the Tevis Cup with an additional award, the Haggin Cup, for the horse in the best condition among the first 10 finishers. Riders may lead their horses and accept the assistance of grooms, etc. Only speed is considered, the one qualification being that the horse stay sound throughout the ride and the morning after. This ride and others similar, through the dedicated work of officiating veterinarians using pulse, respiration, and temperature tests, have developed important and accurate data on the testing of horses for stress and for recovery, data that are equally applicable to other strenuous horse sports as well.

Wentworth and Linda Tellington were among the early participants in the Western States Ride, as well as in other Distance and Competitive Rides. In four issues of the weekly *The Chronicle of the Horse* (Middleburg, Virginia, February 8 to March 1, 1963), they published "Conditioning the Endurance Horse." The following summer they organized a National Symposium on Trail Riding at their Pacific Coast Equestrian Research Farm. In 1967 they brought out the first major book on the subject, the *Endurance and Competitive Trail Riding Manual,* which contained over 200 pages. It was largely a collection of previously published magazine articles. It sold out in six weeks and has become a much-sought-after collector's item. Their inscription on a treasured copy presented to this writer reads in part: "We can already see material for an additional 50 pages!"

In the eleven years that have since transpired, the Tellingtons have seen material for many more additional pages. In this book they set forth in depth the various types of Rides; measuring stress and recovery; selecting a horse; feet and shoes; training and conditioning; physical therapy; back problems; equipment; feeding; and riding the contest. A final chapter deals with certain leading Rides. This book maintains the authoritative status of the earlier manual to which it adds the scientific developments of the past decade and experiences gathered from many leading competitors and organizers.

ALEXANDER MACKAY-SMITH

Preface

The first version of this book appeared in the spring of 1967 in a heavy paperback form with post binders, mimeographed pages, and some photocopies. It looked more or less like a giant notebook, and there was a misspelling on the title page. What an embarrassment! Still, the composite of the best information we could gather was between those covers, and many friends seemed to appreciate the effort. It was sold out in six weeks.

When, in recent years, copies began to command as much as $25 in dog-eared condition, it seemed time to do it over again. Hence this book, which we present for your approval. The original manual was much more informal. Instead of a Preface we simply included a letter to the reader. Nostalgia compels us to repeat this letter here because the essence of what we said then appears to stand the test of time.

Dear Reader:

Whether you are an old acquaintance (which is most likely) or a new member of this strange fraternity of nuts, who like to ride long distances on horseback—rain or shine—may we say it's fun to be together, even indirectly through the pages of this book.

In some ways, it has been very hard work to assemble the material in this book, but you may be sure it has been much fun. Many, many times we have had to stop and laugh or fall into long-winded reminiscences when old arguments were rekindled. Then there are pages made indelible in our minds for the depth of experience which they reflect—when some good friend was lost on the trail for 15 hours, or another won the "dirty-shirt award." The trail grows a bit longer every year, and with the inevitable dimming of memory comes the inevitable embellishment of the truth!

There is one truth, however, which cannot be embellished. It is truly fun to ride. It is fun to get out in the wide-open spaces. It is fun to get together with people who like to do these things. And so, as our friend Wendell Robie says, "Let's ride—really ride."

Although you will find that the manual has been completely reorganized and expanded in this volume, we have been careful to retain every bit of the original information as long as it still applies. Furthermore, we have added much that was not in the first manual at all. For example, there are sections covering shoeing, tack (with particular attention to saddles), clothing, travel, and physical therapy.

It is customary in a Preface to list those people to whom the authors feel an obligation. We tried this and came up with more than nine pages. So we simply skip that. Our friends know well how much we appreciate their help and guidance over the years.

We have barely tapped the tremendous reservoir horses represent as a medium for experience in a world in which we are daily harassed by the technological monsters we have created to "make life easy for ourselves." Endurance riding is anything but *easy*. It requires a great deal of time and patience, a considerable quality of horsemanship, and a very good horse. We hope that this book, the sum of much effort by many people, many wonderful experiences, many heartbreaks, and thousands of miles of riding from sea level to 12,000 feet, from 40 degrees below zero in northern Canada to the hot deserts of the Southwest, will have been found to be worth your while.

Two Special Acknowledgments

KERRY RIDGWAY, D.V.M.

We call your attention to Chapter 4 in Part I entitled "Condition —Meaningful Judging" and Chapter 2 in Part III entitled "Back Problems in Distance Horses." These chapters were originally developed by Dr. Ridgway as professional papers for presentation to the American Association of Equine Practitioners. Dr. Ridgway reflects many years of successful experience in judging and riding in a variety of endurance and competitive trail rides. He was one of the veterinary examiners on the Bicentennial trans-America ride from New York to California.

Kerry has very kindly donated these chapters to this text, and we feel very grateful that we can pass this information on to you.

2. Kerry Ridgway, D.V.M.

CHARLES BARIEAU

Many of the photographs appearing with this text were made by Charles Barieau. He has been a profound influence in endurance riding for over twenty years, and is a member of the Board of Governors and official photographer for the Tevis Cup Ride. A friend and confidant of many editors of horse magazines, Charles has done much for the development of this sport. He was an organizer of the American Endurance Ride Conference and an early promoter of the magazine that was called *Saddle Action*. He travels extensively to cover rides all over the western United States and has a file of photos which tell stories that are simply priceless.

3. Charles Barieau

The exact list of his photographs in this book is as follows:
Nos. 1, 2, 3, 5, 6, 7, 8, 9, 10, 11, 12, 15, 26, 38, 39, 40, 41, 45, 48, 49, 50, 52, 53, 54, 55, 56.

Unless specifically credited, all other photographs were taken by Wentworth Tellington.

PART 1

The Contest

1

Endurance and Competitive Trail Riding: An Overview

Beginnings

There are two specific forms of long-distance riding competitions: competitive trail riding and endurance riding. The U. S. Cavalry rides shortly after World War I from northern Vermont to the Washington Monument in Washington, D.C., which were strictly military occasions within the fraternity of breeders and users of candidate horses for the Cavalry, may be called the first organized endurance-ride contests in the United States.

The earliest contest of the kind we know today was, no doubt, the outgrowth of these Army rides. We refer to the Vermont 100-mile-in-three-day ride conducted by the Green Mountain Horse Association, which has become a tradition in the American horse scene since Dr. Earle Johnson led a small group of horsemen over the course for the first time in 1936. Since that time we have seen distance rides organized first on the East and West coasts and then in many areas of the midcontinent until today there are well over 100 contests to choose from all over the country in which riders may participate in all seasons of the year.

The Australians picked up on this sport when both the Tevis Cup Ride and the NATRC rides were in their infancy in the early 1960s. Shortly thereafter, regular annual events were scheduled in England as well, and activities are opening up now in Europe.

Objectives

This book aims to bring under one cover sufficient information for a person or group of persons to become effective participants in any phase of endurance or competitive trail riding in which there may be interest. It goes without saying that, as in any other field of activity, reading is not enough. It is necessary to have experience. But experience is a long and expensive process if a person has no basis for understanding and no opportunity to take some advantage of the experience of others. This book is, therefore, a compilation of the experience of many people in all phases of this sport. We trust that the reader will be able to build upon this as a foundation: to run a better ride, to select a better horse, to train more effectively, to judge with an extra increment of precision, to compete with more effectiveness, or just to observe with a greater sense of appreciation.

As direct participants for several years in all phases of endurance and competitive trail riding we feel qualified to assemble this information. We do believe, nevertheless, that there is much more progress to be made, much more to be learned, and much room for improvement in our knowledge and in application of that knowledge. It is reasonable to assume that if we exchange ideas freely and openly as the years go by, and if we consider each other's views with an open mind, we can expect to raise the general levels of this sport to a very high degree.

In certain places in this book a reader might get the impression that we are taking issue with some individual horseman. This is never the case. We may take issue with some idea no matter how prevalent it may be or no matter how high the source of the idea, but our objectives are always focused on one thing: improvement. We respect traditional views in many instances, but never because they are traditional. If some view has been endowed with the status of being traditional but is now subject to improvement, we do not hesitate to rebuild. As a case in point, although one of the authors was a cavalry officer and did participate in long marches, one slightly over five hundred miles, he sees little application of the Cavalry principles to modern civilian long-distance riding if for no other reason than that the civilian rides as an individual, while the cavalryman rides as part of a large group. The civilian's primary mission is riding. The cavalryman's primary mission is not riding but fighting, either directly or, in the case of reconnaissance missions, indirectly.

The Good Old Days

Not long ago, a few decades at most, there were those very skilled, natural horsemen who, with years of practical experience, would "eyeball" a horse and tell you if he needed worming, or who would touch him in a few significant spots and then stand back to render a verdict that might affect the decision of a purchaser in the hundred-thousand-dollar range at a big sale of racehorses. In another circumstance, an old-time horseman might simply get to a point riding up a hill when, as a result of "experience," he would stop to let the horse "blow." Many horsemen still follow this pattern, but they would never again win an endurance ride with such tactics! Where a man, at best, might have thought to check the horse's eyesight by waving something in front of his eye to see if he blinked, today the quality of eye examination parallels in many respects that of a human exam. Furthermore, it is not uncommon to see a prospective expensive racehorse examined in detail with a stethoscope or even an electrocardiogram to evaluate his basic systems of blood circulation and breathing. Much of this new view of evaluation of condition at rest and under stress results from the experience of veterinarians and sophisticated horsemen in competitive trail rides and endurance rides since 1955. What a change in a short span of twenty years! We can think of no period in horse history in which so much development of specific knowledge has occurred; yet there are a few basic notions that have not changed:

Two Basic Factors

1. Quoting from the original manual, "The primary lesson, difficult to learn, and more difficult to apply, is simply this. Not every horse was born to be a winner. Find a good one. Do not try to make a winner out of your horse just because you happen to own him."

2. The second lesson is that no horse has a chance unless you treat him right. This does not mean mollycoddle the animal. As in anything else, you have to know what you are doing.

Few, if any, have ever won with any consistency unless they knew what they were doing.

It is within the framework of this experience and these basic lessons that we have written this book, and with the assumption that you share with us the desire to approach, if not achieve, a degree of perfection in selecting horses, in training and feeding them, in organizing a ride, in competing, and in judging.

Endurance and Competitive Trail Rides Compared

There is a basic difference between an endurance ride and a competitive trail ride; the competitive trail ride does not approach the limit of capacity of a trained horse or rider. It simply invades the province of stress sufficiently to differentiate between horses for purposes of selection. The endurance ride, on the other hand, approaches the limits of stress for horse and rider to the point where there is little doubt about the selection. In each case, the welfare of horses and rider is a function of the intelligence, experience, and objectives of the rider and the quality, knowledge, and discreet resoluteness of judges.

Endurance rides, by our definition, would include contests of 25 miles or more in one day (approximately 100 miles maximum) and would have no minimum time limit. The 25 mile distance has much in common with a regular horse race, and consequently is in a somewhat specialized category. Distances of 40 miles or more contain more of the characteristics we have come to recognize as traditional endurance rides.

Competitive trail rides, by our definition, consist of contests that are of sufficient length (rarely less than 15 miles, but rarely more than 40 miles) in one day, that cover a span of time ranging from 4 hours in a single day to 3 days, and in which the maximum approved average speed is about 8 miles per hour but more frequently close to 4.

We said in the 1967 manual that we would guess there might be 200 horses qualified for an endurance ride while there were probably more than 1,000 qualified for a competitive trail ride. Today there are several times that many in both categories, with about 225 horses showing up for the Tevis Cup Ride, and well over 1,000 competitive trail-ride horses active in California alone.

It is our opinion that almost any healthy horse could be conditioned to do a respectable job in either a competitive trail ride or an endurance ride, and for this reason these rides offer a fine opportunity for the competitive-minded horseman to improve his knowledge and skills in training and conditioning without having to find a highly specialized horse. The *winning* of an endurance ride, on the other hand, would require the selection of an unusual horse—so unusual, in fact, that it could very well be of little use in any other kind of horse competition.

The training involved in competitive trail riding falls within the range of reason for nearly anyone interested. A few hours devoted to riding three or four days a week is usually sufficient. The training involved in endurance riding, however, is relatively tedious and time-consuming, and requires a considerable amount of *personal* physical conditioning on the part of the rider.

The quality of horsemanship required depends more on the type of competitors than on the type of ride. A group of excellent horsemen riding a competitive trail ride would give an individual more competition than a group of poor horsemen would give an individual rider in an endurance ride. It is our experience, as you would logically expect, that the percentage of high-quality horsemen is somewhat higher among those riders who have engaged in more than one of these rides. No one knows what kind of a horseman will try one of these rides once, but by the time you see a rider being successful in about three rides you may count him as a knowledgeable horseman.

Competitive trail rides, especially as organized under the auspices of the North American Trail Ride Conference, offer excellent circumstances for learning horsemanship, while endurance rides, especially of the caliber of the Western States Trail Ride (the Tevis Cup contest), offer a maximum challenge of Olympic proportions.

Ride and Tie

Since 1970 two new forms of long-distance competition have emerged. One is a rather short but very demanding event called a "ride and tie" race. This was innovated by the Levi Strauss Company in San Francisco and has now established itself as an annual event. The basic historical idea is that in the old days of developing the West an occasion could arise when two men had to share a horse and cover country at the same time. It could be, as you might imagine, that one man's horse was hurt or lost, and the two simply had to get along with one animal. If they both tried to ride they would make very little distance and relatively slow speed. If, on the other hand, one man ran and the other rode and they took turns, things might go better. The modern ride-and-tie race starts off with the runner and rider leaving the starting line together. At a predetermined point, generally selected by the rider's appraisal of the runner's ability to cover the ground, the rider ties the horse to a tree or post and takes off running. His partner catches up to the horse, which has had some opportunity to rest for a few minutes, leaps on, and passes the man on foot. He then eventually ties the horse some distance ahead. This leapfrogging continues over a total distance varying from thirty to fifty miles as a rule. There are categories of competition for contestants in certain age ranges, combination teams, women's teams, even teams for people in their sixties. We have good friends who enter this contest regularly and are well over sixty!

The other new form is called a marathon race and is mentioned briefly in Chapter 2.

4. Walt Stack and Hugh Bryson crossing the Ride and Tie finish line to win the "Century in the Saddle Award." Walt, then 71, started running at 58 and now has finished 61 marathon races, including the Pike's Peak Contest! Hugh Bryson at 60 has several endurance rides to his credit but has just started to run. At the moment this photo was snapped by Lynda Walker, these two happy types had just run or ridden *42 miles* in a little over seven hours!

The Tevis Cup Ride

There is much reference in this book to the Tevis Cup Ride or, as it is otherwise known, the Western States Trail Ride. We have referred to this contest deliberately for several reasons. This is a very well-managed and well-seasoned "experience" with the best-kept records of any endurance or competitive trail ride we know. The records are not only well kept, they are also circulated after each year's contest for the benefit of the contestants and of students of these events. And since one of the authors is a member of the Board of Governors and the other has been a successful contestant on several occasions, we have an intimate knowledge of this contest, which we believe it may be helpful to share.

Obtaining Information

We have accounted for several other rides in detail in the last part of this book so that the reader may gain some feeling for each of them. For anyone who wants specific information about a specific ride, we suggest he contact the management of that ride. To obtain an address, write to the NATRC or the AERC or to the trail-riding editor of *Western Horseman*. The addresses of all these organizations and a few others are printed in the Appendix.

Points of View

We must appreciate the simple historical fact that this sport, if you go all the way back to the Army contests, is still only about fifty years old. The Green Mountain Ride (grandfather of rides of this kind) is only about forty years old. The North American Trail Ride Conference and the Western State Trail Ride Foundation are both about twenty-five years old. Then we have the AERC, the most recent organization, which is not yet ten years old.

It is understandable that people coming into this sport should expect rules more or less like horse-show rules, grievance committees, ideas of what is fair and what is not fair, stipulations about ages, weights, and many other things. Competitive trail rides have made concessions to this kind of thinking in many ways by giving out a variety of awards and having very intricate rules. Endurance rides, on the other hand, have tended to follow a more simplistic formula with very few rules and very few prizes.

Some people like to receive "points" for entering many rides and covering miles, and there are organizations that have this kind of prize thinking at the core of their charters. The result has been the creation of splinter groups and organizations all over the country. One ride may be "sanctioned," another may not be. The idea of "sanctioning" is to encourage a rider to come because his participation will count toward an annual rating of one kind or another. You may win a good ride, and if it is not sanctioned or if you personally have not paid your dues to the appropriate organization, you simply won't count on the final roster.

We see both sides of the coin, but we tend to favor the simple way of doing things with a minimum of rules—just the very best veterinary examination that money can buy. Speaking of money, most of the old rides, except for paying the veterinarians, have been operated largely with voluntary help. Today we see paid secretaries in some instances, and heavy fees, especially in the cash-prize rides. Then we see the officers or directors of some organizations being financed out of ride funds to make trips and otherwise conduct business. It can be argued that these activities tend to improve the sport or that particular event but there is also the argument that they tend to allow for a new "commercialization" of the sport.

2

Managing a Ride

Rides succeed when management makes adequate preparations, and rides fail when management does not. The operation of a well-run endurance or competitive trail ride is not conducive to making money. Management must have other objectives than the production of income.

Organizing

The following comments first appeared in the mid-1960s in our column "Let's Go," a regular feature at that time in *Western Horseman,* and were reprinted in *The Chronicle of the Horse* by permission of the editors. It is now updated with occasional comments comparing statements made roughly ten years apart.

How would we organize a ride?

First, we would invite a half dozen or so riders who might be interested in putting on an event to join us some Saturday morning with their horses to take a ride of about twenty miles, just to see how it feels to ride together for a goodly distance. We would follow this day of riding with a good chuck wagon type of dinner by a big fireplace where we could talk over the whole idea.

If we encountered some enthusiasm and support, we would plan a similar group outing for a month or six weeks hence. In the meantime we would establish some framework for an informal organization. One person would have been designated to get information from whatever sources are available, such as the North American Trail Ride Conference or managements of established rides or any other organization with experience that might be of assistance. Another person would have been designated to accumulate information on training horses for these events. Two people would have been designated to lay out a more or less exact twenty- or twenty-five-mile course to follow on the next ride. Two other persons would have been delegated to social and business aspects of the next meeting. Everyone should be expected to chip in about ten dollars each for their own food and for a few useful guests and to have a small budget to pay for postage and incidental early-on expenses.

The next ride-meeting would include ten riders or more if possible. The dinner should include the local veterinarian and his family, the officers of the local horse club, a few townspeople who can help, and the local forest ranger or his equivalent. All in all, you might expect thirty people or more at the second meeting.

This time, several firm decisions could be reached, and the whole thing jelled into a working organization, associated with or subsidiary to the local horse organization. It's not a bad idea to commemorate some historical event or known horse achievement. It is not necessary to offer a big cash prize. The Tevis Cup, for example, is retained by the Western States Trail Foundation. All you ever get is your name on it. The prize for all riders who complete the ride successfully is a buckle.

Since these remarks were originally addressed to people in response to numerous requests for assistance in organizing rides when there were not so many, we would observe today that circumstances are substantially different than they were ten years ago.

In addition to the NATRC (North American Trail Ride Conference) there are several organizations of rides both by type of ride and by region, such as the American Endurance Ride Conference. The name here indicates that the organization deals with endurance rides while the NATRC deals with competitive trail rides. We have already discussed, and will refer elsewhere to the basic differences between these two types.

Marathons

A third type has developed recently, which some call marathon racing. The fundamental difference appears to be simply the overall length of the ride. While endurance and competitive trail rides are rarely significantly longer than 100 miles, marathon rides or races are being organized in the 500-mile range. During 1976 there was an effort to stage a marathon race called the Great American Horse

Race, a Bicentennial idea that "didn't fly." There were innumerable problems involved in this big promotion, which one would have to say will probably plague managements of any marathon type of horse race. First, this particular race was to commence in late May and continue on until Labor Day, a time span of about 100 days. Just think of the horrendous expenses in paying good judges for such a thing, the virtually impossible policing and managing problems, and the overall logistics. All of our successful contests are centered around a single locality with much volunteer assistance. The judges are needed only for three or four days at the most, and the trail can be managed with ease. But a long cross-country event presents staggering problems by comparison, with no logical source of money to pay obvious bills that ordinary ride managements don't even have to worry about at all. This highly publicized event attracted a great many people who were not well prepared or experienced but who nevertheless dreamed of winning the $25,000 cash prize that was offered in the promotional literature. Four days after the event started, with contestants having come from as far away as Australia, the management announced it had run out of money. Several times in the next few weeks the race was salvaged by various impromptu maneuvers, and the contestants' will to cross the country one way or the other persisted. This is no place for reiterating the whole story. The lessons for management are:

1. When you count all your costs you will find that in 1978–79 the price in U.S. dollars per day to stage an endurance ride of any kind will be at least $1,000. If you consider The Tevis Cup Ride as a 3-day experience—judging, riding, and judging again—you would think we mean $3,000. However, we will hazard a guess that this ride costs more like $20,000 when you think of awarding about 120 buckles worth about $76 each. The entry-fee income is about $15,000 and they tell you this would not finance the event. Basic Lesson: To run a marathon race for horseback riders you will need a minimum of $10,000 start-up costs and 1,000 per day for the duration of the contest.

2. When you offer large cash prizes you set the stage for an entirely different attitude on the part of the contestants whereby horses can suffer seriously while the individuals succumb to a mental state that might be called "racing fever."

In a "final" session somewhere in Missouri, the contestants split into two groups, one continuing the "Great American Horse Race" largely self-financed on the assurance that there really still was $25,000 to be shared among the top riders when they arrived in Sacramento.

When the original race stopped for the fourth time in mid-July, the splinter group, a rather small contingent, organized on short notice a happy and successful experience known as the Pony Express Ride starting at St. Joseph, Missouri (the original Pony Express starting point) and ending in Old Sacramento, California (the original destination). They followed as faithfully as they could the original trail through back country with much help from historical authorities and simply offered buckles and a bronze statue of a Pony Express rider for trophies.

Time alone will tell how marathon racing will develop in the United States. There is no doubt that for those who can find the time and can afford to stay away from a job that long, a marathon race under good management and good judges over country as interesting as the old Pony Express Trail preserved through central Nevada would certainly be an experience never to be forgotten.

Questions

An early consideration of your management group at the first really organized meeting is: *What kind of ride can your group present?* Would it be essentially for fun? Would it be to give people from afar a chance to ride in interesting new country? Would it be to present a unique challenge to horse and rider? A very legitimate reason to organize a ride is to make something of this kind available to local people who might otherwise have to trailer a considerable distance to participate in a similar event.

The next consideration is: *When can you schedule your event so it will conflict as little as possible with other similar contests?* The kind of event affects this decision to some extent. For example, if you contemplate a 25-mile competitive trail ride, you could easily schedule it on the same weekend as any big 100-mile, one-day endurance ride in essentially the same area as long as you didn't try to use the same trail, because you would be appealing to entirely different contestants. This, of course, raises the third consideration.

What kind of contestant would you be attempting to attract? Here there are more choices and considerations than one might, at first, expect. For example, the Virginia 100-miles-in-3-days event held annually in the spring is open only to members and occasional guests of an old Virginia riding club who enjoy this vigorous outdoor social event in an elegant setting. The NATRC rides, on the West Coast primarily but continuously spreading out over the country, are open to anyone who wishes to join. Here there is an announced interest in promoting better horsemanship. The Tevis Cup Ride is different things to different people. Many contestants come year after year, some of whom achieve the distinction of receiving a 1,000-mile buckle for completing the ride successfully ten times! A small group of relatively local people start each year in the hopes of winning the Tevis or the Haggin Cup. A considerable number, sometimes coming from very long distances away, hope to place in that elite group called The Top Ten. There is another type of rider whom you can find in each year's starting lineup. This is a person who may or may not ride a great deal, but who has heard about this grueling, demanding challenge and wants to see if he or she can really do this thing. When such riders stand up at the banquet to receive their buckles you can see that they often ache all over but feel an exuberance and sense of achievement that is indescribable!

The chances are very good that the kind of ride you will want to manage will be what your own local group would like to do best themselves. Here it is interesting to note that a large number of riders in the northwestern part of the United States have decided that the regular NATRC-type ride is not quite enough challenge for them while at the same time they do not feel like going all out in a 100-mile-one-day experience. Consequently they have formed their own regional group called The Rocky Mountain Competitive Trail Ride Association, with contests in Hamilton, Whitefish, and Missoula, Montana, and Salmon, Idaho. Again we refer you for names and addresses to the Appendix.

During 1977 in the United States there were about ten endurance rides of the 100-mile-one-day type scheduled in various parts of the country. There were almost 70 endurance rides of 50 miles or more and a few 25-mile contests. For a time in the late sixties and early seventies, the 25-mile contest appeared to have some favor, but it is a type of ride that is being phased out now. One reason is probably that it may be attractive to a certain kind of rider once or twice, but it soon ceases to be the challenge that the longer rides are. Another is that from management and judging points of view it poses some hazards since riders often feel they can press a horse harder because of the relatively short distance, and there has to be tighter policing to be sure no horses are hurt.

Do's and Don'ts

1. Do try to organize a ride that will be repeated year after year. You may be disappointed in the number of entries the first year, but if you keep it up, each year will bring more encouraging results. The Western States Trail ride began in 1955 with five riders. Now, internationally recognized, it is host to about two hundred starters annually.

2. Do not try to put on the biggest, toughest ride in the world the first year. You can make your ride into a big rough-and-tough event, and more power to you; but do it on the basis of actual experience with good controls all the way or you will never attract real horsemen.

3. Plan far enough ahead (at least six months) to allow for announcement time and then for potential contestants to prepare for the contest.

4. On all possible occasions prior to your ride, send as many delegates as you can to other rides to compete or help judge by offering secretarial assistance or just to observe and get acquainted. Every ride can stand more "assistants" and would be grateful. They are invariably very generous in helping newly organized rides, by giving you free publicity over the microphone and introducing you at the awards dinner. You can hand out circulars, get to know the people who are interested, meet the managers, and in all ways get the swing of things.

5. Do give full attention to the judging and the care of the horses. If you convince riders that they and their horses will benefit by participating whether they win or not, you will get entries. They will benefit in a number of ways if you plan right.

Four Fundamentals

First: The people who come to your ride should find a good welcome and a place for the horse where he is safe and can be well cared for. Stabling is not necessary, but there should be provision for good parking for horse trailers with room for the contestant to put up his own portable stall if desired on ground that will not be rocky or, in the event of rain, too muddy.

Second: Riders should have real assurance that the contest will begin and end on time. People coming considerable distances have to plan their time carefully.

Third: They should expect to meet other horsemen in an environment conducive to "swapping a few lies." On the entry there should be clear instructions regarding the location of your headquarters, etc., so that strangers arriving will know where to go in town. There should also be clear announcements regarding the preride briefing, which riders will expect. Then you should plan a preride coffee, no-host dinner, or breakfast, and an awards banquet with clear statements regarding the wheres and whens.

Fourth: Entrants must be convinced that the contest will be judged intelligently. Here it is worthwhile to get a senior judge who has considerable recognized experience to work with the local people. The NATRC and The American Association of Equine Practitioners have lists of veterinarians with such experience. It is better to spend several hundred dollars on this item in the budget than to buy the fancy hand-tooled leather or silver prizes. Every good endurance rider we know would go much farther to ride over a good course under the eye of a good judge with a bag of peanuts for the prize than they would to ride a poorly planned course under an inexperienced judge with a silver saddle for the prize.

Without wishing to emphasize failure we would call your attention to the fact that failing to evaluate your own locality and the kind of people who are likely to come, or how much time and energy it really takes to stage a good contest, or perhaps most important of all, failure to appreciate the value of a good judge, can be the source of much grief.

The Trail

Regarding the trail itself, you should have it clearly in mind and be able to provide a map along with the contestant's entry blank. The trail should be clearly marked. Pick a bright color of flagging. Most rides use the kind of flagging that surveyors use. This can sometimes be confused with local construction flagging, so you have to take that into account. There are some conventions in flagging that have come to be accepted in this sport:

5. It pays to be well organized. This picture, taken at a stop during the Tevis Cup Ride, shows how well these people can do it in a very practical fashion. Hurried riders and crews can easily find their way around in this situation.

6. The show goes on in this sport—rain or shine. This is the judge's group at a stop in The Drake's Bay Ride—very wet, but *still well organized.*

Before a junction in the trail hang *three* flags about ten feet apart to indicate a change in course. About two hundred feet after the change in course, hang *three* flags in the same manner. These are called confidence markers so the rider feels sure he is on the right trail.

Indications about two miles before regular rest stops or judging stations should be clear by use of a sign so stating or other understandable marker.

Markers generally should be hung no farther apart than one-quarter mile; and signs indicating distance traveled every five miles are very helpful.

Finally, the rider should know, by good markers, when he is two miles from the finish line.

Depending on weather and time of day, a cool drink or a hot cup of coffee sure is appreciated at the end of the ride!

Because of the potential for getting spread out on the trail, any ride needs at least two qualified judges. Generally, good managements figure on one additional judge for each additional twenty-five riders beyond the first twenty-five—that is, for twenty-five or less, two judges; for fifty or less, three judges; for seventy-five or less, four judges, etc. If there are circumstances of terrain, difficulties to get around, or unusual potential for spreading, more than this minimum number of judges would be required.

Think Ahead

The best thing a manager can do in preparing for a trail-riding contest is to sit down and quietly "try it on for size" in his mind— that is to say, imagine the whole thing is done and ready for execution. For example, think along the following lines:

How much time will really be needed for advance publicity? If you send something to *Western Horseman,* and they will use it (unless it is a conventional paid ad), the lag time is as much as eighty days depending on their publication deadline dates. The other horse magazines are about the same except for *The Chronicle of the Horse,* which comes out every two weeks. You can get a current list of all horse magazines in any library. A part of this same question is: Who will hear about your ride and how will they? Then imagine that someone writes to you about the ride. To whom will he write? What will he receive in the way of specific information and an entry blank?

Imagine that ten days before the ride you have heard from no one. What will you do, and how will you do it? Imagine, conversely, that you have one hundred firm entries when you only expected twenty-five or so. What will you do, and how will you do it? What are your cut-off points? Consider how much space you have for various numbers of horses at check-in areas and for veterinary checks along the way.

Imagine the day is at hand. Is your trail well marked? Who did it? What did he use? How did he know what to do? How do the contestants know where the trail is? Are you ready for the briefing session? Along with all the basic information that must be presented at the briefing, are you ready to deal with smoking on the trail and littering? Have you set a good example by marking the trail well without painting the beautiful rocks in your nearby forest with red, white, and blue paint? The trail should be identified in such a way that a contestant, on the basis of papers and maps you have given him, with no word from anyone, can determine the starting point, follow the trail easily, and find the finishing point without time-consuming personal assistance by members of your staff. Who is going to meet the contestant? How will he find out where his horse will stay? Where will *he* stay? How does his horse find something to eat? How does the rider? Just in case there are necessary last-minute changes in rules and instructions (due to weather, for example), how will you pass the word around? How do you announce a special briefing session? Where is the judge? How is he supposed to know what to do? Where does he stay, and where does he eat? Who is going to help you and the judge meet the numerous problems that are bound to arise during the contest?

The contest is on. A rider is hurt. What preparations have you made for this eventuality? Someone else is lost despite your well-marked trail. Someone else is late, but wants to start out anyway. What do you do about that? One of your official cars breaks down. Where is the spare? As the ride progresses, how do you know everyone is all right? There is a very fast rider and a group of slow ones now separated by three hours' time or twenty miles of distance (perhaps even considerably more). What is the judge supposed to do now? Someone reports that they have seen a rider beating his horse. What do you do about that? You receive a report that "a horse is down with colic." Where is the person to help in that situation? At the end, two riders are reported missing. How do you find them?

The ride is finally over and all these problems are pretty well straightened out. Where are the awards? How long is it going to take to select the winners? Is the occasion for award-giving in hand? How do you let the world know what happened? If this is not carefully planned, the news will be so stale that no one will care much anymore, and the net result is that you lose a great deal of value in the preparation for the next contest.

This brings us to a basic point. It takes a year or at least several months to prepare for a contest. The next one begins while this one is still going on. During the contest, if you take notes, you can accumulate the experience necessary to guide you for the next contest so you do not make the same mistakes twice. If you trust your memory, you will fail.

With this blast of admonishment, you might just be making up your mind that you will never put on an endurance or competitive trail ride! But wait. Let us try to unravel the picture enough to be able to plan and execute with as little confusion as possible.

Here is a check list that results from several years of experience. It is divided into sections based upon the time before the event, very much like a military plan of operation. Having examined the list to determine what aspects are applicable in your given situation, it might be worthwhile to photocopy some for your group.

Manager's Check Lists

I. Approximately one year prior to the planned date of the ride:
A. Have the written opinion and encouragement from at least three persons with experience in this type of competition to the effect that your project should be successful as described.
B. Have selected three key people who can work together:
1. Host (Hostess)—Responsible for publicity, entries, awards dinner (if held), accommodations for horses and riders, preride meetings.
2. Trail master—(Although this position might be occupied by a lady, it often involves much lifting and heavy work.) Picks and marks the trail and produces map including indication of elevations; supervises trail during contest; is responsible for strays and accidents and all unforeseen situations during the event.
3. Competition supervisor—Writes rules; finds and hosts judges and gets them around during the competition; is responsible for

timing and reports, finding and instructing secretaries; turns in final report promptly to host for publicity.

This is the "bootstraps" stage of the operation. As a rule, it is somewhat spontaneously established with the logical persons more or less naturally coming to mind as *general manager, host, trail master, competition supervisor,* etc. It is at this time that exploratory meetings can be set up with visiting experts to give advice on conditioning horse, feeding, etc., at which times the idea of the forthcoming trail ride can be promoted. In this way enthusiasm will be aroused and prospective contestants will be more likely to prepare adequately for the contest rather than discover some of the necessary points of conditioning after the ride is all over and they were eliminated because of improper or inadequate preparation.

It is also at this time that the support of some local organization to sponsor the contest is solicited. At least this aspect of the situation is considered and accounted for in some satisfactory way.

II. **Approximately nine months prior to the planned date of the ride:**
   A. **The trail master has selected the trail and can advise the group about its character sufficiently for the competition supervisor to have a preliminary entry blank and a general announcement.**
   B. **A list of acceptable judges has been obtained.**
   C. **A tentative set of rules has been drawn up to send to experienced persons for their comments.**
   D. **Preliminary announcements have been sent to magazines, etc. Letters to ten or fifteen individuals who are known to "get around" have been written announcing your intentions and soliciting their support.**

At this meeting it is common to begin to form committees around the three key people already selected so certain jobs can be spread around. Naturally, the meeting divides itself into two parts:

First: Reporting on what has been done.

Second: Looking ahead to what is supposed to be accomplished before the next meeting.

It is possible that the central group may wish to meet more often than once every three months for various reasons. But this quarterly system is still a very good idea, and might well be accompanied by a general, public meeting with a speaker or movie describing the training of endurance-ride or competitive trail-ride horses, or the uses of TPR readings in training or judging.

III. Approximately six months prior to the planned date of the ride:

    A. The host, trail master, and competition supervisor have each selected and have in attendance at the meeting the people necessary to help them discharge their duties.

    B. A final trail map is completed in draft.

    C. The final rules are completed in draft.

    D. The entry form is completed in draft.

    E. Aspects of liability have been considered and an appropriate form for competitors to sign has been composed. This particular point has become more and more significant each year and should be given careful attention. Some attorneys recommended incorporating; some believe that waivers of any kind are dubious.

    F. Necessary permissions to travel over the land along the trail have been obtained in an adequate way.

    G. Facilities for horses and riders have been determined for the period before, during, and after the ride.

    H. Anticipated requirements in communication and transportation have been accounted for.

    I. The judges have been selected and have indicated their willingness to serve.

    J. Emergency facilities for horses and people have been arranged.

    K. Brochure describing the event, posters and other materials necessary to promotion are ready to print.

    L. Repeat notices to magazines and newspapers have been sent out.

    M. Entry fees have been set on the basis of anticipated expenses. Reserve funds have been arranged for to cover possible losses.

    N. Sources of trail-marking materials have been found and anticipated quantities of materials established.

    O. Sources of rider identification materials have been found—that is, competition numbers to be worn on chest or arm. Horse identification has been established—that is, spraying a number on the hip or otherwise establishing a positive, rapid means of identifying the horses.

It is easy to see that there is a lot to do at this time, six months before the ride. This is one of the key periods to success. It is quite possible that an active group could condense the time prior to this. But you really need this last six months for magazine publishing time, rider preparation time, and other things that just can't be made to happen any faster. One cannot overemphasize this list or the six-month time involved.

It is at this stage or within the next three months that as many people as possible in your management group actually ride over a trail duplicating the contest experience as nearly as possible. There is no substitute in discussions and planning for actual trail experience. And the trail itself is the prime thing in any trail ride.

IV. Approximately three months prior to the planned date of the ride:
A. Arrangements completed for the check-in, guiding, arrivals, general rider assistance, and awards-dinner location.
B. Trail map, rules, and entry forms printed.
C. All trail problems including rest stops and judging stops established, along with route for vehicles to follow, etc.
D. Finance plans and contingencies set.
E. Repeat notices to magazines, local radio stations, TV, and newspapers.
F. Careful arrangements for timing and reports have been made. Forms for keeping track of contestants during the contest have been approved and are ready for printing. And the timing system has been set up.
G. Arrangements for emergencies have been made and reviewed.
H. Final arrangements for the accommodation of judges have been made and the judges advised.
I. Arrangements for awards dinner are completed and menu established. This includes clean-up.
J. Plans for recovering rider identification markers are set.
K. Responsibility for final publicity material is clearly established with deadline dates in consideration of news media in the local area.
L. Final-reminder memo is ready to send to potential contestants. This is the time you remind the contestants of your final briefing sessions before the ride, and necessary changes or other last-minute interesting information. This is one of the most useful tricks we know of to increase the number of contestants.

Management must not overlook the fact that, even though this sport is growing in popularity, the total number of persons in a given area who are seriously interested in this form of contest is usually not large. It is possible to contact these people by personal letters and indirectly other people interested by word of mouth from the people you write to. Broad, general advertising is not only expensive but also quite unnecessary. The Tevis Cup Ride is now such a big and famous event that personal correspondence with individuals is virtually impossible. Nevertheless, that is the way it grew. When we first became interested in this event, we received detailed personal information from Mr. Wendell Robie, Drucilla Barner, and John Rogers. That big ride did not just happen by accident. It results from the careful, close attention of very high-caliber managers and a great deal of personal attention to details.

Months before the Tevis Cup Ride each year, persons interested receive a nice little newspaperlike announcement telling about the ride, its history, the previous winners, interesting persons, rule changes, trail conditions, etc. They also receive a letter containing entry blanks and preliminary veterinary requirements. After the ride, contestants receive an elaborate form showing the basic physiological status of all horses in the contest.

This unique form has many values to the ride management: 1. It is excellent basic publicity. 2. It gives instruction and information. 3. It is conducive to taking the contest seriously and thus encouraging contestants to prepare better. 4. It promotes better care of the horses.

Perhaps for newly established rides such a form is too elaborate, but we feel that any ride that considers itself a going thing owes this kind of post-mortem information to its contestants. Naturally, this cannot be given to the contestants unless the management has provided excellent judges and a fine secretarial staff that can produce this type of information in the first place.

In light of experience since the original manual was published, we would recommend to all managements, including the Western States Trail Ride, that a record of the temperature, cloud condition, humidity, and wind be set out as part of the record for appropriate locations at appropriate times of the day. This would be of great assistance to serious students of fine points in evaluating situations and conditions and comparing ride circumstances.

V. One week prior to the planned date of the ride:
A. Host—Publicity, entries done. Awards and awards dinner ready. Accommodations for horses and riders ready. Check-in station is ready and personnel identified. Pre-ride meeting place is established and time set.

B. Trail master—Trail marked and checked; emergency personnel ready; cars checked out; communications set.

C. Competition supervisor—Last-minute changes or ground rules set; final notice to judges has been sent and acknowledged; timing set-up checked; final report and all forms ready. Final check of trail; rider and horse identification ready.

D. Check-in Point and Pre-ride Meeting and Pre-ride Inspection— Various committee chairmen and appropriate persons know who is going to be at the check-in point, who is going to deal out contestant numbers, etc., who is going to assist judges in pre-ride inspections. Host, trail master, competition supervisor, and others are briefed on who says what and who introduces whom and who is responsible for what at the pre-ride meeting.

If you have come through this stage with all flags flying, you may rest assured that your ride will go well. At this point we are reminded of the famous story about General Lee being found asleep under a tree by a young soldier in the middle of a battle.

"General, sir," the lad shouted, "the battle's on."

"Yes." General Lee lifted his tired head and smiled. "I know. I've already fought this one."

7. It's a good idea to have the ceremonies move right along at the banquet. Riders like the occasion, but they are a bit tired and have to head toward home. Keep the awards rolling.

3

Judging a Ride

Background

No phase of distance riding has changed more rapidly than the judging. Only 40 years ago the only significant contest of this type in the whole United States was the Vermont 100-Mile-in-3-Day Ride. Although not acquainted with the detailed history of that ride, we feel quite certain that no one in attendance was equipped with a thermometer or a stethoscope. In the military rides of the previous decade, which this ride was designed to commemorate, no one made any observations of TPRs.

The first record of this aspect of judging, as far as we know, is the effort of certain veterinarians associated with the Davis Campus of the University of California; and one of the first individuals to undertake stress observations in terms of temperature-pulse-respiration was George Cardinet III, D.V.M., working with the School of Veterinary Medicine.

In the five years from 1919 to 1923, the Army Endurance Ride for the U. S. Mounted Service Cup constituted the best-documented and most carefully judged competition known in America up to that time. The horses covered 300 miles carrying a minimum weight of 245 pounds (of which 100 pounds had to be dead weight). The race covered 5 days of 60 miles each with a minimum time of 9 hours and a maximum of 13 per day. The total time to win was about 45 hours, which, of course, means that winning riders each day came in right on the minimum time of 9 hours. How much faster they might have gone, no one will ever know. The simple fact is that judges watched to see if any horse was in stress and acted accordingly. They watched to see how much the horse needed to eat and

8. Dr. Murray Fowler, a professor at the University of California, briefing veterinarians at the 1968 Tevis Cup Ride. This was the first year no temperatures were taken for the record. At the right is Dr. Schinichi Nomura of the Japanese Pentathlon Team, a guest veterinarian that year.

drink, and they did pay close attention to dehydration and weight loss. These, quite obviously, were primary military considerations, and this contest was ostensibly to determine what kind of horse would be most useful to the U. S. Cavalry.

In the past 20 years, judging fatigue in horses has become a very sophisticated combination of science and art. We must keep in mind that where the veterinary examiners or judges use these various parameters to determine the state of welfare of the horses engaged in contests, riders use almost all of the same parameters in a different way during training and while engaged in the contest themselves. This requires some thought.

The judge knows only what he sees or feels when he makes the observation. He has little direct interest in the "history" of the horse in question. His whole attention is focused on what will probably happen to the horse in the next few hours after he examines it. The rider-trainer-contestant using the same parameters has a much broader view of things and considerably different objectives.

Judging is the focus of this chapter, but we suggest that riders go over this material carefully. In the chapter on training and conditioning, much of this material will be reviewed from the point of view of the contestant. We suggest that anyone interested in judging may derive some benefit from reading that chapter as a parallel to this one.

Measurements

Pulling out a horse's skin with your thumb and forefinger and watching it recover its contour to determine dehydration is one of the oldest prime observations. If the skin snaps back, all is well; if it returns to normal configuration slowly, watch for trouble in the near future. This observation is still very useful. Our modern contests do not allow any opportunity to observe food intake, interesting as this might be. Even if it were possible, it would probably still be regarded as essentially meaningless because trainers and riders have such divergent opinions of what to feed in the first place. There are too many parameters for just one day's observation.

Speaking of parameters brings to mind a basic scientific consideration that has, in times past, been a subject of considerable attention by German and French cavalry people, and has been discussed occasionally in articles in magazines such as *The Chronicle of the*

Horse. In considering large horses vs. small ones, scientifically oriented military minds have resorted to elementary principles of physics. Without going into technical detail, we would like to advance one idea commonly referred to as "the square law of nature." You know that a falling object increases its speed in direct proportion to the square of the time it falls. At the end of one second it is falling at the rate of sixteen feet per second. At the end of two seconds one might think it would be falling two times as fast, but it is not. It is falling *four* times as fast, or sixty-four feet per second. In another simple physics equation we observe that impact force is a function of MV^2, where M equals mass and V equals velocity. Again the square law of nature.

How do these concepts of physics apply to endurance riding? Let us consider a one-mile race on a regular track. No one is standing there "judging" the horse in terms of TPRs or anything else—just the clock. The horse is expected to recover routinely, and just about every contestant always does. How about two miles? The same. A steeplechase? The same. Somewhere along here we run into the rider "rating" his mount, but the horse is essentially wide open and is expected to recover routinely the way we might if we ran as hard as we could for a few hundred yards. But interesting things happen as the distance increases up to a hundred miles in a few hours.

We have noted that one good endurance horse recently ran 10 miles in 34 minutes and showed basic recovery of pulse to 40 beats per minute after 30 minutes of rest. That is not represented as any kind of record, just something we happen to know. Many current endurance horses could probably do that. The point is: What could that horse do in the *next* 10 miles? We would all instinctively agree he probably could not go quite as fast and would probably require longer to recover to a 40 pulse.

It is easy in judging to fall back on certain safe absolutes like *TPRs—temperature, pulse, and respiration.* Consider temperature. We have observed horses in trouble with temperatures of over 105°F, so we would simply eliminate a horse in the future with a T of 105.1°. Observing a horse in trouble with an outgoing pulse of eighty, we would arbitrarily pick some number less than that . . . possibly 78 in 1960, 74 in 1965, 70 in 1970, or 68 in 1975. These are very close approximations of judging opinion at the Tevis Cup 100-Mile One-Day Ride.

Distances and Times

More recently we have seen the development of 50-mile endurance rides and 25 mile contests. The 25 mile contest verges on being a straight out-and-out horse race, and is often won in a total elapsed actual riding time of about an hour and a half. 50-mile contests are won in approximately four hours and thirty minutes of actual riding time. 100-mile contests are won in something like 11 hours of actual riding time. In a 25-mile contest we feel that one regular veterinary inspection stop is absolutely necessary for the safety of the horses, and spot pulse checks somewhere in the last half of the ride are very useful to control overexuberance on the part of some riders. The 50-mile contest, as a rule, will include two appropriately spaced one-hour check stops with two interpolated spot checks where the pulse must return to some arbitrarily established maximum rate, often thought to be 68, before continuing. The 100-mile contest usually requires three stops of one hour and several spot checks depending on terrain and weather conditions. The point is that much deliberate planning by experienced people is necessary to establish appropriate stops for rest and judging purposes, and there is no set formula.

Limits

While a judge might find an outgoing pulse of 68 safe enough for any stop in a 100-mile contest, he could very properly determine that, given the same amount of time to rest, a horse should show a recovery pulse of 64 or even better in a 50-mile contest, and 60 or better in a 25-mile contest. The point is that the rider is tempted to hold the "throttle" open for longer periods in the shorter rides as he senses less obligation to rate, and trouble can build more rapidly. Consequently, the only thing the judge can do is call closer limits to compensate for this natural tendency on the part of the contestant. While the requirements for good outgoing "readings" of all kinds have become more rigid and the numbers have dropped from a pulse of 80 plus to 70 minus, records have been broken again and again in all ways.

One is tempted to speculate about the limits of all this. We can imagine that as trainers and riders develop more skill, records will continue to fall while the judges may hold maximum outgoing pulses to 60 and respirations to 40. The winners over the years in the Tevis Cup Ride show TPRs far below these limiting standards. At the 40-mile checkpoint, for example, the average outgoing pulse of a good horse is about 50 with a temperature of 100.5°. At the 65-mile check we find outgoing pulses of 60 with temperatures of 100.5°. At the 85-mile check we find outgoing pulses of 64 or less with temperatures of 100.5°.

In view of the continuous 100.5° temperatures, there has been a trend recently to ignore temperature, relying only on PRs (pulse and respiration), probably because temperature is a nuisance measurement to make and so infrequently reveals anything that the combination of pulse and respiration will not cover adequately. It is our opinion that, although this observation may fall completely into disuse with many ride judges, it is a very significant observation for trainers in preparation for rides. We shall, therefore, reserve further comments on temperature for the chapter on training.

Records

Within the stringent limits now imposed we may someday expect to see a horse cover 25 miles in slightly over one hour riding time, 50 miles in three hours, and 100 miles in ten. Times change. In 1960, every knowledgeable rider in this field of sport would agree that "100-mile contest in a year was enough for any horse." Linda's good horse, Bint Gulida, cracked that idea wide open in 1961 by finishing the Tevis Cup Ride in the top ten (actually No. 6) and then, only five weeks later, winning the Jim Shoulders 100-Mile Ride by such a wide margin that the second place-horse came in 5½ hours later. Since then, riding two 100-mile contests in a single season has become old hat.

Consider the Arabian gelding Witezarif, AHC 25667, owned by Donna Fitzgerald. In 1970 this horse won both the Tevis Cup Ride and the Virginia City Ride, both 100-mile contests, and in the same year won the Blue Mountain 50-mile ride. In 1971, after winning the Derby Ditch 50 and placing third at Castle Rock (50 miles), he placed fourth in the Diamond 100, won the Tevis Cup (100) again and placed second at Virginia City (100). The record is well covered in the literature of the American Endurance Ride Conference. Suffice it to say that in many cases when this horse did not come in first, he won the trophy for Best Condition. In 1969 at

Virginia City he won both trophies! His career record, still accumulating after tieing for first at the Tevis Cup Ride in 1976, winning the Virginia City Ride again, then not finishing the Tevis in 1977 but winning the Virginia City Ride a month later, now shows about 20 wins in about 4,000 miles of competition, with about 45 completions. This is, by far, more miles, more wins, and more completions than any other horse has achieved in endurance-ride competition.

So much for the overall picture of judging endurance rides. Competitive trail-ride judging has not undergone anything like this kind of change, primarily because these rides do not invade potentially dangerous areas of stress. Nevertheless, their judging technique reflects the experience of veterinarians in the more rigorous contests.

All of us interested in this sport owe a debt of gratitude to the small community of veterinarians who have given so much of their time, and have concentrated their training and abilities on the project of developing technical as well as more refined general parameters for judging these contests. The progress of this sport in the past twenty years simply couldn't have been possible without them. And the knowledge of horses under stress, which has been accumulated and assimilated by horsemen as well as by the medical profession, has been of inestimable value to the future welfare of horses.

Judges

The balance of this chapter is devoted to specific comments on judging for the benefit of non-veterinarian judges and trainers. In general, management is well advised to have a veterinarian in the judge's position first, last, and always. It is hoped that he will have "done his homework" relative to this sport, because it is admittedly a very specialized field of knowledge. From the point of view of "liability," a veterinary judge represents a valuable safeguard for management.

Nevertheless, a few good horsemen (by this we mean individuals with *actual experience* in the saddle in endurance and/or competitive trail riding under competent judges) are of considerable value to the progress of the ride. Because of their riding experience, they are often able to observe things that a veterinarian might not be expected to pick up unless he is also a good rider. The winning horseman-judge can use his knowledge in these highly esoteric ways without neces sarily giving away his own personal-training or riding secrets. We reiterate that *actual equine experience* for your judge is a must. Most veterinarians are more specialized in dogs and cats and consequently would have to do considerable work to be qualified in this field of judging.

Rules

Different kinds of contests require different tactics and techniques of judging. Judges and contestants should be accurately and adequately informed in advance by management what kind of contest is proposed. There is absolutely no quarrel with the management that decides to let the time winner take all the prizes with no other consideration for selection, provided the contestants and the judge know that is what is desired. Similarly, there is no quarrel with the management that decides to let the winner be determined on the basis of how he rides, how well he cleans his horse, or anything else, so long as the rules are clearly understood by judges and contestants.

1. So, first of all, require the management to show you a good set of rules, one with which you agree without equivocation. If the management cannot do this, then by all means turn them down, because you are exposing yourself to nothing but trouble and grief.

Assuming that the judge is going to be involved in an endurance or competitive-trail ride of the type that has developed in the past twenty-five years in the United States, we find it simple enough to define several cornerstones for establishing the judge's tactic and technique.

Cornerstone A: The degree of difficulty that has become popular in endurance rides in the United States is of such a nature that every reasonable modern technique for determining fatigue available to the judge should be pressed into service. There is absolutely no room for guessing or "eyeballing" or otherwise estimating without sound basis for decision. This means it is necessary to examine telltale membranous tissue (in the nostrils, gums, and eyes particularly). This also means that consideration of both relative and absolute temperature (under severe conditions), and certainly pulse and respiration (under all conditions) are necessary, including the character of the heart sound, even though there is still much to be learned in this area.

Cornerstone B Observing horses, like human athletes, during and after stress periods has taught us the fundamental lesson that there is a considerable difference between fatigue and sickness. *The key consideration is the rate of recovery.* It takes time to recover from being sick. It also takes time to recover from being fatigued. But in the first case, significant recovery is measured in weeks or days, whereas in the latter case, a significant recovery is measured in hours and not infrequently in minutes. Therefore, we should not only be watching for specific condition at any given moment in time, but also the rate of change in condition. A poorly conditioned horse, for example, will become fatigued sooner than a fit horse. A poorly conditioned horse will also require more time to recover. Time is a significant factor in trail-ride-competition judging in a uniquely characteristic way. If a contestant with a good horse comes in to a check stop in a hotly contested 100-mile-one-day ride and is vetted out in 35 minutes while some other contestant is vetted out in 45 minutes because the judges are pressed or for any other reason, the difference in apparent recovery could be very critical. Given well-conditioned horses and tight competition, precision of judging must also include precision timing. This is a very important point for management to have in mind.

Recapping the first two cornerstones of judging, we find that *the judge has to have time to feel the contesting horse to his satisfaction —with his hands, his thermometer if necessary, and his stethoscope, but there must be precision in all respects, especially in the time factor.* This brings us to the second rule of good judging.

2. The judge should be satisfied that management has made proper provisions for placing him in a good position to observe the contestants on several occasions during the contest. He should also be satisfied that he can get close enough with enough time to do the job.

Cornerstone C: Disagreeable situations should be avoided for the simple reason that in the long run they never help anyone and serve absolutely no constructive purpose. Yet disagreeable situations can and do arise during contests of all kinds. It is worthwhile to consider carefully the source of these situations and try mightily to set things up in such a fashion that they are as infrequent as possible. This brings us to the final, basic rules for judges.

3. *In the case of disagreement among judges:* Before judges agree to do the job in the first place, it should be clearly understood by all that there is a senior judge whose word is final in all cases. Disagreements among judges should not be publicized because this only serves to undermine the confidence of contestants in the whole sport.

4. In the case of disagreement between a contestant and a judge:
The judge should solicit the opinion of another judge as soon as possible in any doubtful decision. The rules should so state that if any two judges agree on a decision, that is final. There is not enough time or energy during these contests to handle disagreements in any other way. Many judges feel, as the result of disagreeable experiences with certain kinds of rare contestants, that a contestant can be disqualified at any time with the specific concurrence of opinion of any two judges.

5. Management and judges should make sure the contestants are just as familiar with the rules as the judge is expected to be. It should be understood that the rules are the final point in any discussion or disagreement, and the judge is the sole interpreter of the rules on that occasion.

6. The judge should be satisfied that management will stand behind him in a pinch.

Since most of these cornerstones and rules are largely a matter of discussion between the management and the judge during the time the judge is considering the offer to judge the contest, we shall assume that these considerations are properly accounted for and all is well. This leaves us nothing more to do about judging than to attempt to bring interested persons up to date on the techniques that good judges have developed in the past few years for differentiating among horses subject to adequate degrees of stress in endurance and/or competitive trail riding.

Techniques

We do not attempt to set down specific standards or even specific techniques because, obviously, circumstances such as the season of the year or the geographic location of a given contest must be taken into account. Our point is to explore the art of judging enough to allow newcomers to appreciate some of the fine points and old-timers to reconsider the subject with an organized overview. It is also invaluable to any contestant to understand as much as he possibly can about judging so he can present his horse in the most favorable light possible at all check points. This unique relationship between judge and contestant, handled in the open way that it is, has been largely responsible for the laudable progress in setting new records while at the same time setting new standards for the safety of the horses.

Under the heading of "co-operation both ways" we have observed that in competitive trail rides, with no exception that comes to mind, the judges have done all they could to help each and every contestant complete the ride with as much style as possible. This is a truly remarkable state of affairs, for which we can only salute every competitive trail-ride judge we have ever known. Endurance-ride judges cannot be quite so "generous," but they are still remarkably co-operative with the contestants and will help in any way they can. The judge-to-judge and judge-to-contestant relationship in this sport makes most other sports pale by comparison!

No matter whether a simple award is given for arriving at the finish line first, subject to the horse being in reasonably fit shape after the contest, or whether the judge is expected to pick the most fit horse from a certain designated group, based on time of arrival, age of rider, weight of rider, type of horse, or anything else, the problem is essentially the same in every contest of this type. *The judge is expected at some predetermined point in the contest to be able to pick the horses on a 1, 2, 3 . . . basis to the Xth place on the basis of fitness and readiness to go on.*

The judge who will be most successful (and least embarrassed after the ride is over) is the one who has taken the time to develop adequate systems for determining degree of fatigue in a horse in a contest in which fatigue is the prime aspect.

The systematic acquisition of data during a contest involves careful planning on the part of both judges and management and a considerable amount of dedicated assistance to the judge during the contest on the part of capable, well-briefed secretaries. Currently the maximum spread of information that a judge might reasonably collect would be:

1. A good general description of the horse. This is frequently done by use of an outline of a horse on a piece of paper that has space for the name of the horse, the rider's name and address, and the contesting number. It would also contain space to state the age, type, breed, height, weight, and other specifications of the horse. Certain blemishes, marks, or old injuries, etc., can be recorded on the outline in certain kinds of contests in which riders are encouraged to declare any sores, wounds, etc., which could be observed to the horse's detriment later in the contest if not known to exist beforehand.

2. A planned report sheet, which allows for entries of general observations at the judge's discretion in columns or otherwise, as well as more routine observations at each check point.

9. At a well-managed endurance or competitive trail ride the horse may be expected to get a more thorough physical exam than at any other time in his life. Here we see Richard Barsaleau, D.V.M., having a close look. When Dick is not judging, he will probably be found "among the top ten" just about every time he rides. That's experience!

The North American Trail Ride Conference has excellent sample judging sheets. Many other well-established rides have more or less similar judging sheets, and are usually happy to help a new ride. Although they will volunteer this kind of help, it is courteous to offer them some reasonable contribution to help defray expenses if you don't simply join up as a member.

The preliminary examination: We have found that it is worthwhile to have a systematic way of looking at the horse. A judge could, of course, adopt any order he chooses, but we have found the following procedure to be quite satisfactory and, therefore, offer it with our reasons for this order.

1. Stand back and look at the head, noting the general character of alertness and quick readiness to respond to outside stimuli by responsive movement of the head in general and of the ears in particular. We would expect the eyes to be bright without seeming the least bit glassy. We would complete this phase of the examination by having a look at the eye, nostril, and dental tissue, and by a wave in front of each eye to be satisfied that the horse is not blind. We have explored this subject in more detail in the chapter on physical therapy, and therefore do not go further into detail here except to say that in most cases this examination can help in spotting any drug influence in the candidate.

2. Standing at a little distance from the horse (at least twenty feet away), take in the whole animal with the eye. Be conscious of the impression the animal makes about his tendency to be well balanced and catlike or poorly balanced and clunky. Have him moved about on a straight line away and toward you, in circles both ways, to detect any tendency to favor one leg over the others. Of course, the obvious thing is to note any bobbing of the head in rhythm with the movement of the legs. Beware of the possibility that two fronts or two hinds may be sore and not be able to show much individual signs of soreness through any significant bobbing of the head. In cases of doubt, resorting to hoof testers is not a bad idea. The judge must also be alert to the handler's way with the horse. *Much can be concealed by a knowledgeable handler.*

3. A detailed examination of each leg and each foot is a must for the endurance-ride judge. Careful feeling for heat or soft spots or minor swellings or resistance to flexion in joints, etc., is an integral part of this phase of the examination. A trail-ride judge who does not do these things is either not sufficiently trained, experienced, or interested to do a good job.

4. The pulse and respiration are taken. Do not worry if the horse has already done the required moving around. If he is in condition, this amount of activity is quite incidental. The pulse can flutter or increase sharply momentarily. It is wise to wait a few seconds after finding the pulse to be sure you are getting a steady pulse.

With regard to respiration, the judge can sometimes get a reading rather nicely by asking the handler to hold the horse while he stands at the side in front of the flank and counts breaths by watching the lower belly in front of the flank. It is worthwhile to listen with the stethoscope and hear the pattern of breathing. It takes only a moment to hold the stethoscope at the windpipe as well as on the chest cavity to spot any restriction in the breathing.

At subsequent examinations in the course of the contest, the judge may very well skip some of the detailed aspects characteristic of the first look, but he will, as a rule, follow the same order in making certain observations. This is very helpful to the secretaries who are attempting to help him. He will be looking for any obviously abnormal conditions—pulse in excess of 150, respiration in excess of 150, or convergence in rate of pulse and respiration, or a characteristically bad respiration such as panting or broken wind. But the judge is not instantly alarmed at any observation taken immediately after a horse arrives at an inspection station. Some horses can be emotionally oriented to the contest and reflect this in excitement that is observable with a stethoscope. Their riders may have brought them into a check point too smartly, or there could have been some problem with another horse. Any number of situations can bring about high readings at a check-in. The significant thing is to note the rate and degree of recovery.

Converging rates of pulse and respiration can spell serious trouble. If you assume an at-rest pulse of 40 and a respiration of 20, you see a ratio of 2:1; a horse coming to a rest stop could easily have a pulse of 100 and a respiration of 60 or 70 and be in a very normal range. After 30 minutes these figures would probably recover to 60 and 30 respectively, still in the range of 2:1. As a horse approaches the limits of fatigue for his present condition, the respiration will rise faster than the pulse into undesirable ranges. For example, the respiration might go up to 120 while the pulse is also at 120, and in certain situations you may observe an inversion of the ratio in which the respiration exceeds the pulse. In a suspected abnormal case it is a good idea to let the horse rest for five minutes and have another look after some brief opportunity to settle. If the respiration rate remains high, be prepared to observe that individual closely, because respirations should begin to recover even in the first five minutes after arrival at a check point. At the outgoing time the respiration might not approach the ideal 1:2 ratio with pulse, but it should be clearly less than the pulse, and if you have arbitrarily selected a "cut-off" pulse rate of 70 or so, you are probably judging in a safe range, all other things being satisfactory.

10. Part of the continuous pattern of gaining new knowledge for the benefit of horses everywhere. Here we see a patient contestant waiting to have his blood pressure taken.

Recoveries

A horse in good physical condition will begin to recover his breath so fast that you can count it going down while trying to get the respiration rate. It will perceptibly slow down right while you are counting. This is one of the most reliable single indicators we know that "all is right with the world." Although the pulse is a bit slower to go down, it follows the same pattern within five or ten minutes.

Pulse. The pulse is best taken with a stethoscope. The earpieces of the stethoscope are bent in such a way that when placed in your ears the earpieces should aim at the center of your head, not the base of your skull. This is how you can tell you are wearing them properly. The diaphragm or listening cone is held lightly but positively against the horse's skin. Do not rub it against the grain of the hair. In moving from place to place on the horse's body, you may slide it lightly with the grain of the hair, but you will be obliged to lift it rather than attempt to slide it against the grain of hair.

Stethoscopes vary from the simple "Army surplus" variety in the ten-to-twenty-dollar range, which are perfectly satisfactory, to electronic models with amplification by electric means, which may cost several hundred dollars. We have found that the electronic model is useful in helping beginners to detect particularly interesting sounds that they might not be able to pick up with a simple mechanical stethoscope. Otherwise, the simple models are fine, and almost indestructible, which is an important consideration around a stable.

The heart sounds are best heard when the diaphragm is placed on the near side of the horse behind the elbow. In foals, the point may be a bit higher, but still well forward on the side of the body behind the shoulder. The pulse is normally a solid-sounding two-beat sequence, with the second beat being somewhat louder than the first. There should be a neat space between the beats. A ka-plunk—ka-plunk—ka-plunk would be a phonetic description of the sound with the normal intervals for a healthy untrained horse. A poor heart sound would be a light kaplunk—kaplunk—. A trained horse over age 4 and under age 20 will probably range from 30 It has a very positive quality. The overall pulse rate in a healthy horse over age four and under age 20 will probably range from 30 to 44, with stallions running on the low side, geldings slightly higher, and mares on the high side. A pulse of 40 would be close to an average.

With training the pulse tends to become slower as well as more positive, and may be as low as 24 or 26 in some great athletes. It is not uncommon for a trained horse to have an at-rest pulse of 24 to 32. This means a contraction of the heart about once every two seconds. The big muscle can do a great job with practically no strain working at this rate. A pulse of 60 at work is still very good. This means a contraction of the heart muscle once a second, still very comfortable. A pulse of 150, on the other hand, means the heart is contracting 2½ times a second. It is obvious that at that rate there isn't much time for the "relaxing" phase. What muscle is going to "relax" 2½ times a second?

The pulse may also be taken visually or with the fingertips. These observations will be of a surge of blood moving through an artery causing a slight bulging in the tube as the crest of blood passes. The points on the body where these observations may be made are: first, along the jawbone where the artery comes up from the throat latch area and crosses the bone. This spot is found with a light touch of the fingers. You would be wise to use the hand you normally do not use—that is, a right-handed person has a bit more sensitivity in his left hand, and vice versa.

Another excellent spot is in a groove on the underside of the tail, approximately four to six inches from the root. This is particularly convenient because you can get a pulse with your fingertips while waiting for the thermometer reading. You can also observe respiration by watching the flank from this position. Finally, you have a direct sensation of the rhythmic agreement of pulse and respiration. They will not be the same speed, but they will be in some rythmic relation such as 40:20 or 40:30 or 40:36. This last reading would be both rare and not very good. You can imagine any natural combination up to 100:50, 100:60, 100:66, 100:75, 100:80, and we stop there.

Quality of the Heart Sound

The heart can beat too hard as well as too fast. A "plunk" in the stethoscope might be all right, while a "thump" would not be. When there is excessive pressure on the valves and heavy pumping, the stethoscope will yield sounds suggesting a leak and a driving contraction. A phonetic description of the sound might be a th-h-h-*ump*—t-h-h-ump-*ump*. This is the last stage of identifiable sound before the horse gets what we call thumps. In this stage the heart is not necessarily moving too fast, but so violently that you can see the thumping through the side of the horse from a distance of several feet away, and you can actually hear it while standing that far away. We have indicated in Part IV, Chapter 1, the emergency measures a horseman should take in this situation.

Skin

The condition of the skin is a unique clue to the condition of the horse if you can read it. There is no part of the body that loses its elasticity and tone faster than the skin in sickness or in fatigue. A good horseman can get a book full of information by grabbing up a handful of skin and just feeling it. So feel a lot of horses in varying condition and you will tune your own hand in a way that defies any book. Watch for leathery texture or the feel of a chamois. Stiff is bad; flexible is good.

The skin can have varying conditions of moisture from clammy, disagreeably moist and cold, to very hot and dry. Different parts of the horse can have different skin temperatures simultaneously, such as a cold shoulder and hot legs, or a strangely cool flank and a hot belly. We cannot go into the ramifications of these skin observations here, but we do feel an obligation to call your attention to the amazing ability of skin to give you messages about your horse's condition.

Transitional Tissue

The mucous membranes in the nostrils and eyelids should be salmon pink in color. If they are light, almost white, the horse is probably anemic from some disease or inappropriate food. Paleness in the membranous tissue in the gums suggests poor blood over a long period of time. In the eyes and nose, redness is to be expected after severe exertion as long as there is no fever (which can also cause redness). Liver problems are reflected by a yellow color in these same membranes. Blue suggests that the blood has not oxidized properly and contains an excess of carbon dioxide. Red spots or streaks in these membranes are often associated with infectious diseases or blood poisoning.

After a horse has exerted himself extensively, all of his faculties slow down. He cannot recover as fast as he might. This includes how the blood performs in removing used materials and replacing them with fresh. If you observe a deep red or brown tone in gum tissue and you press with your thumb hard for three seconds or so, the color, whatever it is, should be restored in the same amount of time that you pressed. Given the colors indicated here, if the time is slower, the horse is approaching his limit.

With all of these observations it is an excellent idea to keep in mind what each condition would appear to be in a healthy horse in a good state of fitness. For example, the skin would feel soft and firm, not leathery or weak, and it would snap back smartly when you pull it out. Similarly, the gum tissue would appear nice and pink and would recover its color almost instantly after you stop pressing on it.

You will become very skillful after you have observed many horses in various states of fatigue while keeping in mind what a fresh horse would seem like relative to any observation you wish to make.

11. Long after most of the riders are sound asleep the judges wait for late arrivals. Judging takes a lot of effort as well as expertise. This is the Washoe Lake stop in the Virginia City Ride.

4

Condition—Meaningful Judging

By Kerry Ridgway, D.V.M.

Much has been written about the value of pulse and respiration in evaluating the condition of competitive horses. These values have become so ingrained that they have come to be placed on an undeserved pedestal of infallibility.

I have ridden and judged too many horses with good P&Rs (pulse and respiration) who were "out of gas," some with many careful miles left in them and some that didn't have two miles left before having to hang it up for the day.

These animals will show P&R failure in a more subtle way. They lag behind or just hang at higher acceptable limits with no ten- or fifteen-minute change.

Therefore, in the judging, especially of competitive horses when stress is not as great over a given distance and a given numerical score is required, it behooves us to evaluate the many other, more subtle, factors of condition available to us. When combined with pulse and respiration, a much more meaningful evaluation is afforded.

These factors include, but are not limited to, the character of respiratory quality (including auscultation), state of hydration, musculature evaluation, impulsion and co-ordination, character of sweat, gut sounds, mucous membranes, and attitude (willingness). With a list like this, why hang your hat on P&Rs only?

Let's spend a few minutes on some of these facets to see what is necessary to put them to work for us.

Respiration Quality

We have all witnessed the horse who arrives at a given check point with a heaving or gasping or very slapping type of respiration indicating that the animal is having a more difficult time bringing the needed oxygen-carbon dioxide exchange to ideal levels. Another type is the animal who must breathe very rapidly because it breathes very shallowly (pants) in order to effect recovery.

These may very well recover to acceptable limits with the ten- or fifteen-minute recheck. It is my contention that these animals are not as efficient and desirable from a work-output standpoint as the animals who breathe deeply and regularly in the recovery phase and can be scored accordingly.

Those with slapping, heavy, gasping, irregular, or otherwise stressed respiratory character will often exhibit congestion if carefully auscultated by an experienced veterinarian.

Hydration

Hydration is a characteristic widely used and abused. The common practice is to pinch the skin and record the level of hydration. The fault here lies in the whens and wheres of such practice. The practice at best gives limited data, since many horses have poor skin response under ideal conditions even before the event starts. Thus a few guidelines are in order.

The skin response is best in skin areas near the heart and becomes slower and slower the farther up the neck toward the ears one progresses. To be of any value it must be evaluated preride and written down as a baseline.

The neck and head need to be straight. If the neck or head is curved toward the examiner, the response will be slower and conversely if bent away will be more rapid. The skin should be tested at the shoulder, lower neck, and midneck.

This response must then be co-ordinated with the saliva present in the mouth. The horse with poor skin response but copious saliva present *cannot* be considered significantly dehydrated since saliva production is one of the first things to cease as a mammal undergoes dehydration.

Musculature Evaluation

Much can be learned by careful pre-ride visual and "hands on" evaluation of muscle tone. A subjective evaluation is based on muscle firmness, definition of muscle groups, and overall weight status. Decide whether the animal is underweight or overconditioned. The latter denotes an animal that has been overfit and has no fat reserves to draw on. Thus he metabolizes his own protein when in stress, leaving him with a short, dull, "burned out"-looking coat.

More ideally, the well-conditioned horse should have firm muscles that stand out in definite groups. He should have some firm fat palpable over the ribs. Slight rib outline may still be discernible. His coat should exhibit gloss and the appearance of healthy hair. When this type of animal moves, the musculature should appear to contract and relax smoothly without the appearance of jiggling or muscle-boundness.

The horse with excess weight will usually move with the musculature seeming to almost flop around.

Once you have made your subjective evaluation, record it on every horse on a one-to-five scale. You may use one rating on palpation and another one the way he moved with respect to muscle and fat covers if you wish further breakdown. Refer back to the initial rating every time you see this animal to see if your evaluation continues to correlate with his performance.

The horse who arrives at a check point with tremors, typically in the muscles of the lower shoulder, flanks, or thighs, has experienced more stress than those who do not. This I feel to be true even if the tremors do dissipate within the recovery period allowed and can be scored accordingly.

At the ride completion, fairly deep palpation of the muscles of the croup, posterior thighs, chest, and shoulders will often reveal muscle soreness. The horses with such muscle soreness will usually move in a more rigid, stilted, and shorter-gaited manner. With a practiced eye and hands you have then added one more valuable parameter to your evaluation of condition.

Mucous Membrane and Capillary Refill

Much has been said, written, and utilized in evaluation of these characteristics, so let's just review the highlights.

It is imperative that a pre-ride check be noted of membrane colors and the number of seconds required for the capillaries to refill after firm thumb pressure is exerted to the gums for a few moments.

Are the membranes of the eyes injected? Is there any evidence of jaundice? Is conjunctivitis present? Remember, many horses trailered in open or dusty trailers will have a lot of irritation present by the time they arrive at the base-camp site.

Are the membranes of the mouth a healthy pink or is there evidence of anemia? Horses on high carotene (as in fresh alfalfa) diets and many Appaloosa horses will have a slight normal yellowish color imparted to them.

As the ride progresses the capillary refill may change from a normal one-to-three seconds to a stress-indicating five-to-ten seconds. This gives the examiner valuable stress-condition data on what is happening to the horse's circulation and toxemia status. The stressed to sick horse will progress through stages of congested membranes to jaundiced or cyanotic membranes. In addition, the scleral vessels of the eyes may become enlarged, dark, and tortuous —that is, injected—as stress progresses.

Bear in mind that these must be evaluated against initial examination for comparison, so I emphasize again: Put your findings in writing.

Sweating

The sweating mechanism is the horse's best means of maintaining normal body temperature. Look out for the rider who tells you he has a really tough endurance or competitive prospect because it never works up a sweat. He is either very unknowledgable, has an unconditioned horse or a horse with a problem, or is an unmitigated liar.

The unconditioned horse will generally exhibit a lathery type of sweat often with an unpleasant odor. In contrast, a better-conditioned animal will sweat a clear and often copious sweat with a not unpleasant odor.

Lack of sweating in a hot, stressful situation is prima-facie evidence of dehydration and impending fatique. It should be recognized that the first sweat even in a well-conditioned horse may be somewhat frothy due to accumulated dirt, grooming oils, and other foreign material on the skin.

Gut Sounds

As a horse enters into long-distance stress, its cardiovascular system becomes primarily concerned with oxygen and nutrient transport to tissues and transport of metabolic wastes from musculature. To accomplish this, circulation to the gastrointestinal tract is lessened and peristalsis decreases as stress increases. The highly stressed equine will have a total absence of bowel sounds. Monitoring abdominal sounds through the course of a ride can then provide the examiner with valuable evidence of the state of condition of the animal. Moreover, it provides a valuable basis for advising the rider as to whether the horse should be fed at all during or immediately post-ride.

The horse with an absence of peristalsis is basically unable to effect digestion and would be prone to colic (especially if easily fermentable foods are consumed).

Attitude, Willingness, Co-ordination

Even though these factors are basically subjective, to the experienced eye they can be the most valuable of all in evaluation. This is true because they encompass how all the previous mentioned criteria are affecting the individual equine. All previous criteria provide the refinement necessary to predivide a scoring system, and these three provide the insight necessary for allowing the horse to safely continue the ride. They are sufficiently self-explanatory so that only a few statements need to be made.

Attitude in the resting horse can be very misleading since many excellent horses go into a state of total relaxation or even sleep at examination points. One must, therefore, place his emphasis on the horse's attitude when he is trotted out. This may even require that the evaluation be made under saddle rather than "free" trot out.

Lack of co-ordination will usually manifest itself in the tired horse as shortened stride, increased stumbling, toe-dragging (especially of the hind feet), increased interference, two-tracking or cross-tracking (feet crossing midline while in forward progression).

In summary, we've tried to define many factors that can be utilized in scoring the horse in condition category. It cannot be too strongly emphasized that one should not hang his or her hat on any *one* criterion but must

Evaluate the Entire Horse!

Rider Name _____ Horse Name _____ No. _____

	Preliminary	1	2	3	4	5	6
Pulse and Respiration	P/R P/R (Incoming)						
	P/R Recheck						
	P/R Recheck						
	P/R Recheck						
Mucous Membrane and Capillary Refill	Cap. Refill (sec.) (sec.) ___	___	___	___	___	___	___
	A ☐ Membrane OK	A ☐	A ☐	A ☐	A ☐	A ☐	A ☐
	B ☐ Injected	B ☐	B ☐	B ☐	B ☐	B ☐	B ☐
	C ☐ Toxic	C ☐	C ☐	C ☐	C ☐	C ☐	C ☐
	D ☐ Cyanotic	D ☐	D ☐	D ☐	D ☐	D ☐	D ☐
	E ☐ Icteric	E ☐	E ☐	E ☐	E ☐	E ☐	E ☐
Hydration	Skin Resp. (sec.) (sec.) ___	___	___	___	___	___	___
	A ☐ Saliva Present	A ☐	A ☐	A ☐	A ☐	A ☐	A ☐
	B ☐ Saliva Absent	B ☐	B ☐	B ☐	B ☐	B ☐	B ☐
	C ☐ Slight Dehyd.	C ☐	C ☐	C ☐	C ☐	C ☐	C ☐
	D ☐ Moderate Dehyd.	D ☐	D ☐	D ☐	D ☐	D ☐	D ☐
	E ☐ Marked Dehyd.	E ☐	E ☐	E ☐	E ☐	E ☐	E ☐
Bowel Sounds	A ☐ Normal	A ☐	A ☐	A ☐	A ☐	A ☐	A ☐
	B ☐ Minimal	B ☐	B ☐	B ☐	B ☐	B ☐	B ☐
	C ☐ Absent	C ☐	C ☐	C ☐	C ☐	C ☐	C ☐
Respiratory Character and Quality	A ☐ Deep and Regular	A ☐	A ☐	A ☐	A ☐	A ☐	A ☐
	B ☐ Shallow or Irregular	B ☐	B ☐	B ☐	B ☐	B ☐	B ☐
	C ☐ Panting	C ☐	C ☐	C ☐	C ☐	C ☐	C ☐
	D ☐ Labored	D ☐	D ☐	D ☐	D ☐	D ☐	D ☐
	E ☐ Pulmonary Congestion	E ☐	E ☐	E ☐	E ☐	E ☐	E ☐
Musculature	Muscle Tone *(ALL CHECK POINTS)*						
	EXC. GOOD FAIR POOR						
	☐ Excess Weight Muscles OK	A ☐	A ☐	A ☐	A ☐	A ☐	A ☐
	☐ Good Weight Tremors	B ☐	B ☐	B ☐	B ☐	B ☐	B ☐
	☐ Under Weight Muscle Soreness	C ☐	C ☐	C ☐	C ☐	C ☐	C ☐
	☐ Over Conditioned Muscle Cramps	D ☐	D ☐	D ☐	D ☐	D ☐	D ☐
	Coat Quality: Tying Up	E ☐	E ☐	E ☐	E ☐	E ☐	E ☐
	EXC. GOOD FAIR POOR Azoturia	F ☐	F ☐	F ☐	F ☐	F ☐	F ☐
Sweat	A ☐ Yes	A ☐	A ☐	A ☐	A ☐	A ☐	A ☐
	B ☐ No	B ☐	B ☐	B ☐	B ☐	B ☐	B ☐
	Character:						
Coordination	A ☐ Excellent	A ☐	A ☐	A ☐	A ☐	A ☐	A ☐
	B ☐ Good	B ☐	B ☐	B ☐	B ☐	B ☐	B ☐
	C ☐ Fair	C ☐	C ☐	C ☐	C ☐	C ☐	C ☐
	D ☐ Poor	D ☐	D ☐	D ☐	D ☐	D ☐	D ☐
Attitude and Willingness	A ☐ Excellent	A ☐	A ☐	A ☐	A ☐	A ☐	A ☐
	B ☐ Good	B ☐	B ☐	B ☐	B ☐	B ☐	B ☐
	C ☐ Fair	C ☐	C ☐	C ☐	C ☐	C ☐	C ☐
	D ☐ Poor	D ☐	D ☐	D ☐	D ☐	D ☐	D ☐
Temperature							

PART II

The Horse

12. Cougar Rock is the name of this Arabian stallion, son of Bint Gulida and Bezatal, two of the greatest specimens in this sport. He is shown here in 1974 being held by Ed Johnson's wife at Squaw Valley. On this occasion Ed piloted this horse into the Echo Hills vet check with a pulse of 64 and respiration of 44, about as low readings as anyone has ever seen among the top contenders. He was in first place at that time, but Ed had to give in to pain from previous injuries in a horse-training accident, and pulled out 15 miles from the finish line. This represents an ideal endurance horse with breeding closely related to Arabs that won the Army tests during the 1920s.

1

Selection

Selecting an endurance horse is not a complicated process, but it is specific. You must first have a distinct impression from some distance, then at close range, that the horse is bold, unafraid, and a winner at heart. Horses of this type have a certain way of looking off across the country. They are not necessarily the dominant beasts in the pasture, but they do not take backtalk from other horses. They are not prone to be herdbound. They seem to enjoy working in new country, and generally give the impression of being observant. Curiosity is a good sign. As a rule they seem to like people, and, when trained, will go where they are aimed without being foolish. They are never reluctant unless something specific such as a shoe is bothering them, and, when asked, will go like the wind without urging. In competition, the horse has no tendency to stop unless you signal him to do so.

Where to Look

Before we go further into this subject we will call your attention to the fact that we are now talking about endurance horses. As we have already intimated, we feel that any decent horse ranging in size from a reasonable pony to a good-sized hunter would be potentially satisfactory for competitive trail riding as long as he conformed generally with our specifications. Because endurance riding is more specialized and more demanding, we must concede that Arabian horses have, as a breed, done very well. There have been winning Thoroughbreds, Quarter Horses, Appaloosas, and crossbred animals, so we repeat that the fundamental qualities are what you should be looking for regardless of anything else. Thinking in practical terms, we probably would not go looking for our ideal horse in a big, fancy stable where the horses are essentially mollycoddled and overfed from birth with little if any opportunity to practice the "art of *enduring.*" These places are obvious sources for the country's finest show horses, but the difference between show horses and endurance horses is, to put it bluntly, chasmal. It is a strange fact that although Arabian horses have proved themselves over and over in this sport, probably due to their thousands of years of heritage of the toughness of desert sands and winds, American breeders of Arabian horses can boast about the breed but take little if any credit for the actual winners.

We are aware that several people have gone into Nebraska and found excellent endurance prospects, paying from five hundred dollars to over two thousand dollars for them. We have also heard of occasional good buys in rural spots in California. The state of Washington, also Idaho, ought to be especially good hunting for top-quality endurance prospects. If you are looking for a horse, it would seem to be a good idea to go to a few of the leading riders in this sport and solicit their advice. Occasionally they have a horse for sale. In this instance, of course, you must know you are probably getting a cast-off for some reason or another, so you should check very carefully. In eight years we tried to produce some tough, high-class endurance horses. We think we had about ten young horses for sale over which we had adequate control as breeders and growers. From the ten we would say we might have produced three qualified endurance horses. We bought and sold many horses, and among forty or fifty, possibly as many as three more qualified endurance horses passed through our hands.

Occasionally a horse that has done well in endurance riding and actually has a working record comes up for sale. In such cases, you have to be sure the horse is not burned out or suffering from some failing condition of the lungs or is not simply weary. Horse tradin's still horse tradin'!

It is a very good idea, when you go shopping, to verify your judgment by soliciting the independent opinion of a good horseman who is not at all involved in the deal.

When we went to look for Linda's great endurance horse, Bint Gulida, we first decided on an Arab as our probable first choice. We traveled over twenty-five thousand miles in three big swings across the country, crisscrossing into twenty-five states, actually looking at over fifteen hundred horses and examining nearly seven hundred in detail. After that experience we wrote an article for the *Arabian Horse News* (January–February 1961) entitled "Twenty-five Thousand Miles of Questions and Answers." Naturally we stopped and visited at many of the most prominent Arabian studs in the country.

At that time all we had to go on was what we had heard about the sport and our practical experience with large numbers of horses traveling up to a thousand miles into the Far North of Canada on geological and geophysical expeditions. We would have to admit that we were accustomed to picking "good likely-looking horses" in "good condition," selected at the start of each summer season from 120 more or less wild ranch horses. In examining the hundreds and hundreds of Arabian horses that were proudly paraded before us in most elegant circumstances, we became aware of the simple fact that we literally couldn't see them through all the fat that so many breeders and judges seem to confuse with substance; yet in their own world that fat seems, unfortunately, to be necessary to winning ribbons. Additionally, many of them had been subject to two circumstances that would almost certainly keep them from completing any rigorous training program. First, from having been ridden too young, there was too much chance that their feet would flatten and lose the necessary concavity that is the source of strength in the one conformational area more punished than any other part of the horse. Second, because they had been stabled in any slightly bad weather, they had been softened so much that only a kit full of medicine would sustain them. And most of them had already been subjected to enough medicines and various drugs for every little problem to support a small pharmacy.

We were approaching a state of disillusionment when we arrived at an isolated horse farm in Iowa. There were about five nice-looking horses in a 160-acre pasture that we noticed as we drove in the yard. The owner was expecting us and had some iced tea waiting. It was a very hot day in July. These horses, it turned out, had been bred under the watchful eye of a very controversial figure, Carl Raswan, and were direct descendants of W. R. Brown's great stallion Gulastra, the source of those horses that won the 300-mile Army races in the 1920s. In keeping with classical tradition, these horses were not ridden until age four. As a matter of fact, the horse that immediately caught our eye was a mare whose total training to that day comprised of being halter broken and allowing her feet and teeth to be examined by veterinarians from the excellent school at Ames. We were looking at Bint Gulida for the first time. She came right over to us and looked us over with just as much seriousness as we were looking at her. She was about four and a half and had never been in a barn, winter or summer. She had never been in a trailer, but she had stood on many a cold winter day with her tail to the wind when it was blowing forty miles an hour and snow was flying through the zero-temperature air. She was well sprung, but basically lean. You could see her. She was well let down. But now we are getting ahead of our story.

13. Witezarif, one week before the Tevis Cup Ride in 1976. Note that he carries a bit more flesh than Cougar Rock did. We think, all in all, that this is probably a better "tune."

Head and Neck

Beginning at the horse's head, let us consider the construction that seems suitable to endurance riding. The mouth should be tight, without any sagging lip. The nostrils should dilate easily and be large. They should be mounted on a face that is clean-cut and joined to a good, clean, wide throat latch for high-quality breathing. The eyes should be wide-set, clear, and large. Be very wary of any liquid seeping out of an eye. If it is coming out of two eyes it may be just a simple localized sickness such as a cold. But in just one eye it could indicate something chronically wrong and related to breathing inside the head. You should be satisfied that the horse can see *well* and has nothing wrong with its eyes. The ears should be somewhat hairy inside, good-sized, and mounted in the traditionally accepted way, not too close together and not too far apart.

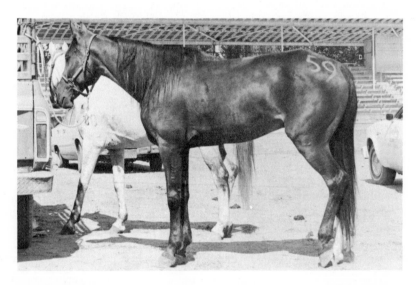

14. Witezarif, the morning after the Tevis Cup Ride in 1976, which he won for the sixth time! He placed second in 1974, first in 1970, '71, '72, '73, '75, and tied for first in 1976 with the horse standing behind him. That horse is Champion, who also won the Haggin Cup for best condition.

They should be characterized by an almost continuous, individual movement, somewhat like a pair of matched but independently working radar antennae, not fixed in any position.

The horse must be equipped with sound, well-constructed teeth, not for the ride, but for getting some good out of the food it must have in the months before the ride. It must have no bad habits such as wind-sucking (cribbing), nodding, or weaving.

The head must be mounted on a good neck of medium to long length. A short neck is not associated with good balance. Many of the winning endurance riders are looking for a long, light neck and a small head. The neck should fit on the shoulders with a clean, well-defined look. The neck that is longer on the top than on the underside (avoiding a ewe-necked appearance) will tie into a strong back. The withers should be well defined to hold the saddle, but not too high. The windpipe in a good neck appears loose with a well-defined jugular groove. Listening at the windpipe you should hear a gentle swishing sound, no rough sounds at all; and there should be no mucous material in the nose, especially in only one nostril.

Body and Legs

The shoulders should be constructed in such a way as to allow a free and easy long stride necessary for sustained speed.

The top line of the horse's body should parallel the bottom line. The ribs should be well sprung. The girth should be good-sized for the overall size of the horse. The distance around the flank, even in training, should tend to be an inch or two larger than the girth in circumference. The horse must not tuck up at all because it interferes too much with deep breathing.

The croup should be medium length and somewhat sloping. A very flat croup, although highly desirable according to some Arabian breeders, is generally a significant fault. A horse with such a croup will have his legs set behind him rather than under him. This generally goes along with too long a loin area often involving a depression in front of the point of the croup, which, in turn, gives a weak back. On the other hand, sickle hocks, associated with too much slope in the croup, are also undesirable, as they indicate a lack of driving power as well as a fundamental mechanical weakness.

The tail should be set clean, not low, and not tucked in. It should ride freely.

We shall go into considerable detail with legs and feet in the chapter on shoeing.

Age

To be ready for training, the horse must be at least four years old. It will take about eighteen months of careful feeding and at least a year of training to be really ready. You may enter one or two light competitions during 'this period for experience for both yourself and your horse, but we would prefer a horse six or eight years of age and would work with the right horse if he were as much as twelve years old. A good endurance horse properly cared for and skillfully handled should be a high-class performer well into his teens.

Size

Obviously the horse has to be big enough to carry the weight. With Arabians this probably means a lower limit of about 14.2 hands in height and 800 pounds in weight. It is hard for us to imagine a horse over 16.1 hands and over 1,100 pounds handy enough to do the job.

Some readers might remind us of Red Camel, a very large horse trained and ridden by Richard B. Barsaleau, D.V.M. This horse, nearly 17 hands and probably weighing 1,250 pounds, placed in the top ten of the American River Ride (50 miles) and in the top ten in the Tevis Cup Ride (100 miles) in 1977. This certainly establishes that the right big horse can do it, but we see this as more of a tribute to Dick's superior horsemanship and dedication to detail than as an argument in favor of a big horse. In fact, Dick chose to work with this horse to see if he could make both an endurance horse and a candidate for three-day combined training.

Natural Freedom

There should be a certain natural freedom in the horse's way of moving, which one would develop as much as possible in training. A little horse has to move his legs so fast that it is hard to get him into an adequate rhythmic speed that can be maintained. On the other hand, a large horse tends to wear down too fast toward the end of the ride.

The Perfect Horse

In summary, it seems safe to say you will never find the perfect horse. Therefore, you will probably do best if you have some firmly established priorities with respect to what you insist on and what you may be able to do without when it comes to the details of conformation and mental characteristics of the horse you want.

Colonel John F. Wall wrote several excellent books on horses in the years before World War II, including the much respected *Practical Light Horse Breeding*. One afternoon, sitting on the big veranda of a fine old hotel in Camden, South Carolina, with a mint julep in his hand, he summarized his ideas of a good horse by saying that a person really is not picking a horse, he is picking a problem. The question comes down to this: What problems are you willing to work with?

The one problem you can do without in all endurance and competitive trail riding is any kind of difficulty whatsoever with the two front legs from the knees down. There must be no problem with interference or weakness of any kind. By comparison, very few problems arise with the back legs.

A basically good body—one that contains a good heart and lungs, with no digestive problems—and one that will hold a saddle properly is a big plus. If you can find a good head on it, so much the better. That body has to drive those legs uphill and down and you have to stay on it uphill and down. So much for the physical characteristics.

Mental characteristics are equally as important. Again it is a matter of simple fact that you are choosing a problem. What kind of problem can you do without?

Choosing a horse is a simple enough process when you think about it.

Good Luck!

2

Training and Conditioning

You would probably agree with the general observation that the sum total of the experience any animal—or, for that matter, any person—has is its training up to that moment. Every experience becomes a part of the pattern of training, and the quality of training depends on how the experiences are accepted or assimilated by the individual.

Earliest Training

With a horse, training—or, if you prefer, experience—begins with birth. Many people, having some element of control over the birth of a new foal, will prepare a special stall, be ready with hot and cold water, towels to wipe the little critter off with, a veterinarian on call in the event of any irregularity of any kind (who will probably be called anyway, just to be sure), and a plan of total vigilance allowing the mare no time to herself at all. We used to be very much that way. We recall a very humorous situation in which a good and very experienced brood mare we had purchased well along in foal (pasture-bred, so there was no idea of the date of breeding) lived with us on a hillside pasture on the Palos Verdes peninsula outside Los Angeles. Night after night, when the occasion was deemed imminent, one of us would spend the night in the barn in a sleeping bag, but nothing happened. Then one morning we were sure the mare was going to foal, so we both kept watch on her as she moved heavily around in the three-acre hillside enclosure picking at any little bits of grass or shrubbery she could find. At a distance there was a good-sized bush just over the top of the rise in the pasture, and she was accustomed to saunter over there behind the big bush and disappear for a little while. Suddenly we realized we hadn't seen her for a while. Panic!

We hurried over the fence and across the 150-foot distance to the bush, and there big as life, our fine old mare was standing eating the last of the placenta. Her foal was propped up on one elbow, very alert to our arrival, looking in our direction confidently as if to say, "Well, Mom, we did it!"

We suppose you could say *we were getting the training* that time. At any rate, we simply decided to leave things alone. Shortly the foal got up, not too awkwardly, staggered a step or two, then seemed to get the feel, and moved straight to the mare's belly. With a couple of firm, commanding bunts, the little creature was "locked on" and getting that first, vitally valuable special fluid that comes ahead of the milk. The mare stood co-operatively until the new foal backed off a step, and then she turned carefully and began to clean off the foal's neck, still wet and sticky-looking. Shortly after that she worked around to the foal's rump, and, with a systematic "knowhow" impossible for a human to duplicate, she began working on the tight anus. Shortly afterward we noted the foal discharging a few little balls of compacted fecal matter—and all systems were go!

That foal was a bold, self-confident little rascal right from the start. He never had any trouble of any kind. No colds, no coughs, no scour, no tangles in the fence, and today we would say we have to *thank the mare, no thanks to us,* because we probably would have made her nervous by hovering over her. We would have taken the placenta away and buried it. We would have wiped the foal off and possibly denied the mare a secretly natural experience vital to the total sense of motherhood. We would have been holding him up, "helping him" find the tit with our do-good drive, and just fouling up the whole natural experience as fast as we humans possibly could.

There are thousands of people in America today who have brood mares. The vast majority of them are of one mind, and the thinking goes more or less along these lines:

1. My horse is too expensive to take chances with. I can not afford to "let nature take its course."
2. It is inhuman not to try to give the "poor" mare every bit of help we can. I could never forgive myself if something happened to her simply because "I didn't care."
3. Everyone knows that many foals are born and turn out just fine

that would almost certainly have died at birth or soon thereafter without modern medical help. If it is available we have a moral obligation to use it.

The greatest horsemen we have ever known take issue with these ideas on all counts; and after years of embracing these ideas in less and less degree, we finally concur with the principle of natural birth, even when the foal dies and could have been "saved." You have to have a good deal of faith in the Creator, but it pays off.

Because of the prevalent attitude of breeders in America we have thousands of useless, sick, unfortunate young horses with weak legs, weak backs, and weak heads cluttering up the equestrian world, needing more or less chronic assistance from veterinarians just to stay on their feet. It is a well-established fact that Americans have generally taken breed after breed of animal, dogs particularly, and brought them to a condition of near total degeneration. If the dog has a long nose, breed for a longer one. If he is inclined to be big, breed him to be bigger. If he has long hair, breed him to have longer hair.

Senator Federico Tesio of Italy is widely acknowledged in horse circles to be a highly successful breeder of Thoroughbreds as he has produced an extraordinary number of winners of steeplechases and flat races and many sires of great horses. He has been known to place several very valuable young colts together in a pasture to "fight it out" when most horse owners would have them separated completely, fearing the slightest scratch, to say nothing of a broken leg! When asked about this, his response was a simple observation that the horses could choose the best one better than he could.

What we are saying is that there is little point in training a horse not worth training; and most horses born today have been subjected to so much weakening experience from birth that among Thoroughbreds the big winners number only one in several thousand each year, while the vast majority break down either skeletally, muscularly, or mentally before they see their third birthday. Among Arabian horses, for every remotely acceptable endurance prospect there are thousands of fat, useless little creatures with no future beyond being a very expensive "pretty pasture pet." These are the stark, unhappy, unpopular-to-say facts. And it is our opinion that there is little use in putting thousands of hours of training into an animal that simply hasn't got what it takes.

If you are fortunate enough to find a horse that has been left to nature's ways almost entirely and has not been weakened by too much indoor living (in barns), too much rich food (pellets, rich legume hay, sweet feeds, overindulgence in supplements), too much protection (shots for every little thing, medication for any reason, blankets, leg wraps, tonics, bracers, corrective shoes, special fly oils or sprays, etc.), you may have a chance to come through a good endurance ride with some joy. If you have to work with a horse that has been subjected to the kinds of experience we have cited, your job as trainer will be much more difficult, and success much less likely.

There is an old saying that a good horse makes a good trainer. *True.* You might think that these remarks should come under the topic of selecting the horse. The point we are making is that a very considerable, if subtle, form of training, most important to a winning horse, actually comes from other horses and begins with his very first experiences in life.

In pursuing this concept of horses training horses before humans get a crack at it, we should give some consideration to a belief held by many old-time horseman and not a few new-time horsemen as well. We are talking about "first foals"—that is, the product of a brood mare the *first* time she has ever had a foal. The idea is that, as a rule, these little horses are not as good as subsequent "products" out of the same mare. There are many subtle considerations here, among them several that come under the heading of training.

Exploring the whole subject would require more space than we can devote here, but we must touch upon all phases of this proposition at least in passing. First, since most mares do not have the experience of living in a band with a stallion, but, to the contrary, are kept away from stallions for fear something will happen to them such as getting kicked or otherwise hurt, the actual encounter at the moment of breeding is traumatic and consequently potentially upsetting to certain glandular and other natural functions that would not bother a more experienced mare. The argument against the first foal starts with conception.

During pregnancy the new mare must undergo remarkable and substantive physiological adjustments to accommodate the foal, which are just "old hat" to the experienced brood mare. Point two against the first foal.

At birth, horsemen frequently observe the mare rejecting the strange thing she has produced and "needing help," the very kind of help we have already criticized. Point three against the first foal.

In the months of suckling, the mare, in the presence of other mares in the brood pasture, either is overprotective or pays little attention to her progeny. She never allows the little creature to explore, or conversely, she lets some other larger horse literally run the poor little thing to death. A more experienced brood mare makes a more stable mother and allows for a balanced set of experiences for her offspring, which means far superior training.

Once weaned, a little horse is very fortunate if he can live with a few of his peers in a big pasture with some older horses, especially if the older horses were once good performers. Retired "old pros" can teach a young filly or colt a great deal in the first two years of their lives. They make invaluable "baby sitters."

If you are fortunate enough to be undertaking the training of a four-year-old horse that has already been trained by some fine horses from birth, your job is much simplified. You will be working with an animal that is just naturally self-confident, surprisingly experienced in strange little ways you will come to appreciate if you are sensitive, and, to top it off, loaded with good sense. If, on the other hand, the horse was "helped" into this world, protected from life in the raw, including other horses, protected from germs —protected, protected, protected at every turn—you can ride your heart out and probably never even finish a real endurance ride; more probably you won't even get to the inspection the first day! You will be staying home taking care of a cold, or his navicular bones, or something strange that you and the veterinarians can't quite figure out.

Early Experience

Now, as we go into the training that involves the intercourse of experience between horse and rider, we say: *A good horse is a good horse.*

If, for any reason, as long as you are reasonably skillful, the horse does not progress, or seems to develop weakness, or needs special attention, *get another horse.* You truly can't make a silk purse out of a sow's ear.

The difference between a competitive trail ride and an endurance ride must ultimately dictate significant differences in the training pattern. We will present all phases of training and presume that you can differentiate among phases based upon your objectives, the rides you want to enter, and the terrain and weather conditions you and your mount will face.

Considering a few differences between the two basic kinds of rides, we first note that the shorter endurance rides require speeds, often over very rough country, that would leave any competitive trail-ride management, judge, or contestant gasping with disbelief and disapproval. The longer endurance rides involve the strange experience of traveling hard and fast after dark, a situation never encountered in competitive trail riding. We have seen "experienced" trail riders literally frightened to the point of getting off their horses and stopping completely in a 100-mile, one-day ride because they had never thought to ride at night and they simply didn't dare to go on, even on a good, clean trail, to say nothing of slipping and sliding on a truly precarious trail where you or your horse could get seriously hurt, and you really do have to *depend* on your *good, fully trained* horse. Then, too, there is always an element of sportsmanlike gentlemanliness in competitive trail rides, especially among the old-timers. But this takes on a somewhat different color in big endurance rides, again especially among the "regulars" at the top end of the list. They have consummate respect for each other, but they give no quarter.

As a trainer, you can learn enough about judging and acquire a stethoscope and a thermometer so that you can measure a few distances and try various techniques with your horse to see what the shortest time is that you can cover 25 miles or so and have the best possible recoveries. You will eventually try galloping up a hill and then observe how long it takes to recover enough to go on within the frame of requirements that judges will impose. This compares rather well with how drivers of race cars work things out or motorcycle riders prepare for dirt contests. The proof is in the pudding, and training will certainly require you to be almost as good at judging as the judge you will ride for. He in turn must know almost as much about training and riding as the trainers and riders do.

Preparing for competitive trail rides is a bit more difficult than for endurance risks because you don't come down to the wire in the same way. There is room for opinion under these conditions, and your best bet is simply to get your horse in as good overall condition as you can, but do not set him up so high that he frets along the trail because he wants to go faster. He must present himself to the competitive trail-ride judge at all times as a well-conditioned gentleman. Experience at a few rides of your choice, and observing who wins, are invaluable in refining your training tactics.

There was a time in the early days of endurance riding when the horses were expected to be a bit "wild" because of their background and the nature of training. Not uncommonly you would see a horse while being inspected by a judge take a shot at him with a back foot. Today this does not happen and should not happen. In most cases such a horse would be eliminated by the veterinary committee before he started the contest. The endurance horse of today is actually tougher than those of twenty years ago, and also much better mannered as the sport enjoys the refinement of maturity. In the "good old days" the riders just jammed along. Today, to win, everyone knows you have to check your own horse's TPRs with precision, and as trainer, you won't like it if every time you insert the thermometer in the rectum you get your teeth threatened by your own horse!

Endurance involves hardship, and the horse must be conditioned in his mind to hardship. He must have the capacity, like a tough human, to "grit his teeth and pull through." Perhaps the most singularly significant training value in this respect is to let the horse stand out in all kinds of weather. We always did this, and never had a horse in training sick with any kind of medical ailment whatsoever. We must note, however, that a competitive trail-ride horse is often judged on appearance, and standing out as much as an endurance-ride horse does might just mean that he would not even place because he would look too scruffy. The reader will, quite obviously, have to use some judgment.

Endurance riding means covering country, and we should concentrate on making every ounce of energy work in a horizontal direction in the line of motion. The horse must learn to move with a daisy-cutting action over even country, and with a smart, effortless, nonstumbling motion over uneven ground. These lessons are closely associated with urging on the part of the rider. Make the horse move out at all gaits. Give him experience at good speeds over a wide variety of terrain. In general he will begin to conserve energy when he becomes a bit tired, but not too tired.

Endurance riding leaves no time for questioning where to go, so the horse must develop great confidence in both himself and his rider. A good exercise is to set out on a straight line in more or less open country and at some predetermined point, known only to the rider, turn at some angle, known only to the rider, and head off in another direction. This should be done at a brisk walk until the horse moves precisely on a straight line unless given a positive signal to turn. There should be no weaving whatsoever. When this is accomplished well at the walk, increase the gait to a slow sitting trot. The work is not complete until you can do this at near breezing speeds.

Having selected our ideal endurance horse and arranged the circumstances for as much "education" as possible from other horses before he comes to us for specific training, we come to the point of breaking or starting the individual. Since this book is not about general training, we shall touch only briefly on those aspects of breaking or starting that are particularly important to the endurance horse.

Further Development

First, boldness is desirable. Because our mount must have a lot of self-confidence, it follows that he must have a lot of self-respect. Therefore, *nothing,* absolutely nothing, in his early experience with his first rider should erode his sense of dignity. No throwing around, tieing him up, nothing that will have the least effect of letting him feel beaten or defeated. You may be very sure that no Kentucky Derby winner was ever made to feel defeated! And your endurance horse should be similarly respected.

Second, because endurance riding is an extremely disciplined sport, your horse should be trained, in due time, to do exactly what you want him to. He will allow you to throw the halter rope over his back, and he will step into the trailer on command. No fuss. He will drink out of anything from a rushing river to a paper cup. Ideally, he will lie down and relax when you ask him to, but for most people this can verge on a circus stunt, and so we make little point of it. The ultimate objective is to achieve a maximum efficiency through relaxed discipline; and as we have already pointed out, you have to use good judgment as you go along.

In the name of relaxed discipline we should point out that the trainer and/or rider should *like* the horse. If the horse is likable, the trainer and rider will naturally forgive him when he makes a mistake and will tend to be more relaxed. It is hard to imagine a successful team with a horse, however good, that the trainer and rider does not like more than he likes most horses. Moreover, it follows that this situation will produce a happy horse; and don't ever think a happy, well-disciplined, relaxed horse won't impress the daylights out of any judge! When the chips are down, the relaxedness and good discipline will not only pull the horse through the tough spots, but will also give him a clear edge with the judge perhaps even in a subconscious way, which can mean the difference between going on and being held back. This difference is sometimes a hair-line, razor's-edge proposition, and a likable horse will always enjoy a subtle advantage.

In the original manual we presented "an 18-month training program" for taking a 4½-year-old from scratch and building him up to being a prospective winner of a 100-mile-in-1-day ride as a 6-year-old. This was, of course, simply an idealized statement. We combined what we did with what we would have done had we the opportunity to do it over again and presented this as well as we could. The actual experience culminated with two 100-mile-in-1-day rides about 6 weeks apart. No horse, to our knowledge, had attempted two such contests in a single year up to that time. Most horsemen agreed then that one contest like that in a year was enough! Without any expertise other than several years of general experience and some good training from people like Colonel John F. Wall and Will Caywood, we trained as well as we knew how. A few days before the Tevis Cup Ride, Bint Gulida had a chance to go over the trail with Marko B, Ernie Sanchez's great winning horse. She then rested a couple of days and competed. Ernie almost won again! Bint Gulida could have placed second in all probability, but, knowing she was going, without precedent, to another contest 1,800 miles away and only 6 weeks from then, she was not pushed at all. She came in sixth. After 6 weeks of essential resting and easy riding, we took the mare to Oklahoma and won by the widest margin we have ever heard of up to this day—5½ hours!

This immediately set a pattern, and many riders in subsequent years unhesitatingly began to enter, and even win, more than one 100-mile-in-1-day contest. So we have changed this training chapter completely to reflect these new experiences. We feel that, today, training can be seen as more complex without being impossible. A good trainer can easily plan to enter a few lesser contests as part of the training. Then when he has the horse about as fit as it can be, he has a different training problem, that of maintaining a high level of fitness and eagerness almost constantly with peaks to match the dates of competitions. This, as the saying goes, makes it a "whole new ball game."

A word of caution. We have observed, as judges have, that many riders overtrain. This can be spotted by watching for various common signs of weariness. The animal's muscles and wind may be in great shape, but he is simply tired of it all and he shows it in the way he moves, stands, and thinks. One of the reasons Arabians do well in endurance riding is that they are smart. But we feel quite sure that in a very long race involving group discipline for many days, where you cannot choose your own way of going except within very narrow limits, the ideal horse would be a rather dull one, "a horse," as the famous Joe Back of packhorse fame would say, "that just don't care."

Meanwhile, because this sport involves considerable travel, and because the locations are often very remote, much attention has to be given to the problems of moving your horse and keeping him in circumstances that are often quite difficult. For handling these phases, which must be integrated thoughtfully into the training program, we refer you to the chapters on feeding and travel.

A Four-month Program

Let us imagine that we have picked up a good horse, green broke, and reasonably sensible at age 5. We have 4 months to get ready for a 100-mile, 3-day ride, 40, 40, and 20 miles. The average elevation is 2,000 feet and the total difference in elevation on the trail is 3,500 feet since there is a real mountain to climb on the second day. You will have to hike right along. Although the third day involves only 20 miles, you still have to count on averaging about 7 miles per hour to be considered. This is about par for many eastern rides and a bit more difficult than most western rides of this kind.

Speaking broadly, we want our horse to learn to be a gentleman who will go out and cover a good stretch of rough ground smartly and be looking for more. We want him to be a smooth ride with the ability to conserve his energy.

Starting on the first day of beginning training, we practice with consummate patience getting on and off until our horse *stands still* like a statue unless you give him a specific signal to go somewhere. Some people think the horse has to be a fiery charger. We think there is no harm in good discipline at this point. Let him get worked up later on in a self-controlled way or he just might use up too much strength jumping up and down.

We also begin to accustom him to being examined all over— legs and feet, belly, vital parts, dock, eyes, ears, nose, and mouth. We do not wrestle him down to do this; we simply practice great patience. We do not make the mistake of earing him or twitching him or snubbing him or in other ways trying to dominate him. We solicit his confidence. We do not do this because we are trying to be particularly humane, even though it is the humane way to go about it. We do it because our future winner has to *feel like a winner* and not like a beaten-down slave, a deadhead, or in horsemen's terms, a dog. We picked this horse because he was a winner type. He had that look in his eye and that way of standing in the pasture. We do not want to knock this out of him now or at any time (even during the heat of the contest).

When we finally get down to the business of riding after 10 or 15 minutes of handling and standing still, we encourage him to *move off smartly* at a good, long-striding, swinging walk. This gait alone may require our fullest attention for the whole 4 months. But it cannot be overemphasized because it is the most important thing our horse needs to be able to do in competitive trail riding. There is nothing more impressive to a judge than a good free walk at any time during the contest because the judge knows this is how you cover ground and not only save energy but also frequently gain strength when the chips are down!

Right here, at this most preliminary stage of training, we must point out a subtle difference between endurance riding and competitive trail riding. The big walk will impress the judge in competitive trail riding. The endurance-ride judge would not be influenced except to use this observation as an indication of how the horse is reacting to the grueling pace of the competition. So work for the big walk—5 to 6 miles an hour. You may ultimately want to train your horse to let you hang onto his tail (a common practice in endurance riding) while you both work your way up a big hill. If he can walk 6 miles an hour, he can slow down to suit you, pull you along, and really rest at your meager pace of 4 miles an hour.

Thinking about fast gaits and big strides and keeping rhythm going, it should be self-evident that this training can best be accomplished if the saddle is comfortable and the bridle, such as a simple snaffle, is uncomplicated or has no bit at all. And in tacking up as well as grooming and all other actions around a horse, there is a certain frame of mind that good trainers seem to have. It is manifest in the way they move and speak: usually not quickly but steadily, with not many words; always firm, always sensible, always sensitive; no wasted motion, no wasted emotion; lots of patting and encouraging, but no "loving" and "kissing."

To avoid boredom for both rider and mount, you walk a half mile or so to loosen up; then where the going is good you break into a good, free, exuberant trot, like a happy moose. So far we are not considering any unusual terrain. This stage comes a bit later. Right now you are working on normal, back-country conditions, relatively flat and decently wide, like a Jeep trail or an ordinary country road, not on pavement. You do not pit your green horse against any severe tests of strength, balance, or nerve. You are simply hoping to get him off on the right foot with a willing, confident, co-operative attitude so he will move along with freedom and interest in being alive and seeing country. Changing diagonals at the trot is very important to be sure of symmetrical development of muscles and balance and strength of back.

Galloping is fine, but not too soon or too much. Gallop to establish rhythm. Gallop to have a good time. Change leads regularly for the same essential reasons you change diagonals. But for a long time, lean on the trot for most of your speed and distance, and while doing this, make every effort to improve your own trotting technique. You should be so well balanced that you *never* need the reins for support. You should come down comfortably but *never* hard. Make the trot the smoothest, easiest, lightest experience possible for both yourself and your horse, like ballet dancing.

Whenever it is time to go, *go at the most comfortable and efficient and rapid speed that the chosen gait will allow.* This would be not less than 4 miles an hour at the walk and 8 miles an hour at the trot. The ideal speeds would be controllable between 4 and 6 for the walk, 8 and 13 for the trot, and 12 to 20 miles per hour for the gallop. We rely on the trot, but do not hesitate in the shorter rides to gallop considerable distances, changing leads every mile or so, and changing diagonals at the trot every half mile. Where a good endurance horse would fight you if you held him to a 4-mile-an-hour walk or an 8-mile-an-hour trot or a 12-mile-an-hour gallop, you would want your competitive trail horse to travel this way willingly when he has to come into check points within a minimum-maximum time limit. In thinking about the 100-mile-in-3-day ride, we have to give our horse the experience of striding out and of going at good speeds. But for preliminary general training, other aspects have to be considered, and there is still a difference in training for an endurance ride. You can appreciate that a good competitive trail-ride horse could probably never win a big endurance ride; and conversely, a good endurance-ride horse would not win a competitive trail ride. What is the old saying? You can't have your cake and eat it too.

Broadening Experience

Now that we are beginning to have an eager traveler who will let us listen to his heart and lungs and let us examine his feet to our heart's content, and look up his nose, and take his temperature, we go looking for some hills.

Out in the hills we look for the little narrow creek crossings, the narrow trails, the logs across the trails, a bridge or two, the expected obstacles, and we introduce the horse to all of these with the same firm patience we used in making him stand still for mounting. If he seems to want to refuse to go through that water or over that bridge or into that narrow place, hold him firmly but with not too tight a rein, facing the "problem" without fighting him. Soon (within thirty seconds to two minutes normally) you feel him relax under you because he is getting bored. He cannot give his attention to that "scary thing" ahead for much longer. You move him closer, letting him sniff and smell, maybe even snort, to his heart's content. Hold him lightly but firmly facing up the trail until he relaxes and will continue in the direction you have chosen.

Whipping him only reinforces his idea that the obstacle is scary. Holding him quietly to the task will create future good habits. Often going out on the trail with another well-trained trail horse is the quickest way to success. This is especially true if you want to teach a horse to swim. So much for dealing with individual obstacles. It's like the story about Paderewski and playing the piano. It is not the moment of the concert; it is the six hours a day of practice. For you, sensitivity is more important than strength.

Moving up and down hills at various speeds, you give your horse time to figure out how to put his feet down. Give him a free rein whenever possible and let him use his head. Remember that you can go fast uphill and down if you do it right. Going down, if you encourage your horse to bring his back feet under him and raise his head and neck to keep the weight off the forehand, you can trot at a good speed, and you won't hurt his front legs with bucked shins or anything else. The trick is to take your time. Let the horse have a chance to figure things out. Be light in the saddle and encourage him to get his feet under him when the going gets tough.

Going uphill is very useful as both a wind builder and as a muscle builder. Galloping evenly uphill (not lurching or lunging) and trotting within close limits is an excellent wind builder, and, of course, the most positive experience the trainer and rider can have when it comes to sensing rhythm. It is a big mistake to let your horse lope uphill until he wants to stop from fatigue. You do not want to set any bad habit patterns, nor do you want to set any permanent psychological limits.

There is a way a horse seems to dig his feet into a hill at a good, hard-driving walk that is very desirable in training, and equally in certain difficult situations on a ride. In the early stages, it is a good idea to stop long before the horse wants to while climbing—say, every two minutes or so for 20 or 30 seconds. Good judgment in picking stopping points pays off. Watch ahead and pick a shady place, a level spot if possible—any better-than-average spot along the trail. If you don't find one conveniently, turn the horse on the hill until he is standing sideways. If near a cliff, be sure he is facing the drop, not with his rear to it. Feel him from the saddle. When you become accustomed to feeling him from the saddle in this very positive experience you will find you can develop your own ability to sense him in more subtle situations later on. There should be no signs of heaving, blowing, shaking in the legs, panting, or any evidence of loss of interest in the surroundings or what he is doing. Take it easy, but be firm. In a few easy experiences the horse will grow remarkably in his ability to go up and down short, steep pitches or long, steady grades. You can tell how much he can do if you know your TPRs well. Again, we suggest you be sure to read the parts of this book that review these factors from the judge's point of view. In the early stages you should be particularly careful to watch for the relationship between breathing and the pulse. Your horse at the beginning would probably have a resting pulse of about 40 with respiration of 12–15, a ratio of 3:1. Working hard, a PR of 70–70 is close to a top limit. Letting your horse have time to build himself up pays off. Do not overdo it in the early stages. We do not want to baby our animals, but we must not defeat them psychologically either. Here again is where your good judgment cannot be substituted by any words of wisdom in a book.

After your horse has come up a good stiff hill about a mile long, but is still essentially fresh, push him smartly over any kind of ground. If it is even, he will begin to daisy cut; if it is uneven he will pick up his feet. Plowed ground is excellent footing for this exercise at first. By taking advantage of this combination of a hill and either good or bad footing, you can develop valuably efficient feet and conserve energy remarkably.

Refinements

At about this time in the training program, we attempt to develop as much smoothness as possible. This is done by making sure to maintain even gaits. Do not let the horse wander around. Where it is possible, ride in precise straight lines across the country to some predetermined point and then pick another straight-line course in another direction to another point. In this way the horse learns that you have the rudder hand, and he soon concedes you the piloting. This point has to be modified somewhat for big endurance rides because of the problem of traveling at high speed in the dark. Here the horse, because he seems to be able to sense quite well when a human can't see at all, is better off when allowed to pick the course than when trained to obey the rider's rein too closely.

The more time you get in the saddle at this stage, the better; and the more you use your legs and weight and the less you use the reins, the better. By using your legs we do not mean to kick the horse in the sides. Use of legs is confined to the slightest type of pressure with the calves and thighs and a slight but positive adjustment of your weight with relation to the horse's back—slightly forward to impel the horse forward, slightly back and down to slow him or stop, centered and light in the saddle to keep him doing whatever he is doing, whether it is standing, walking, or running. You could even think of these basic body positions like a gear shift.

The next significant step to develop the required smoothness is to concentrate on rhythm in all movements. Again, the cornerstone of the technique is a sympathetic but firm discipline. Having worked on even gaits so the horse does not move smartly for a short distance and then bog down slowly to a snail's pace only to be perked up again like a dude horse, we really achieve more than even gaits. We achieve a certain businesslike attitude on the part of the horse that will be very valuable in competition.

We now approach the small obstacles on the trail with the same frame of mind. Presumably we have passed the period when everything is scary. Now the horse will cross that little creek or that log, but too often there is a tendency to do it unevenly. The horse slows down perceptibly on the approach, then jumps the object and lunges forward after clearing it. We want him to move into the problem at an even speed, step over the obstacle or into it, and move away with the same evenness. This has nothing to do with "testing it to see if it is safe" and all that sort of thing that horsemen talk about. This is simply a case of learning to be disciplined and workmanlike as opposed to being undisciplined and silly about things along the trail. Every silly move, like stumbling, takes precious energy that the trainer must work to save.

One of the great secrets of rhythm may now be applied, which is the secret of rhythmic breathing. Ride to a good little hill with a flat place at the top. On this special occasion, let the horse, after being reasonably warmed up, gallop up the hill at his own speed. This is very important, because you want to sense the speed and rhythm that he himself selects. At the gallop, because it is fatiguing going uphill, he will adopt a motion that is in precise rhythm with his breathing. Count the cadence, "1, 2, 3, 4 . . . 1, 2, 3, 4. . . ." When you get to the top of the little hill, keep counting at the same rate. Change gaits to the trot and work to make the posting match the rate of counting established during the brief galloping phase. The horse will still breathe in rhythm with the trot and soon learn to do this himself. With luck, you can do this in one good try. It should not require more than four or five efforts to establish the idea in the horse's head. Then he will see how much easier it is to go, like a human athlete, in rhythm with his breathing. This trick alone is worth 20 miles or 2 hours in a one-day contest! And it is just as valuable in a competitive trail ride in terms of condition of the horse along the trail or at the end of the day. It is one of the greatest secrets that has come out of endurance riding. The Indian riders we know do this naturally. And there is a suggestion in *The Horse of Blackfoot Indian Culture,* a Smithsonian Institution publication, that this trick of rhythm was one of the reasons why the Plains Indians were able to outdistance the cavalry so often. There is no doubt that bareback riding at high speed just naturally puts rider and horse in tune with each other, both in breathing pattern and use of weight.

The whole subject of breathing for both horse and rider is, of course, vital in big competition of many kinds: hitting a polo ball; jumping a big fence; breaking out of a gate. All winners have a distinct pattern of breathing in these situations, whether they realize it or not. The trick is that mastery of the pattern early through understanding saves much time and energy during the training phase. Controlled breathing affects the attitude of the rider's whole body and in turn can be used with almost hypnotic effect to encourage a horse in a frightening situation.

We might think of training as dividing itself into 4 parts: (1) learning, (2) practicing, (3) conditioning, and (4) competing. Competition is a phase of training as surely as learning, since you and your horse will both learn every time you compete. Generally, we might think of the learning stage as one of concentration, and consequently probably not involving any really long sessions. The learning stage would ordinarily involve 4 or 5 sessions a week of 1 to 1½ hours each. With the average horse this could go on more or less continuously for 2 months. Then you would want the horse to take a bit of rest, perhaps a week off. You would then move into a practice-conditioning phase in anticipation of that 100-mile-in-3-day contest we have been aiming for. If we are looking forward to a 100-mile-in-1-day contest, by comparison, we would have the same 2-month learning phase at first, but follow this with a second 2 months of learning/practicing. This would involve 4 or perhaps 5 days a week (depending on the individual), with occasional rides of up to 4 hours on weekends or other convenient times. After 4 months we would get serious about the endurance horse and go into a practice-conditioning phase of 2 months, for a total of 6 months from the start, during which we might even go to a 50-mile contest just to get the feel of things. We might note that it is unwise to take your horse to too many short contests if you are preparing for a long one, because habits can form whereby he thinks he has done enough after some relatively short distance.

Rating and Practicing Distances

We are now moving out of the learning into the practice stage. Only two more points need to be made to round out the picture of training for competitive trail rides: (1) practice rating, and (2) be sure you have ridden as far as the contest requires and at the speed the contest requires at least once before the contest begins. Many people make the mistake of practicing over some relatively short distance. Then when the contest comes, the horse seems geared to the practice distance and gives out before the end. Another frequent experience is that the horse's back is not tough enough because of the short practice times, and it develops heat bumps after wearing the saddle for the time required by the contest, a problem that crops up frequently in competitive trail riding.

About rating, one could write many pages, but it would all add up to one thing. Pick a measured distance—say, five miles. At five miles per hour you could cover that distance in exactly one hour. Try it. If you come to a ditch, and the horse takes a few extra minutes to cross it, *make up the time*. Get to the end of your course on time no matter what the problem was and do not be satisfied with any excuse whatsoever for either yourself or your horse. Make yourself conscious of time by doing this often over a variety of distances. This will also contribute to the horse's attitude—a certain sense of urgency that will make covering the ground ultimately much easier than if you have to keep after him during the contest. Do not worry about his manners. He can be brought to do these things and still be a perfect gentleman.

It is ideal if you can have a course of 20 or more miles that is clearly measured and marked every 2 miles. Then you can plan to cover this at various speeds during the training program to help give you the feeling of estimating. The normal experience is to discover that every minute counts and you have to be conditioned not to waste time. It is far better to control the rest time by not wasting time along the trail than it is to be lax about details and have no time to rest when you really need it.

It is a great thing to be able, from time to time, to let out the throttle over a good distance. Endurance horses really like this. Some endurance riders say they like to test their horses once in a while over 20 miles or so. They cover the first 10 miles in between 30 and 40 minutes, depending on going conditions.

You will notice, if your training is proceeding well, that in approaching obstacles and in moving up hills your horse will work with his head surprisingly low. Do not discourage the horse from working with this uniquely low head carriage, which he will attempt to adopt naturally. It is like the specialized stances required for many sports and very valuable to the horse in this kind of contest.

15. Pat Fitzgerald tailing his horse in a 100-mile ride. Heading the official AERC list of riders in terms of total miles in endurance competition, Pat is well worth watching. This is not only a good example of tailing, it is also an excellent example of tack.

Leading—Driving—Tailing

The accompanying illustration shows Pat Fitzgerald "tailing" a horse up a steep hill. This is a practice that seems to be unique to endurance riding and is done quite often.

A good trainer will always have a horse that, early on, will lead well. This is useful on many occasions. It helps in loading a horse in a trailer. It helps in getting a horse around some obstacle that makes him wary. It is useful when he is sick. It pays off when you present your horse to a judge. We feel that having the horse lead well is, therefore, critically important.

Driving from the ground is also a worthwhile exercise. Many people even start horses by driving them first. Simply put on a bridle and possibly a saddle. Feed long lines from the bridle through the stirrups of the saddle back far enough so you can stand behind the horse and drive him while walking just as though you were in an old-fashioned buggy. Some endurance riders have extra-long reins so they can do this going up long hills.

This brings us back to tailing. Having a horse that will lead well and also drive, you may now simply use a halter rope or other long rope or a piece of leather or nylon the way Pat is doing in this picture. Grab the tail with the same or the other hand and scramble uphill behind your horse. The horse can actually rest while pulling you uphill this way, so everyone gains. You keep making forward progress, stretch your own legs, get up that nasty hill, rest your horse, and actually make pretty good time, all in the same maneuver. Be sure your horse can do this. It's a good trick.

TPRs

It is presumed that when you first selected this particular horse for training, you had a qualified veterinarian listen to the horse's heart and lungs to be sure they were sound and not bothered with some defects. It is interesting to note that if the heart and lungs are checked along with temperature at rest, and then the horse is exercised fairly smartly for only 10 minutes, any significant irregularities will almost certainly reveal themselves to a trained ear with stethoscope in hand.

Let us consider precisely how to make certain routine observations.

Temperature is observed with a thermometer. There are a variety of types of thermometers, from plain, old-fashioned glass models to very fancy, fast-working, metal-cased instruments. The price varies from about $5 to $50 or more. The inexpensive ones are perfectly satisfactory, but deserve a few comments about their use. Make sure you have a veterinary type, which is somewhat more heavily constructed than a similar instrument for humans.

If the thermometer you use requires a minute or more to do its job, and you find it inconvenient to keep your hand on it, you should probably tie a string to the little hole in the end so you can fish it out if the horse should work it in too deep because of some pressure from his tail. This rarely happens, and if you do lose the thermometer inside, there is still very little danger, since the horse's muscles are designed to extrude material from the rectum, not pull it in. The thermometer is almost certain to fall out. The worst that could happen is that you have lost a good instrument. The thermometer will tend to fall out a bit more frequently with the string attached. There seems to be just enough weight to cause it to slide out on many occasions when it would otherwise have stayed in.

It is not a bad idea, after reading the temperature, to place the instrument back in the rectum again for 15 seconds or so to be sure the reading is the same.

The actual placing of the thermometer is easily accomplished. Shake it down. Lubricate the tip a bit, most commonly by spitting on it, and after pulling the tail to one side with one hand, insert the thermometer with the other. If you do this smoothly and with no fuss, the horse will not give you any trouble. Try to stand very close to the horse's hip—not directly behind him—while doing this. This horse is unlikely to kick. He is more likely to simply try to move away or jump around or clamp his tail down. If you keep in close, you contribute to the horse's calmness, have more control, and are in a much less vulnerable position if he should try to kick. . Most horsemen wipe the thermometer, if necessary afterward, with the horse's tail hairs.

The normal to be expected for a healthy horse is between 100.0° and 101.0° F. We have seen horses with apparent normal temperatures as low as 98.5° and others as high as 100.6°. It behooves you to take your horse's temperature several times and get to know him personally. The temperature will vary some, depending on the time of day or how soon you take it after sleep. In the morning it tends to be about at its lowest—98.0° or so, rarely lower than that. Sickness is indicated as a rule if the temperature is lower than 98.0 or higher than 102.0°. That is in a horse at rest. The lower reading would be particularly serious in a horse at work, while the higher reading would be regarded as a good working temperature.

We have indicated the techniques for cooling in Chapter 13. It is generally wise to change temperature slowly until you become very skillful and your horse has experience in these things. Changes at the rate of one degree per 10 minutes are about as fast as you should shoot for. Until you have skill to avoid shock, you would be better to work at the rate of one degree per 20 minutes.

The technique of observing the pulse is given in Chapter 3, but here are some further comments and suggestions.

When you watch a judge take a pulse you immediately see he usually counts for 15 seconds and multiplies his reading by 4 to get the rate per minute. Many people conclude this is the way to do it. For the experienced judge working under the time pressure he must accommodate at a one-hour stop this is the best he can do, but it does not allow enough time for anyone to consider the quality of the pulse, which we regard as just as important to the trainer as the simple rate. We strongly advise that in taking both this reading and the respiration that you *dwell* on the observation. Take your time. Really listen. Really feel. You will be amazed at how much you can learn in a purely empirical way, particularly when you know what your horse has just been doing and what his other signs are. The judge does not know your horse or what it has just recently been doing. He only knows what he finds right there on the spot. You know much more than he does about the "circumstances"—that is, who just gave you a hard time on the trail, or that you felt your horse tying up only 5 minutes out of that stop and had to give up half an hour waiting patiently for him to "get it together" before coming in. If you really know some additional aspects besides knowing your horse, you have a great advantage.

The pulse may be felt or seen in the center of the chest when a horse is working. Very skillful riders can see this pulsebeat on a competitor while riding alongside or very slightly ahead, and, knowing their own horse's pulse or probable pulse, make a determination to challenge your horse by inviting you to "ride along" at a higher speed than you should at that time and consequently setting your horse up for an unfavorable judgment at the next rest stop. These very subtle things can happen, and judges will never be able to know when they happen; only contestants will, and among them, very few.

The pulse may also be observed between the bulbs of the heels. This may be difficult to detect by a beginning observer in a horse at rest, but if you trot a horse about 10 minutes and then place the tips of your longest fingers lightly in the cavity between the bulbs of the foot you will feel the surging pulse. This is very useful in detecting strains to the feet or legs while working. If, while riding, you feel your horse may have just twisted an ankle or suffered a bruise, you can feel a throbbing pulse in this area of the foot that is unique to that particular leg within 30 seconds of the injury. This can happen during western riding practice involving quick stops and quick turns. It can happen during jumping from landing hard or hitting a pole or quick turning. It can happen while hacking along a road and stepping on a bad spot, in a hole, etc. The horse will give a strong wince of an involuntary type as opposed to stumbling or otherwise having momentary trouble with one foot.

If this throbbing, digital pulse is picked up, the foot should be cooled promptly with water (within 15 minutes) or at least not worked anymore. Lead the horse rather than ride. Walk the horse rather than trot. You stand a good chance of helping him recover right then as opposed to letting the situation turn into a limp and lameness and a lay-up of from 3 days to a month. In the cavalry we wore big yellow scarves around our necks, which served many useful purposes, such as keeping dust away from the back of our necks. But in this situation we poured a few tablespoons of water from a canteen on the scarf, which was wrapped loosely around the lower leg. Counting on an entropically adiabatic phenomenon where the air, your water, and the scarf appear to be at the same temperature, the effect may be to cool the injured part enough so that you can go on within a few minutes and completely avoid further difficulty.

The easiest way to find the *respiration* is to stand just in front of the horse's flank and watch the movement of the side of the belly. If it is very low (under 10 breaths per minute), it may be necessary, while you are first learning, to put your hand lightly on the lower belly to feel the rhythm.

Another way to spot respiration is to stand at his head and observe the movement of the nostrils. The problem is that a horse often sniffs or holds his breath, making it impossible to get the job done.

The at-rest respiration will vary from as little as four to perhaps 30 or 35 before you suspect sickness. An at-rest respiration of 60 would be regarded as a sign of illness or something not right. It pays to know the individual horse in interpreting these observations. It also pays to couple the observations of pulse and temperature with the observations of respiration. A high respiration (70) with a normal pulse could indicate momentary fear or suspicion. A high (70) respiration with a pulse of 70 would suggest a fever or an imminently developing fever or colic. This condition with a normal temperature would indicate that fever is soon to come.

The respiration can have varying character. The conditioned horse's is deep and clean and very hard to observe at rest, because the deepness is concealed apparently longitudinally inside the body and does not require transverse variation in the rib cage. Whatever the strain, the respiration will give the impression of being deep and clean with no rasping sounds or other irregularities, certainly no coughing.

Veterinarians use the word auscultation to describe a way of observing respiration. This simply means pressing your ear or stethoscope against the horse in revealing places. The air goes in and out of the lungs with a very fine soft sound. Naturally this sound is intensified with exercise, but it still has a certain soft character if all is well. The technical name for this sound is a vesicular murmur. Sometimes this murmur can disappear if the horse is sick, but we are not concerned here with sickness. In the early stages of inflammation of lungs or air passages this murmur can become rough and harsh. If you apply your ear over the lower part of the windpipe in front of the breast bone and hear a harsh blowing sound, you are hearing what is called a bronchial murmur, and all is well if you have just been exercising your horse. If, on the other hand, you listen to the lungs themselves in various places with your stethoscope and hear the same sound, your horse may have some kind of lung ailment and a veterinarian should be called. If you listen along the windpipe and hear gurgling sounds that are called mucous rales, you are dealing with a potentially serious problem, which again indicates veterinary assistance. A shrill sound, almost like a whistle, might be heard, indicating very dry conditions. You might also hear a sort of friction sound like two rough surfaces being rubbed together. All of these odd sounds are undesirable. Listen for the soft vesicular murmur, and if you hear anything else, beware.

Assuming the sounds are all right, it is somewhat difficult to get the individual breathing faster than 80 breaths a minute, and more often the rate can be kept below 60. Given a few moments to rest, the horse that breathes this way can seem to go on effortlessly, all day long, with occasional stops long enough to take that one big, deep breath and get ready to go again.

The ability to recover by relaxing and taking one giant breath is characteristic of a well-conditioned horse. You often observe them after a stiff climb, breathing hard and deep. You stop and look around, both of you enjoying the scenery and the feeling of being alive; then your horse draws his body up under you with a big breath, and suddenly you realize he is quietly waiting to go on. That's a winner—in winning condition.

Another pattern of breathing is a panting sound as though the air just starts to go down his windpipe and comes back out without really getting to the lungs at all. This is almost what is going on. Under these conditions there is little exchange taking place, and if you were to observe the membranes in the horse's nose at that moment you would probably find them bluish instead of salmon pink. A horse that persists in this breathing pattern without improving is better left at home. A horse with good potential, on the other hand, that is allowed to develop this pattern, is in the hands of a trainer who might be better off taking up tiddlywinks because he apparently has no feeling for athletic activity.

Although we have, as judges, observed respiration rates in working horses as high as 200, a rate virtually impossible to count, our experience as trainers and competitors is different. Our best horses have rarely breathed faster than 60 breaths per minute at any time during the contest.

Basic Physical Problems

For all persons interested in the condition of a horse we recommend *Know Your Horse,* revised edition, by Lieutenant Colonel W. S. Codrington (London: J. A. Allen & Co., 1971). Although we do not subscribe to many of his remedies, we feel that his descriptions of normal structure and functions of the horse as a background for diagnosing various difficulties are superb.

Here are the characteristic experiences of trainers while observing TPRs in the course of the training period:

1. Temperature will rise more or less steadily during early training states. For example, on a 20-mile ride in 3 to 4 hours, if the temperature is taken every 5 miles, in theory you would expect something normal (say, 100.5° F) at the outset. At the first 5-mile check, temperature, 102°; at 10 miles, temperature, 102.5°; at 15 miles, 103.0°; and at 20 miles, 103.5°. By comparison, the temperature readings in the trained horse will in theory read like this for the same 20-mile course now covered in 2 to 3 hours: At the 5-mile mark (slightly higher), say, 102.2°; at the 10-mile mark (slightly lower than for the untrained horse), 102.2°; at 15 miles (still low), 102.2°; and at the 20-mile mark (starting to rise very slowly), 102.5°.

The basic idea is that an untrained horse will reveal a straight-line increase in temperature while a trained horse will show a rise to a working level followed by a long plateau at a constant temperature, which will finally begin to climb as the horse approaches his limit. You, as trainer, will observe your horse working up to an operating temperature just like an engine, rather soon, and hold this operating temperature for a long time, whereas the same horse originally showed you his temperature just going up and up the farther he went in direct proportion to the stress.

Of course, the trained horse will finally show a sharp rise in temperature as he approaches his own stress limit and becomes fatigued. Just before becoming exhausted, the horse will, as a rule, show a lowering of temperature. To inexperienced people this could seem as though the horse were in great shape. If, in training, you take him to the point where his temperature starts to go down from some normal working high such as 103°—that is, while you are still making forward progress—you have probably pressed too hard. No harm is done if you stop soon enough. But still, this is positive evidence that you were probably carried away and training a bit too fast. At this critical moment you may also observe that his ears have stopped that "radar" movement you have come to expect. His eye may even be a bit glassy. He may not be so interested in the surroundings as usual; and simultaneously he may

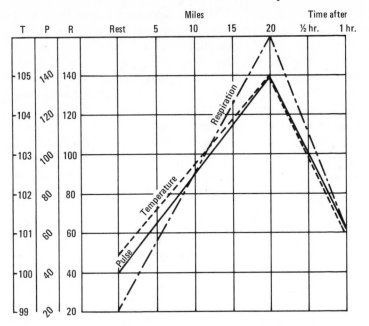

Fig. 1. This is a **hypothetical** graph to indicate the character of TPRs for an unconditioned horse. We have theorized what would be logical readings for an unconditioned horse attempting to travel 20 miles in three hours over average country.

You would see a temperature approaching 105°, a pulse in the 140 range, and a respiration in excess of 140. When the respiration exceeds the pulse, a judge would call this an inversion. This condition is to be avoided.

One-half hour after arriving at the 20-mile mark you would expect recoveries as shown, and an hour after, you would expect recoveries into a safe range in any healthy horse.

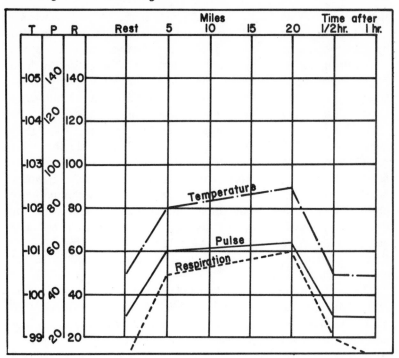

Fig. 2. This is a **hypothetical** graph to indicate the character of TPRs for a horse that has been conditioned properly for about three months or more. Note that all of his at-rest readings except temperature are lower as a result of training. At the five-mile mark he will have developed a "working temperature" slightly higher than an unconditioned horse, but he will have achieved a "working range" of TPRs that he can hold for a long time. This we call the "plateau"; and in competition we would take full advantage of this by holding a very steady and rhythmic delivery of energy.

Note the near complete recovery in only one-half hour. Finally, while the unconditioned horse needed three hours, this horse may be expected to do the job in only two.

step unsurely or unevenly, even stumbling here and there where he usually is very sure-footed. To the rider this stage is often revealed by the horse seeming a bit rubber-legged. Even though we are emphasizing TPRs at this time, we must not let attention to these limited scientific observations blind us to the many, many useful general observations that serve to reinforce our judgment and verify the conclusions that TPRs encourage us to draw.

2. The pulse of the unconditioned horse at rest will be slightly higher than it will be after proper training. Let us say the horse reveals a resting pulse of 40 as an untrained candidate. After being fitted up he may have a normal at-rest pulse as low as 34. It would be surprising if it were not somewhat lower than the ordinary pulse. The pulse will climb more or less steadily with work for the unconditioned horse, but for the trained horse it will rise quickly to some working speed and hold there for a surprising long time. A pattern like the temperature—temperature and pulse are closely related.

The unconditioned pulse might theoretically follow this pattern: at 5 miles, 65; at 10 miles, 90; at 15 miles, 115; at 20 miles, 140. This is a continuously rising pattern. Generally we know today that no benefit derives from working with a pulse of over 80 as a rule, but in the early days we established these figures before we realized that it is more efficient to train in lower pulse ranges.

We are assuming the same 20-mile conditions in terms of time as we did temperature. The conditioned-horse pulse might follow this pattern: at 5 miles, 60; at 10 miles 60+; at 15 miles, 60+; at 20 miles, 65. The plateau will be plainly apparent, but the inevitable rise with fatigue will still show. It will be lower, and rise less fast, but it will have the same basic character. The curves on the graph will be in the same family, in other words. The trick is to work in such a way that this plateau stage is made to last as long as possible for both pulse and temperature.

Evenness of movement, seriousness of purpose, confidence in his own ability, experience to sustain him through potentially frightening situations, and interest in going on all go to improve the pulse chart.

3. The respiration of the unconditioned horse will usually be considerably higher at rest than that of the conditioned horse. On

a 20-mile ride in 3 hours the untrained-horse respiration might follow this pattern: at rest, 20; at 5 miles, 55; at 10 miles, 90; at 15
miles, 125; and at 20 miles, 160. This is a theoretical picture, of
course, and these readings are highly undesirable. An untrained
horse, like an untrained man, will start puffing immediately.

The trained-horse respiration might follow this pattern: at rest,
6 to 8; at 5 miles, 50; at 10 miles, 50+; at 15 miles, 55; at 20
miles, 60. Again we see this same plateau pattern with the rise
at the end.

Of course, we would normally expect temperature to be the most
consistent measurement, changing more slowly than the other observations except near the limits of stress, when it can change up or
down with alarming rapidity. Pulse is next in steadiness. Respiration will move up and down considerably with speed of travel,
rate of climb or descent, frightening experiences, humidity, temperature of the day, apparent quality of the air itself (breezy or
very close), and the state of the digestive system.

We have not seen a horse whose temperature ranged over 105°
who did well in competition, even though no particular harm
seemed to come until the temperature rose to over 106°. Any
temperature over 106° in our experience indicates nothing but
trouble.

A pulse of less than 30 is so rare that it can indicate trouble in
most instances. Our attention was called to the amazing 26 pulse
recorded for an Epsom Derby winner a few years ago and reported to us by Alexander Mackay-Smith. He goes on to say that
some rare horses' pulses are even lower than this. In checking
hundreds of horses in various states of training, we have never
seen anything like this, and would have to chalk it up as unusually
rare. A low pulse of 32 sounds to us ideal and almost always goes
with a "good heart sound." This sound is characterized by a unique
distinctness, no light tick, no muffled quality, no irregularity of any
kind, with a good space between the systolic and diastolic beats.
Although the rate may increase, this quality of sound will remain
constant for any good horse in good shape. A pulse of over 100
does not go with a winning horse, although you may not be in
trouble until the pulse is considerably higher, possibly as high as
140. In recent years veterinary judges have discovered some ab-

normal heart sounds in some very good endurance horses and learned that these sounds do not indicate trouble per se; but we, as buyers/trainers/riders, would not want to be bothered with this possible trouble any more than we would with any other observable problem. We would get another horse.

When to Rest

There are old sayings to the effect that it takes much longer to build a horse up than to run him down. With slow-moving pack horses in the Far North working 100 days or a bit more, we had to watch closely to be sure they did not "loose bottom." It is customary on a big pack trip to give the animals a few days off every so often to graze and "put it back together," to use the current vernacular. Racehorse trainers, to consider the other end of the spectrum, have the same notions. The only difference is the time frame.

Feeding, training, and conditioning go together. Here we find the first real differences between competitive trail riding and endurance riding. In training for the toughest competitive trail ride in the United States you would have about the same learning/practicing stage and somewhat the same practicing/conditioning stage; but, of course, the actual competition is very different. Therefore we find ourselves at this point having to consider very divergent training procedures. You simply do not want your horse to be too eager for the slow, NATRC competitive trail rides or he will not be willing to go as slowly as you must go to stay within the minimum-time limit. If he is too well conditioned and too hotly trained he will strain so much resisting your restraints that the judges will not like what they find. Again, your good judgment must come into play.

Getting back to the idea of running your horse down, the idea involves all conditions, from long periods of time to a very few minutes. If you are working your way up a big hill, and have 30 miles to go after that, you are much wiser to spend a little extra time making sure the respiration stays in a normal range than pressing "till the horse has to blow," as the old-timers used to say. You will have spent so much horse if you let the respiration go out of sight that you can never make up for it on that day. By holding the breathing down, you will have saved a lot of horse to make it over the 30 miles beyond the hill. When we get to the part on riding the contest, we will tell you something about how experienced contestants can "have a bit of fun with each other" on a big endurance ride.

Enough to say that you have an excellent chance to do well in any contest if you are ready for it. In this case, being ready means knowing your horse. At the Indianapolis Speedway, or in a big boat race, or in any other contest involving speed, it is vital for the driver or pilot to know his car or boat or airplane or horse. It's all the same. And what can be known by understanding TPRs is so clearly valuable that a rider/trainer can hardly afford to do without it in this sport.

Some Danger Signals

It is probably useful to review those conditions observable by TPRs that indicate shock or near shock.

A temperature pattern as follows: rising to a high in excess of 105°, and rapidly falling. This is especially alarming if the temperature goes into a subnormal range.

A pulse pattern as follows: Rising, often with irregularities introduced that reflects stress, to a high in excess of 80 and then not showing recovery after half an hour of rest. A pulse rate of 10 per cent to 20 per cent lower than the horse's known normal at rest pulse. A pulse characterized by a heavy throbbing so that the heart seems to thump. A pulse characterized by a fluttering.

A respiration pattern as follows: a rate of X (say, 40) after work followed by a rate of X+ (say, 42) with a half hour's rest. While most respirations will go down immediately when you stop, you will occasionally observe a rise for a minute or two if you stop too fast. But a respiration that is higher after a half hour of resting is an indication of real trouble. There are two other kinds of respiration trouble: a panting accompanied by a rocking of the body that persists after 10 minutes of rest; and any breathing that seems convulsed or associated with strong contractions of the stomach muscles.

It is not a bad idea to have the competitive horse accustomed to take vinegar or oil or strong beer without resistance. In certain situations that can arise with some suddenness, the trainer could help the horse with a natural substance of known potentialities of efficacy. Many a hard-working horse has been saved from over-strain by a good shot of ale, for example. Let us imagine that you have been working your horse for some months and are generally pleased with the progress. You decide next Saturday to take him out for a good 40-mile spin. Your target time is 4 hours. The first 20 tick off beautifully. You rest a while, possibly 30 or 40 minutes, and then take off again. But at around 35 miles, the horse seems to be fading. You stop to check him out. PRs are not really too bad—a bit higher than you thought, but not really bad. You check him over, and suddenly are aware that his eyes are not looking out at things. They are inward-looking. He is not paying attention. Here a good, old-fashioned horseman's ob-servation tells you that TPRs may be in a reasonable range for the moment, but the horse is under more strain than you expected. You ease him home over the last 5 miles and get him in a good situation. That is the time for the ale! In the old days, many, many coach horses forced to move out at speed for one reason or an-other, were unhitched at the tavern. The passengers went in to have a glass of sherry by the fire while the horses went into a warm barn and had a bucket with a pint or so of ale offered while being wiped down and groomed. It was a most common finish for a race with the highwayman.

On another occasion, you have waited the usual time after feed-ing to take your horse out for a good spin. This day, for some reason or another and unbeknownst to you, the horse is not digest-ing quite as well as usual. Whereas we all know he needs to have digesting time for the blood in his stomach to do its work, this day the blood should be able to stay on the job a bit longer, but you are now requiring his system to do two jobs at the same time. A few miles down the road, the TPRs are not bad, but he just doesn't feel right to you. You get off and check again. Could be a bit of extra sweat, or perhaps not as much as usual. Something is differ-ent. Not quite right. You can't really diagnose anything specific, but he simply isn't performing up to scratch. What actually has hap-pened is that food, which ordinarily would be processed in his stomach, is not moved along the way it should. The digestive process has been prematurely disrupted on this occasion, and a situation something like conventional colic is developing. Here a good shot of half apple-cider vinegar and half vegetable oil (about a pint) can help rectify the situation in less than fifteen minutes.

In many situations while working with tired or overstressed horses, a trainer/rider can find himself and his mount so far from veterinary attention that he has to be ready with some simple basic remedies. The primary remedies, of course, are rest; slow, gentle movement; keeping the animal warm; being very calm; protecting the individual from any kind of weather extreme if at all possible (that is, getting in out of the rain, out of hot sun, out of wind, etc.). At night be sparing in the use of harsh lighting, especially if it is a limited form like a flashlight.

Conditioning and Competing

Most of the subject of competition is covered in the chapter on riding contests, but we feel that since many early rides may be considered as part of training and conditioning, we should consider a few final points, especially as they apply to the endurance horse.

It is not enough that your horse learns to be very rhythmic and go up and down hills properly if he is going into an open-ended endurance contest. You have to anticipate that riders, as in any race-oriented contest, will try to put you off in one way or another. You and your horse have to be prepared. These aspects of the contest are very minimal if significant at all in competitive trail riding, but they can be problems in endurance riding, especially in the very beginning and at the end. You might call this phase of training/conditioning, practicing discourtesy. Most riders traveling along together practice a number of "trail courtesies." These might include combinations or variations of the following experiences:

You all come to a gate. One rider gets off, opens the gate, and lets everyone through, then moves through and closes the gate. Normally it is courteous for everyone to wait until the gate closes and the rider is remounted and ready to go

Or,

A rider has some trouble with his saddle or other equipment and has to stop for momentary adjustments.

You should have your horse ready for any form of "discourtesy" you can imagine in any situation even remotely resembling these circumstances. You have just stopped your horse on the trail, thinking you are quite alone. You have to relieve yourself. You move over behind a bush just a step off the trail and try to "get things done" as fast as you can with your pants in one hand and the reins in the other. Suddenly a horse shows up moving slowly along the trail, but the rider sees you. He instantly, for whatever reason you might think, gallops right by you and speeds away. It could be that he didn't want to embarrass you. Your horse "jumps out of his skin." It's a case of your pants or the reins, and your horse goes charging down the trail. Could happen.

In most trail situations riders will try to guide their horses in such a way that they do not interfere with each other. During an endurance contest you may have your rhythm down pat and be moving very well on the "best horse in the contest" and you know it. You come up behind someone who is much slower, who happened to start in a heat before you. This person is a friend of another person who is your only real competition. For some reason—narrow trail, bad footing, any reason at all—you are held back two minutes, throwing your whole rhythmic pattern way off. In the meantime the slow horse has been resting before you came up behind him. You and your horse are impatient. Now you try to pass. The slow horse moves out at a good gallop, throwing your horse even more off his carefully controlled pace up to that time.

What to do about these situations? They are rare occurrences on competitive trail rides, but "old hat" on endurance rides among those people contending for top honors.

The answer is to practice with a friend so your horse can get some "experience" in these situations. You could easily anticipate them in your imagination and then do the best you could during the ride. But your horse needs a very odd kind of training in order to be counted on in these extremely annoying circumstances. So you and your friend go for a ride together. He drops back a hundred yards or so and you get off. He charges by on a prearranged signal. Your horse jumps and frets. You calm him and hold him. Then you reverse roles. When you begin to have things in hand, and your "training" is coming through, undo the girth on your saddle and go through the whole thing again. With a few chances to "work your training magic" on the upset horse you will have him standing still for you in all kinds of "pants down" situations. Remember what we said when we started this chapter. Practice getting on and standing very still. Well, this is more of the same thing. Having a fiery beast in this situation is very embarrassing! Naturally, you will do the same thing with an open gate where the horse has to move with you to follow the gate and be co-operative.

Finally, practice that ultimate control of rhythm so that if you find yourself "boxed in" you can cut back a whole gear or even stop until you can get things together *on your terms* later down the trail. There is a lot of time to "win" in an endurance ride until you get into the final ten miles. But this will be covered in the riding chapter.

Entering a few rides, then coming home to practice fine points that you discover you and your horse have to improve on is the final stage of conditioning and training. Again, we must caution: "Don't be guilty of overtraining." As your horse grows fitter and fitter, you will be riding him less and less frequently. Again, it is a matter of judgment.

Experience will reveal how many little things you have to account for; but it may serve a useful purpose to remind you of a few situations, and suggest through example some of the detail that you must attend to. The check stops are often crowded with other contestants and observers. Your horse has to be very tractable under halter as well as under saddle. You have to be able to lead him rapidly and quietly through narrow places and among other horses to get to a place where you can take some care of him at rest stops. He must be taught to ignore all distractions including large machinery, electric generators at night, and various odd automotive devices. A well-trained horse will be perfectly relaxed while one veterinarian is taking a temperature, another is listening to his heart, and a third is checking his breathing or taking a blood sample. Your horse should drink out of a paper cup, a Coke bottle, a canteen, suck water from a sponge, lick it off your hand, catch water from a hose, or stand and wait when there is no water.

For all of these remarks we should observe that in the hands of an experienced person, a good horse can be conditioned in 3 months to do a satisfactory job in a 100-mile, 1-day contest. On the other hand, to hope to win a big endurance ride you would probably have to take a horse to quite a few contests today to get him ready. 15 years ago it was possible to win a big ride on the first try if you knew what you were doing and had a very good horse. Today things are different. The competition is tough. Many riders have years and years and dozens of contests and hundreds of miles of invaluable experience to fall back on and so do their horses.

Go to the first contest with your hat in your hand. Take care of your horse.

People who have successfully passed that big milestone of actually getting ready for the first ride and completing it with a bit of style will begin to appreciate the sage advice once given by a topflight judge at the Virginia 100-mile, 3-day ride several years ago when asked his opinion about training and conditioning. He said, "Well, let's imagine someone offered a contest in ditch digging. Two men decide to enter. One has never dug a ditch before, and the other has been digging all his life. To the first man I would say, 'Practice digging ditches.' To the second I would say, 'Rest up.' " There is a bookful of wisdom in these words.

3

Feeding

We open this chapter with a direct quotation from Alexander Mackay-Smith's editorial in the May 12, 1972, issue of *The Chronicle of the Horse,* which was inspired by the original rough draft of this chapter sent to him at that time for comment and criticism. (As you can see, it takes quite a while to write a book!)

"Back in the days when the Calumet Farm horses, with one victory after another, were about to break up racing, their trainer, Plain Ben Jones, was asked for the secret of his success. 'Shucks,' said Ben, 'the only hard thing about training a horse is finding out what he likes to eat.'"

Since World War II, scientists and agricultural specialists have made incredible "progress" in feeding food-producing animals—cattle, pigs, sheep, and poultry, for example. One is reminded of an industrial assembly line when thinking about our agricultural giant and the systematic feeding of these animals. The feeding of an *energy-producing animal,* such as a horse, remains, for obvious reasons, an art that science can aid but never replace. A successful program for a food producer may be achieved by reading books and labels, resorting to computers and statistics, but a successful program for the trainer of a horse can only be achieved by *reading the horse.*

In recent years much of the art of feeding and horse husbandry appears to have slipped away for many of us as our attention has been focused on the science of feeding. Where we should have *added* the science, we have tended to *substitute* science for art. We are wise to use the science as well as we can, but preserve the art of feeding; and remember that *food values are as much a function of the condition of the horse as they are a function of the condition of the food.*

Sources of Information

This chapter is a blend of information from four divergent sources:

1. Results of scientific investigations, even though the bulk of this information is obviously devoted to very artificial animal situations and conditions, and has little if anything to do with a natural animal.

2. Esoteric knowledge derived from practical experience of trainers like Plain Ben Jones, Will Caywood, and many other very successful horsemen of our acquaintance, even though all you can say to back it up is, "It won't hurt."

3. Gypsy knowledge, which has much of the character of mysticism and inspiration about it. This would include such human/animal ideas as "entertaining" your horse, perhaps indirectly, with the coarse musical sounds of an accordion or harmonica by the firelight in the evening just before he is expected to go into the contest.

4. Our personal experience in feeding hundreds of horses over the years, including pack animals in northern Canada and athletic horses engaged in a variety of competitions from endurance riding to three-day eventing under controlled conditions at our research farm.

Early in their great book *The Lessons of History,* Will and Ariel Durant said, "It is a precarious enterprise, and only a fool would try to compress a hundred centuries into a hundred pages of hazardous conclusions. We proceed." Considering the insignificance of the topic of feeding horses compared to a hundred centuries of history, we feel very humble, especially when we realize how little we know about this subject. But we proceed.

Effects of Domestication

While on this note of history it might be interesting to consider some observations related to domestication of animals in general that could give us pause for thought. We are referring to R. Thevenin's *Origine des Animaux Domestiques* (Paris: Presses Universitaires de France, 1947). A few quotes may serve to whet your imagination: ". . . many domestic racers have been bred to excel their wild relations in physical powers. This applies among horses to the racing breeds, which have much stronger shoulder muscles than the wild horses . . . reduction of musculature is equally common . . . the character of the skin, one of the most important products of the animal world, is intimately connected with the development of subcutaneous fat . . . the length of the digestive tract, which is increased in domestic carnivores . . . the length of the gut is connected with the change from pure flesh diet to one which includes quantities of vegetable matter. . . ."

Even though these comments refer to changes occurring over many generations, we are brought to wonder, for example, about the very long gut in our horses and the possibility of twisting, various forms of colic that are directly related to this long gut, and the basic idea that a wild horse is probably eating "when he can" while his domesticated cousin is "stuffed two or three times a day" and perhaps needs the long gut for storage as much as anything else. As a consequence of our feeding methods he may just naturally have a propensity to gut problems such as colic.

Some Basic Considerations

First must be having the right horse which means a horse that actually has the potential to succeed. There is an old saying: "You can train a mule for the rest of his natural life, and he ain't goin' to win the Kentucky Derby." The horse must not only be appropriately chosen for the competition, he must also be sound.

Second, we must be sure the horse's system is in good adjustment. A good horse may simply never have a chance because he is so heavily infested with parasites that he cannot assimilate his food. The ecological balance of parasites must be carefully and consistently controlled by an effective and safe parasite program. Traumatic and violent changes in the status of the horse's digestive system resulting from harsh parasite-control programs must be avoided.

Another lack of adjustment could be such a simple thing as that the teeth need floating.

No two horses are alike. Each requires separate study and an individual program, the development of which is the horseman's art. If, like Ben Jones, you can find out what your horse likes, you will be happy "he eats like a horse."

Exercise is the third basic element. The horse must be involved in a well-conceived program of training. In the beginning the physical aspects of his job are undertaken as early in the day as possible and the mental aspects are undertaken in twilight or during the hours of darkness under the most austere conditions of solitude that can be arranged. The secondary phase of training involves work at any time of day, with particular emphasis on working in the heat of the day and in the dead of night in order to be properly prepared for the exhausting conditions of most endurance rides. Professional trainers can usually take advantage of this idea, while amateurs often have demanding jobs or other requirements for their time, which make this ideal virtually impossible to achieve.

Proper exercise can stir the system to new life each day. From the time the foal is born he must have an opportunity to run, really run, to feel free.

Exercise is the cornerstone of good gland adjustment, whether it be the thyroid, the liver, the gonads, the sweat glands, or any of the thousands of other glands in our miraculous systems.

Feeding must be co-ordinated with exercise. Until very recently you could pick up any number of scholarly books on nutrition for man and animal without reading a word about exercise. Nutritionists, even today, concentrate almost exclusively on the solids and liquids that go into the subject's mouth with little regard for anything else, including environment or exercise. We believe you would agree that there is a greater likelihood that a football team will win if they play football and just eat hot dogs than if they eat the finest food in the world and just sit around.

Then, too, the horse should have company and interesting activity in his environment at times other than exercise and practice. He should not be alone. If circumstances do not permit his enjoyment of the company of other horses in conditions where they can mingle, there is rarely a reason why he can not have his own dog, cat, goat, chicken, duck, frog, or something to think of as a friend. Horses have a way of identifying with animals other than themselves. Some even prefer humans.

It is paramount to the goal we desire that the horse does not eat alone under any circumstances. Company is the spice of life at eating time.

The horse should have the sense of being appreciated as an individual. Sincere interest of the horseman in the horse comes through only if the horseman spends some time with the horse with patterns of behavior that the horse can understand. A horse ridden by a rider who appreciates him will give much more than the "dominated" horse, and the rider will enjoy the association more.

Great horsemen often satisfy the horse's desire for personal attention, build the sense of anticipation, and check the individual for state of well-being all at one time by engaging in a period before the main meal of the day, usually the evening meal, when they offer the equivalent of cocktails or even entertainment and a definite social hour. This is the time when they examine the individuals or parts of them in minute detail. One great trainer known to us in the old days would always "sneak" or appear to sneak a little paper cup of karo syrup in the spring to a horse while background sounds of preparing the feed were coming through. This man was one of the top jockeys in the United States for many years and was personally breaking young mounts "out of the gate" at Hialeah when he was seventy-eight years old! Certainly *eating time is probably the most important time in the horse's day.* It is during these times when a horse has the best chance to "put it all together," to reflect on the experiences of the day and compose himself for the anticipated experiences of tomorrow.

Preparing Food

The final condition for assimilating good food is established in the way the food is prepared and served. The most undesirable tactic conceivable is to rush around in the barn and, with no set schedule, throw a flake of hay to the animal that catches him by surprise (not uncommonly arousing him out of a sound sleep) and leave, feeling that the horse will do well because the hay is the best that money can buy.

The horse should have an opportunity to participate in the experience of preparing the meal. This does not mean he should have to get his own hay. But it does mean he should have time to anticipate and build up his desire to eat by hearing familiar sounds for a while—perhaps even an old tractor outside, or grain falling into a bucket. It's also good if he can smell things. The mistake sometimes made is that we prepare feed out of sight or hearing or smelling range of the animals and then virtually throw it into their stalls with no time spent in the vital stage of preparation.

Just as company is the spice of life, so hunger is the spice of food. Happy hunger comes from two things: *exercise* and *slowly developing anticipation* as the digestive juices begin to flow and dampen the inside of the mouth.

While eating, the horse should have the confidence that he can eat as slowly as he wishes and not lose part of his meal because he did not hurry. *The unhurried horse will invariably have better chemistry going for him inside.*

We must interject an idea that is unique to endurance riding here. The nature of endurance riding as well as the traveling to and from contests require that you accustom the horse to eating at different times of the day or night so he will not be thrown off feed at a contest where he must eat at 4 A.M. to prepare for a 6 A.M. start, for example. Therefore, although a regular time for eating is ideal from one point of view, odd-hour feeding is something you should do from time to time to meet this unusual requirement.

Moreover, when a horse has only a stall and paddock available, we make it a practice to whet his appetite by withholding one meal a week, a morning meal so that he will not feel hungry all through the night.

Making Changes

Most of the very successful horsemen we have known over the years prefer feeds that have been processed as little as possible and under conditions of moderate temperature ranges. They offer their own occasional variations such as moist brans, as needed. They are reluctant to make large changes as in, say, roughage. Going from green colors to brown you can change quite rapidly, but going the other way takes time. The best example of this is when spring has come and the grass is up and looking very delicious. The horse has been all winter on cured hay. You turn him out, and within a short time he can founder, unless you introduce him to the grass gradually—perhaps an hour a day for three or four days. On the other hand, you can go from green grass to cured hay without much concern. While we are on the subject of major changes, we should mention that when traveling, you should carry enough feed of all kinds from the previous few days to mix it with what you have to procure during the trip. For example, mix one-third new hay with two-thirds old on day one, two-thirds new hay with one-third old hay on day two, and so on.

Occasionally there is a need to change concentrates or add ingredients to the regular pattern of food. In general we have found that, in anticipation of changing feed in any way, it is best to cut out or cut back the morning meal, then add just a suggestion of the new taste to the evening meal, and subsequently build up to the planned dosage of whatever the new material is over a period of several days. If this procedure is followed, even finicky horses will allow a considerable change of diet.

Nutrition and Health

A well-fed horse with appropriate exercise is unlikely to catch so much as a cold in his lifetime, and we can say this with considerable practical experience and research work to back up the statement. But we should remind you that feeding a horse to win is a never-ending process. Do not think you can leave a horse on any old diet until a short time before a contest, then suddenly switch to a high-grade diet, shoot a quick worm-killer to him, and take off. It won't work.

Much of the quality necessary in a great horse is built over a minimum period of a year (a complete cycle of seasons). Some qualities must be developed from birth and never forsaken in the life of the animal, especially if the horseman is interested in breeding as well as performance.

It takes the whole growing-up period (at least five years for mares and seven for stallions) without a break in continuity to bring the horse to its maximum state of well-being without any let-up or stinginess at any time during the period. There is an old Arab saying: "The first eight years are for the horse, the second eight years for the owner, and the third eight years are for his worst enemy."

Today we see things a bit differently, though we agree about the first two periods. Give to the horse in feed, attention, and training for the first and then take your full measure in the second. But in the third, in a partial state of retirement, the horse can be used in many ways to great advantage into a ripe old age if you keep his feet and teeth in shape and carry on with a good basic feed program. There's nothing like a happy old horse to teach a new rider. He's dependable and he knows people. Reproducing horses can do great things, even maintain high rates of productivity well into their twenties when properly exercised and fed and given a constant flow of tender, loving care.

Now let us consider a brief list of some of the chemical compounds found in good food together with a layman's explanation of their apparent specific values as far as can be determined. But while examining this list we ask you to keep in mind that, important as it obviously is to know how much of a certain substance there is in a given quantity of food, it is really more important to know how much ultimately gets into the horse. You might also go through a bit of an intellectual exercise along these lines: When a scientist gives a name to some substance such as Vitamin A, how much more do you know, being able to say the name, than you did before? If you ask the scientist for clarification, he might say, "Well, all these vitamins are simply complex organic substances occurring naturally in plant and animal tissue." How much more do you really know? We must remember that most of the ideas regarding the value of specific substances such as vitamins or particular minerals are obtained through laboratory studies where control conditions must be maintained; and these control conditions are, as often as not, carefully designed to be quite unnatural.

Vitamin A: Essential for normal growth; prevention of skin and tissue disorders, aids resistance to colds and infection of the mucous membrane of the nose, ear, throat, and lungs; needed for full utilization of calcium and iron; vital for bones, teeth, eyesight and blood.

Vitamin B-1: Essential for healthy nerve tissue, normal reproduction, lactation, good appetite, and digestive system.

Vitamin B-2: Promotes growth, essential for nerve tissue and good eyesight.

Vitamin B-6: Helps prevent anemia, dry skin, skin lesions, and loss of weight; assists in co-ordinating nerve and muscle tissue.

Vitamin B-12: Builds blood and promotes growth; aids in prevention of anemia, nervous conditions, and certain skin disorders.

Vitamin D: Essential for proper assimilation of calcium and phosphorus required for strong teeth and skeletal development; required for prevention and treatment of rickets.

Vitamin E: Helps increase fertility; aids normal glandular functions and helps prevent impaired skeletal muscular action.

Niacin (a B Vitamin acid): Very important for maintaining normal function of the gastrointestinal tract.

Calcium pantothenate (another B Vitamin acid): Aids appetite, promotes growth and general good health.

Calcium and phosphorus: Two minerals indispensable for development of strong teeth, skeleton, and prevention of rickets.

Iodine: Required for basal metabolism due to its importance for proper functioning of the thyroid gland.

Iron and copper: Needed for rich, red blood, prevention of loss of weight and anemia.

Manganese: Essential for proper bone formation, growth, and reproduction.

Cobalt: Required to prevent anemia, poor growth, unhealthy coat, and emaciation.

Magnesium: Essential for sound skeletal development and proper neuromuscular functioning. Considered an aid in adjusting to heat.

Salt: Promotes good digestion and maintains acid-base balance.

As the years pass, a list such as this is bound to grow longer, but we ask you to consider a few facts. First, all this knowledge is essentially not even fifty years old yet, while good men have been raising good horses for over four thousand years without knowing any of these terms or concepts. The very word "vitamin" is interesting. "Vita," of course, is derived from Latin and means "life." "Amin" used to be spelled "amine" because these chemists thought the "substances" they were isolating and studying were indeed "amines." Now they know better, but they are stuck with the name anyway. So to get around a bit of embarrassment we simply drop the "e" and say "amin," which is essentially meaningless. The spelling changed quietly, but the word really should be something else. . . .

The point is that our knowledge is very recent and bound to grow in elaborateness. A classical experiment in nutrition was conducted by Sir Frederick Gowland Hopkins in 1912. He showed that young rats, fed on chemically pure food, ceased to grow, but that growth began again when minute quantities of fresh milk were added. Hopkins concluded that fresh milk contains "necessary food factors" that are necessary for growth and health. Later work distinguished several different kinds of these factors, which are now known as vitamins.

Naturally, when chemists make "breakthroughs" of this magnitude a whole new industry may develop with little bottles everywhere and a great superfluity of TV advertising. Chemotherapy, with its roster of synthetic organic drugs, was given great impetus by Paul Ehrlich (1854–1915), who is famous for his work with toxins and antitoxins and who found an arsenic compound that destroys *spirochaete pallida,* the cause of syphilis in man.

While considering these scientific marvels with due respect, one can only muse about how much we do not know, how much there is to learn, and conclude that perhaps we should go on to seek a fine, broad spectrum of natural foods that may contain even more of those "accessory food factors" so wisely identified by Professor Hopkins in 1912. But while taking advantage of modern scientific ideas about health and nutrition, we should probably still try to *read the horse* even more carefully, more hopefully, and even more reverently than we do the labels.

Roughage

Roughage is, of course, the fundamental food of a horse. Historically, horses have for thousands of years been able to eat green or dry grass in various stages, either wandering free in nature or in a domesticated condition. Over the centuries there has been general agreement that horses fare best when they can pick at rough feed twenty-four hours a day if they wish. When we confine horses, this naturally limits their ability to forage, but we can attempt to compensate for this and satisfy the requirement of the horse's small stomach safely and satisfactorily by feeding roughage a minimum of two times a day. In the case of many of our endurance horses we provide good-quality hay on a free-feed basis in self-feeder mangers that prevent waste.

There is a simple rule of thumb about feeding hay that can be adjusted to fit most horses: To maintain weight, feed 2 pounds of hay for every 100 pounds of weight of horse. In other words, a 1,000-pound horse would eat 20 pounds of hay per day—10 pounds in the morning and 10 pounds at night. If he is working hard or is a little thin, he may eat more. If he is too fat you can cut back a little, but working the weight off is better. We have fed as much as 26 pounds of hay a day to a 760-pound Arabian in training to maintain weight. Another way of measuring hay is to feed enough to keep the horse busy, without wasting it, in eating for 2 hours morning and evening. There is an excellent brief for feeding 3 times a day, but we believe that when you think of the practical problems of most horse owners, 2 times a day is realistic, and the alternative would be a free-feed system.

One cannot be too careful about how the hay is fed. Keeping the hay off the ground is important to prevent waste and also to prevent "sanding," a condition that results from picking up dirt with hay when it is eaten off the ground and ultimately results in chronic colic.

We have essentially two choices of roughage in their natural forms of hays or legumes: hard grass or grain types such as oats, timothy, or similar hard, brown stemmy hays; or softer, leafy types such as alfalfa and clovers or vetches. Some horsemen do well with combinations of these, and some argue that you might choose according to which is the best available—that is, if the alfalfa near you is fresh-cut in high bloom, as it is primarily cut for cattle, you would be better to use oat hay even if it is about the quality of straw. If, on the other hand, the oat hay is devoid of grain or leaf and the alfalfa is a bit older and less in bloom, then pick the alfalfa. Here we would have to say, as we have said many times before, that you must use your own good judgment. When we come to the part of this chapter on "reading the horse" you may find help in making that judgment.

Basically, it is essential to pick hay that is not dusty or weedy. Smell the hay to make sure it has a clean smell, and feel it to make sure it is dry. If you put your hand between flakes of a freshly opened bale and it feels warm and damp, don't feed it. It can cause severe colic.

One more point about feeding roughage should be made. Some people simply separate a flake of hay from a bale and throw it in the manger. It is much better to take the extra ten seconds and open the flake up, spreading the hay in a natural fashion. There are several good reasons for this, including the possibility that you just might find a piece of wire or a foreign object that could be harmful.

Pellets and Cubes

Any kind of substitute for natural roughage in the form of pellets or cubes or concentrated forms of that type should, in our opinion, be fed only if there is absolutely no alternative. Pellets are dehydrated in a highly compact form, which means they must be *re*hydrated by the horse; this requires a major adjustment of the horse's digestive process. He has to get the feed back into something approximating normal condition, and this requires water in one form or another. For a working endurance horse that may be slightly dehydrated in the first place, this process of rehydration of pellets in the stomach can rob him of vital stomach fluids and cause further general dehydration.

Second, the horse can consume a sufficient amount of nutrient by eating less volume than his system should have. This requires another fundamental digestive adjustment.

Third, because he can eat his fill in too little time, he has a psychological problem that manifests itself in eating fences or anything else he can find, including halter ropes, leather reins, anything at all.

Fourth, it appears that good first-class pasture grass or properly cured hay or a combination of these is basically better for your horse anyway.

Concentrates vs. Natural Food

Today we frequently have choices of feed mixes of various kinds combined under formulas created in agricultural schools or big feed-company laboratories. These mixes represent modern scientific ideas about what is best for the average horse in America, and probably will not come up to the required standard you will need for your endurance horse. Some of these mixes are called "sweet feeds" because they contain a sweetener, most commonly molasses. They also contain grains—corn, bran, barley, oats, with possibly the addition of a variety of lesser feed substances such as soya bean and cotton seed. In almost all cases the original natural materials have been ground, chopped, steamed, rolled, crushed, or otherwise considerably altered from their natural form.

An old anecdote comes to mind. You know that about half the world's population lives on rice. Another half lives on wheat. A tiny portion lives on oats because they can't grow wheat or rice. They are the people of Scotland. An Englishman was once putting a Scotchman down by saying the Scotchman ate only what the Englishman would feed to his horse (oatmeal). The Scotchman told the Englishman that he could indeed find no finer *horse* than the *Englishman's* and that oats seemed to do for the *men* of Scotland what they quite clearly were able to do for the *horses* of England.

Oats as a grain have followed horses all over the world as northern Europeans reached out in the empire-building stage of history. True, some horses spent long times on shipboard eating hemp rope with dates, and some others had to get along on what they could find with peanuts as a supplement, but most of the world's horses today enjoy oats primarily and barley or other grains in secondary quantities.

Consider for a moment that you might take two little grains of oat to a great laboratory and say you are ready to pay any price to find out what is in them and what their nutritional capacity is. Just as you pass them to the technician you drop one and step on it "quite by accident." You sweep up the bits. He takes them and the whole grain, but he cannot tell you the difference between them scientifically because he has to *destroy* them both to give you your answer. There is one great fact the laboratory overlooks: The whole oat could have been planted and have made another oat, but the crushed oat never could. That, to us, is a significant difference.

We believe, and here we must confess the exact same orientation as the gypsy in his mystic idea of things, that eating and digesting are intended to be just as secret a process as procreating, conceiving, and growing a baby. When the horse closes his mouth over a blade of growing green grass or a whole seed, something happens that we probably will never discover in a laboratory any more than we will be able to make a horse in a laboratory.

Consider that a foal can do rather well if he has a chance to wander over the earth and eat mostly grass with occasional tree bark, bushes, seeds, and even fruits. With his marvelous secret machinery, easily visible in dissection but still a total mystery to the most knowledgeable of us, he turns grass into hoof walls, bones, skin, eyeballs, teeth, blood, juices of an uncounted variety, hair in his tail and on his side, special tissue around his nose, and muscles —all essentially out of green grass, water, and fresh air.

So we opt without question for a base of whole oats combined with hard grain or grass hay alternated when possible with alfalfa or pasture grass. Your own good judgment based on your experience and your particular geographic circumstances must be your guide. If you wish to put more weight on your horse, add rolled barley and bran to the oat base. The barley has to be rolled since unrolled barley is virtually impossible to digest. In the case of cold weather, cracked corn can be substituted or added to the barley.

Quantity

In terms of volume our thinking has changed over the years. We used to attempt to feed as much grain as we could get our hard-working endurance horses to eat, based on principles of racehorse feeding. This would often amount to a total of 12 to 15 pounds of grain a day in three feedings. Many people still feed this much, but there is a trend, with which we agree, to cut back on the grain and feed more like 6 to 8 pounds a day, depending upon size and condition and, most important, work, as well as the feeling of power in the horse. Donna Fitzgerald tells us that Witezarif gets absolutely no grain when he is inactive or not working; and when he is working hard she may feed only 3 or 4 pounds of oats a day. Of course, this horse is fortunate in having available, 24 hours a day, Yerrington, Nevada, hay, comparable in our part of the country to the blue grass of Kentucky.

It is, of course, absolutely vital to cut way back on the grain on the days when the horse is not worked. The classical idea of feeding a hot-bran mash once a week is a good practice. The hot mash would normally be fed on the night before the rest day. It is made of approximately 3 quarts of wheat bran, 3 to 4 quarts of very hot water, 2 quarts of oats, a little salt, and some "goodies"—carrots, apples, whatever he seems to like. Placed in a pail and covered for about 15 minutes to steam under a gunny sack where your horse can smell the meal in preparation, it can work fine magic.

Supplements and Special Foods

There are a great many supplements offered on the market today. There is also a prevalent idea that if a little is good, more must be better. If you have good air, good water, good roughage, and good grain available you will need very little supplementary food of any kind. If your roughage leaves something to be desired, then you may need trace minerals or specific vitamins.

It is not difficult to get celery, parsley, carrot, or any lacy-top vegetables that your grocer may have that are a bit over the hill for selling in his produce section. Often you can get these free if you ask. Cut up and mixed with a bit of salt, these are very good tidbit changes from the ordinary daily routine.

Kelp is an excellent, natural source of trace minerals and necessary iodine.

Unpreserved apple-cider *vinegar* is one special food we would not be without. We use it in several ways. First, by simply putting a bit of it in the feed we acquaint the horse with the taste. He may not like it at first but he soon comes to like it very much. Whether there is any food value or not is not the point. It is a matter of taste. If you have to introduce a new taste such as an oral wormer, simply add the vinegar, and in most cases the problem of refusal is automatically solved. In the case of water, we put a bit of vinegar in a pail every now and then. When traveling, if the horse won't drink, we simply add a bit of vinegar and he accepts the strange water with no fuss. In fly season we add about one-eighth to one-quarter cup of vinegar to the grain ration each day and the flies do not bother the horse. Our horses get some vinegar almost every day of the year.

Salt, of course, is a must—by far the most important of the supplementary foods. A block is not enough. We also keep loose salt and minerals available on a free-feed basis almost all the time.

Tidbits for training may be varied. Carrot, raw potato, orange peels, apples, sugar or other sweets occasionally, salted peanuts, and dates are only a few possibilities.

Solid, Liquid, and Gas

Considering the diet of horses in physical terms of solids, liquids, and gases, the horse needs all three. He breathes the gases and oxygenates his blood, especially when he breathes deeply (the basic reason for exercise from the point of view of nutrition). The *gas* should be good. Smog can get him just as surely as it can get you.

Good air is a very complex gas and it is much different when the sun's rays are pouring through it, even through a cloud, than it is at night when it is shielded from the sun's rays by the mass of the earth itself. But this is a geophysical aspect of nutrition that few people take into account.

The liquids are, for the most part, water. The horse should have his water clear and clean in a clean container. Too many horsemen slight this important aspect of nutrition. Good spring water or river water directly from the source is a wonderful luxury. So is rain water. But unfortunately the water that comes through miles of concrete pipe and has been "protected" from contamination by various chemicals before it comes out of the tap is little more than a wetter.

As for the solids, we all know this has become a very complex subject with much literature available. Some people enjoy "getting into details." Others just depend on advice from neighbors or friends who seem to know something they don't. In a book on endurance and competitive trail riding we can only hint at the problem of feeding the solids you choose. But we leave this subject with the thought that there is much to be said for keeping things as simple as you can. Variety—quality—frequency. These are very significant words in any feeding program.

Reading the Horse

Animals are equipped with various signal devices which, when readable by the skilled horseman, are just as good as lights and gauges in an automobile to tell how the engine is running and what is going on inside. While we have become accustomed to measuring temperature, pulse, and respiration in trail rides, both as indices in training and as indicators in controlling levels of competition and finally determining superior horses, these same measurements can be used in cases of sickness if you know something of the fundamentals. But there are a host of other indicators, more sophisticated and more subtle than these, which great horsemen since Xenophon's time have passed down from one to another as secrets of their art, and it is essentially this highly esoteric body of knowledge we propose to probe here.

Movement is certainly such an indicator. A horse should walk light on his feet with a certain rolling motion of the hindquarters that calls up the image of a big cat. One can feed a horse an excellent diet—all but salt—and the horse will not have this catlike walk. Add the salt, and the light, powerful character of overall motion returns. For those who enjoy scientific explanations for things, we are told that sodium and chlorine, the two elements in table salt, are minerals that help regulate the water balance in an animal and maintain the acid-base balance. Sodium is specifically needed for muscle contraction and may, therefore, be associated with the observation of catlike motion.

Coat is important, too. The horse's hair should be short and tight in his skin and tend to lie evenly. The hair in his tail and mane will pull out hard after seeming to stretch quite a bit before coming out. When you break a few tail hairs, they should tend to curl up in strange little knots after stretching considerably. A broken hair that just looks as though it had been cut without any feeling of first stretching and that lies flat in your hand, with a possible split, is not indicative of a healthy horse. For the scientifically minded, it seems that Vitamin A and cobalt, among other items, are associated with this condition. Both are common ingredients in vitamin and mineral supplements.

Odor is still another sign. A horse's skin should not smell bad in any way, even when you hold your nose right up close. His breath should not smell bad. His droppings should not smell at a distance of over two feet, and his urine should not have a disagreeable scent. These bad smells are often associated with poor adjustment of certain glands, the liver, salivary, and lymphatic systems particularly. In our modern diets, these poor adjustments more often than not are associated with too much protein in our anxiety to get extra power. Remember, *mare's milk and the great old hays such as year-old timothy are surprisingly low in protein yet obviously beautifully suited to the horse by nature.*

The *droppings* should be firm and round without looking like rocks. They should not be dark and should generally be characterized by shades of brown or tan rather than green, red, or blue. The color of droppings seems to be derived more from the color of the gastric juices themselves than from what the horse eats. Naturally, green grass or alfalfa will contribute to shades of green just as oats and timothy will contribute to shades of tan, but a little experience with these modifications will soon clue a new horseman in on how these colors range and what they signify.

A combination of smelly skin, dark green droppings, weak kidneys, and a lathery sweat can be regarded as overwhelming evidence of straining the kidneys and the whole digestive system by overloading on proteins. A horse remaining on such a diet cannot be expected to hold a peak performance very long unless he is a uniquely stout individual.

Droppings may be either watery or very solid in connection with too loose or too difficult evacuation of the bowel. Loose droppings may reflect a simple problem such as parasites. They can also reflect ingestion of some toxic substances such as polluted water or hay that has been sprayed, fly-repellant materials—many, many sources. It is for the horseman to consider the possible sources. In the meantime, cutting back on feed intake to a very simple diet of hard, brown hay for a few days and administering about one-eighth to one-quarter cup of vinegar may help straighten things out. As our old trainer friends would agree, "It won't hurt." Hard droppings, on the other hand, obviously reflect a need for more moisture in their formation. There are many possible causes for this condition, including dehydration, but again, resort to a simple diet for a few days and administration of vinegar will usually restore a more normal evacuation process. Dehydration can be checked by grasping the skin on the neck and pulling it out. If it snaps back, your horse is not dehydrated. But if the fold of skin pulled out requires a few seconds to return to normal configuration, he is dehydrated and may require salt, electrolytes, and rest. And in extreme cases where these symptoms are associated with fatigue, a consultation with a veterinarian is indicated. He may give the horse intravenous glucose or other substances.

The basic procedure for dealing with either hard or loose droppings is to simplify the diet by resorting to a very simple regimen of *clean* water and hard, dry hay. Carefully reconstruct the dietary intake over a period of days with attention to the effect of each individual ingredient, observing the horse as he reacts to this systematic changing of feed. Keep in mind that overstrain, heavy fatigue, and sudden changes of any kind such as traveling can be responsible in whole or in part.

Although few horsemen would undertake to make such detailed observations, the actual weight of the droppings over a period of a day should exceed the actual weight of the intake of all dry food by about 10 per cent on the average. A horseman might take note of the apparent amount of fecal matter evacuated when his horse is feeling good and working well. Then he is in a position to judge the amount of droppings in a general way if they become too soft or too hard. If the volume increases, the horseman can assume the horse's system is attempting to eliminate an undesirable substance. If the amount decreases, the horseman may assume the system is subject to some interference due to any of a great variety of situations, ranging from improper glandular balance to some outside strain. Again, simplifying the diet is preferable to applying some "instant cure" medication unless there is a considerable rise in temperature. Assuming temperature is holding close to normal, use good animal husbandry. If at-rest temperature rises to two degrees above normal for the horse and is associated with loose or hard fecal material, you have a proper problem for a veterinarian.

In perspiration, the sweat should be watery, should not smell, and should not leave a sweat line of any significance. A horse in obviously bad adjustment will produce a white lathery sweat that doesn't run off readily, dries slowly, and leaves a distinct white, almost gummy stain in the hair. White sweat around the saddle pad or under the bridle is generally regarded as a warning signal of poor balance and improper feeding.

The *urine* should be straw-colored and clear, not brown or black or cloudy. The undesirable colors can come from a horse that has been fed right but is overtired. But in most instances they are associated with too-rich food or toxic ingredients in the food.

There are also such indicators as color of gums, of linings of the eyelids, nostrils; condition of the soft flesh near the anus; the condition of hoofs and frogs; the way the horse stands; his tendency to remain in one place in a pasture—all these things are clues to the state of well-being as we observe the animal. Actually, the list of observations an experienced horseman makes goes on and on, and in a lifetime of study and thinking he begins to respond to his observations with variations in feeding or training or exercise or rest in a way that defies categorizing.

We come now to behavior, the way the horse feels under the saddle and in your hands. The obvious signs that could be associated with feeding programs would be: a tendency to stumble that cannot be accounted for by the condition or care of the feet in a mechanical sense; a feeling of weakness in the back, or a feeling of weak balance so the horse seems more like a bicycle than a solid platform for your weight; a tendency to shy a lot (which may be associated with weak eyes); a quick-rising respiration rate; and a tendency to act resentful to gentle, properly applied controls through the legs, back, or hands of the rider.

Observing the horse from a distance while the animal is not aware that anyone is watching can be revealing if the trainer is prepared *to take time* and let things happen.

On these occasions a horse should appear basically contented, alert, interested in the world around him, and not burdened with anxieties.

As you approach closer, the horse should appear calm but brilliant, self-controlled and aloof, but fully amenable to handling by a competent person, and evidencing a certain kindness and tolerance, especially toward small animals around him.

It would be a bad sign if he tended to pace or weave, and it would be equally bad if he seemed mean toward small animals or resented the skilled, gentle handling of an experienced horseman.

All these aspects we have been observing add up to good mental balance, and good balance should not be confused with either stupidity or docility.

A Test Program

It is common for us to say things like, "I feed 20 pounds of hay per day," without knowing if it is really 20 pounds or not. We estimate by some vague method of splitting flakes or otherwise, but we use specific numbers just the same. Similarly, people using coffee cans or other simple measuring equipment for grain think they know in some accurate way what they are feeding. But in almost all cases we do not really know precisely. The consequence, strangely enough, is that we tend to overfeed in a variety of ways that waste food. In most barns and around most paddocks where horses are fed, one often observes significant quantities of roughage just trod into the ground instead of eaten.

So we should like to recommend a 30- or preferably 90-day program to you, regardless of how efficient your operation is. If you actually weigh the roughage, fine. Otherwise, find a simple bathroom scale and set it in a convenient place where you can pick up a ration and weigh yourself holding it. Then subtract your weight and actually get a measurement of the weight of hay. It's simple and only takes a second. Similarly weigh the grain ration for an individual.

Make up a simple set of *records* and keep track for two days of exactly what your horses are eating.

Measure the amount of water each horse drinks. This is where the old-fashioned pail is far superior to an automatic waterer as a device for warning of oncoming sickness. Many times a horse will crave water or alternatively go off his water when he is in the malaise phase of a sickness, and a horseman will detect this immediately by an inspection of the watering pails.

After two days of careful measuring of hay, grain, supplements, and water for each horse, go through a proper worming procedure, using whichever worming method you prefer. You might even use this occasion to try two or three acceptable worming methods and see which is best for your horse.

Watch the droppings with care and take samples for viewing in good daylight, noting color and character. Note the urine. Each day note the smell of breath and other signals described in this chapter. Enter your observations in your notebook.

Take fecal samples and have them analyzed *after* the worming.

Continue to measure your feeds and be careful not to leave waste.

After thirty days take another fecal sample to be sure parasite levels are adequately low. Check the volumes of feed against volumes when you started. *It is very important that you feed only what the horse actually needs at all times. Do not feed in such a way that there is an accumulation of waste.*

It has been our experience that such a brief, disciplined 30-day trial can change certain patterns of activity for a horseman enough to save him the price of feeding one out of six horses and do a better job at the same time! Furthermore, in addition to doing a better job and saving one sixth of your total feed bill, you will find, if your worming program is a good one and your wormer is properly effective, that you can save another one sixth of the feed. Good management with a top-flight worming program will yield a better horse for only two thirds of the cost of casual horsemastership.

Summary Check List

At all times. Be alert for changes in droppings, urine, way of going, general behavior, heavy or rapid breathing at rest.

Daily. Note the way the horse stands and moves. How does he relate to other animals? Droppings. Tendency to leave food. Condition of lips, nostrils, eyes, ears, anus, coronets, runny eyes or mucus, normal saliva or ropy. How does he eat and drink? Water consumption—how much?

Weekly. Condition of hoofs and frogs, hair. Check skin for scales, sores, quality of flexibility and tightness. Color in nostrils and gums. Observe pattern of use of prehensile lip and pattern of rotation of lower jaw against upper in chewing.

Monthly. Observe the horse at a distance. Try to use the same general location and time of day. If you tried this observation every day you couldn't see subtle changes. Once a month you will be able to pick up significant changes.

Quarterly. Check teeth for hooks. A tendency to eat sloppily and lose grain while chewing is a common indication of poor adjustment of teeth. Take fecal sample or simply worm if you do not use a continuous wormer.

4

Feet and Shoes

One could quote clichés from the literature of horsemanship, going back to Xenophon, regarding the importance of feet. But the simple fact is that we are looking at four rather small structures supporting the weight of the animal, generally around 1,000 pounds, plus his "cargo," which normally runs close to an additional 200 pounds. Since he cannot move on four feet without having at least one foot off the ground and more customarily two, we are dealing with 600 pounds of pressure per hoof as a rule while the horse moves in competition over some of the ruggedest terrain people can find!

Even a good-sized foot does not cover more than 16 square inches in total ground-contact area. This reduces the impact pressure to something like 38 to 40 pounds per square inch; and if you consider hard surfaces and the area of a horseshoe (about eight square inches), the impact pressure approaches about one hundred pounds per square inch. Many scientists and engineers who have studied this situation for military people since 1750 in Germany, France, Spain, and the United States have written reports that tend to summarize the situation as nothing short of a miracle of natural engineering. Today we are asking horses to pound their way over long courses in record times, and the more experience one gains the more one is inclined simply to bow and say, "Allah, I wonder."

Before we get into the technical aspects of feet and shoes, a few general comments may be useful. Farriery is truly an art, and it may be recognized as an art when you see somebody who is able to make the shoe fit the root rather than carve the foot to fit the shoe. The foot has its own natural peculiarities just as a person's face has and may be recognized for its individuality. These peculiarities are not confined to the underside of the foot, but may be appreciated in side or front views as well. They are invariably related to the overall structure and way of going of the animal; and proper trimming followed by proper shoeing of the foot can be very beneficial to the movement, comfort, security, and ability of the horse to cover long distances most efficiently.

Ordinary Growth, Wear, and Proper Fit

Even when you turn a horse out for rest, you must remember that his feet are still growing. When you are using a horse hard, as in endurance riding, the average hoof grows almost half an inch at the toe and slightly less than a quarter of an inch at the heel each month. By comparison, a horse doing less strenuous work will grow the half inch in about six weeks. A good way to tell exactly how much your horse's feet grow is to put a little copper tube around a one-eighth-inch speed drill in such a way that the tip of the drill only protrudes beyond the tube about one-eighth inch to be sure you do not drill too deep. Then drill a hole on the front of the hoof about half an inch down from the hair line (coronet). Measure this distance carefully and make a record of it. Exactly a month later simply measure how far the hole has grown down the hoof from the hair line. The front of the average hoof is about three inches long, so it would require about six months for an active horse to grow out his hoof completely.

Because of this continuous growing you should have a competitive horse's feet trimmed at least once every six weeks, and if you are attempting to accomplish any corrective adjustments, it should be done every four weeks. The idea of taking shoes off a horse during a rest period has some merit, but one must beware of allowing the forefeet to break away, especially if the ground is hard.

The signs that a horse needs reshoeing, possibly before six weeks have elapsed, are: (1) there is a loose nail or a raised clinch. (2) The foot begins to overhang the shoe. (3) A branch of the shoe has been twisted slightly and is bearing on the sole or on the seat of a corn. (4) The shoe has worn unevenly. (5) The horse travels badly, stumbling or interfering, etc.

Occasionally a horse may travel short immediately after a shoeing job. This can indicate that the shoes are too tight, and they may simply loosen up with a few miles and be all right. On the other hand, there may be trouble with a nail being too close to the sensitive part of the hoof wall, in which case each nail should be carefully withdrawn and the shaft examined for signs of blood. If you find blood, force some iodine up into the nail hole with a syringe and do not replace the nail for a day or two. There is no great harm done, but this sort of condition should be avoided. Cutting the foot too short or paring the sole is also a common cause of sore feet after shoeing and can and should be avoided.

Without attempting to go into the subject of feet and shoeing in the technical detail suitable for a veterinarian or a blacksmith, we shall simply address the fundamentals in such a way that you may recognize a job well done or possibly poorly done. First, let us consider the overall anatomy of the foot.

Anatomy

There are four bones in the foot. Beginning at the bottom, there is the navicular or shuttle bone, which lies crosswise inside the hoof and provides the base for the coffin bone, which has special shapes like wings to hold these two bones in a flexible but limited relationship to each other. The next bone in the upward sequence is a short pastern, which forms the link between the bones inside the hoof and the bones above the hoof. The short pastern rises up out of the hoof about as far as it extends down into it. The final bone in this four-bone sequence before you reach the fetlock is the long pastern. Structurally, the three upper bones, the long pastern, short pastern, and coffin bone, bound together and supported by a complex of tendons and ligaments, should form a straight-column when considered both from the side and the front. This column of bones will have an angle to the ground that we shall consider later. The imaginary line that passes through the center of these three bones, beginning at the fetlock and extending to the ground, is called the *foot axis*. This line should appear straight and would normally be parallel to the front face of the hoof. We will note some exceptions to this classical idea with regard to endurance horses when we consider the specific degrees of angle of these structures to the ground.

Basically, when you shorten the toe (or raise the heel) you tilt the coffin bone forward and make the hoof stand steeper. This allows a bit of slack in the tendon that attaches to the upper surface of the coffin bone and consequently allows the fetlock joint to drop down so the long pastern forms a lower angle to the ground. You can readily see that this process would cause the foot axis to appear to be broken upward or forward. Lowering the heels produces the opposite effect, starting with tensing the flexor tendon and increasing the angle of the pastern to the ground. The foot axis at the top of the hoof would now appear to be broken downward or backard.

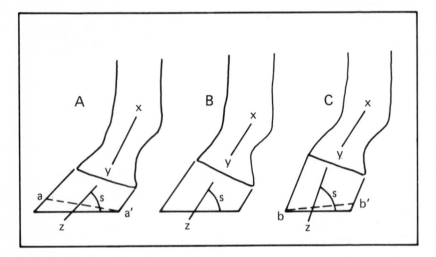

Fig. 3. The foot axis.

The long pastern bone can be angled slightly to the axis of the coffin bone with the short pastern being like a hinge. A flexible relationship can be appreciated like the leaf spring of a car: it should be a straight angle at rest.

In A the foot-axis line (x-y-z) is said to be broken downward or backward at (y). The fetlock is slightly low when the toe is long. By shortening the toe or raising the heel, cutting along the line a-a¹, the face of the hoof will form a steeper angle to the ground and the fetlock will come down slightly due to the relief of strain on the flexor tendon.

B shows the ideal straight foot-axis line x-y-z with an angle of approximately 55°, ideal for the endurance horse.

C shows the foot-axis line x-y-z broken upward or forward at (y) with an angle of 70°. It can be corrected some by trimming the hoof along the line b-b¹, reducing the angle of the face of the hoof to the ground and raising the fetlock slightly.

16. Witezarif: left front foot one week before the Tevis Cup Ride in 1976.

17. Witezarif: left front foot the morning after the Tevis Cup Ride in 1976.

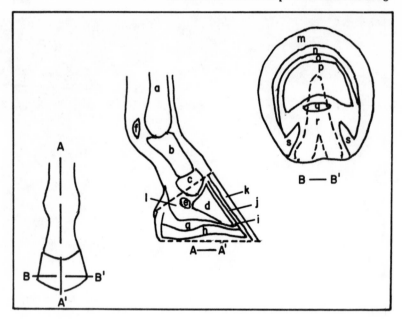

Fig. 4. Vertical and horizontal cross sections of the foot.

In cross section A-A[1], we have left out much detail in order to place emphasis on the structures significant to our understanding of shoeing problems.

The three-bone column that should be straight is indicated by the letters b, c, and d—the long pastern, short pastern, and coffin bone, respectively. This column of bones joins the cannon bone (a) at the fetlock. Mobility of the three-bone column is assisted by the two sesamoids, one at the fetlock (f) and the other inside the hoof, the navicular bone (e).

The plantar cushion (1) absorbs the shock between the weight of the horse and the surface upon which the hoof falls; (h), the horny sole, is the visible part of the bottom of the foot, and (g) is the soft zone between the horny sole and the plantar cushion.

The hoof capsule is a wonderfully complicated structure, but for our purposes we can simply appreciate the visible outside surface (k), which is a horny wall covered in varying degrees downward from the hair line by an impervious material called the periople. We think of this thin-wall covering as extending downward about as far as the nail holes as a rule; (j) represents the white line, that zone of intermeshing of hundreds of leaflike structures that secure the hard, insensitive, horny outer wall to the fleshy, sensitive inner wall (i).

In cross section B-B¹ we show the relationship between the hard, horny outer wall (m) and the white line (n). In shoeing, the nails should enter into the white line (n) and emerge about three-quarters inch up the side of the hoof (m); (o) represents the sensitive, fleshy part of the foot, while (p) gives a different view of the coffin bone. The navicular bone (q) is cradled between the wings of the coffin bone; (r) represents the area on the bottom of the foot covered by the frog; (s) shows how the bars are reflected from the horny wall. Without this reinforcing structure at the back of the hoof wall the hoof obviously couldn't withstand strain at all.

There is a very tough, elastic object on either side of the short pastern bone that is made of gristle and extends from the wings of the coffin bone back to the heels and upward about an inch above the hair line at the back of the foot. You can feel this with your fingers, and these two members of the foot structure are called *lateral cartilages*. They should feel elastic and allow your fingers to change their shape slightly under pressure. If they feel like a bone (indicating sidebone), the horse is probably not going to be able to do much really hard work. These lateral cartilages are related to another tough, gristly structure deep down inside the hoof capsule called the *plantar cushion*, which can dissipate the violent forces resulting from the impact of the foot with the ground under the grueling stress of moving rapidly over rough country. If the lateral cartilage has lost its tone and seems bony, the plantar cushion is probably also too hard; shock can be translated up into the horse's skeleton and cause pain and consequent lameness.

The outer *wall*, the hard, insensitive, visible part of the hoof capsule when the foot is on the ground, is connected to the bars on the bottom, which gradually disappear near the point of the frog. The angle between the wall and the bar in the horizontal plane is called the buttress. The lower edge of the hoof wall, to which the shoes are attached, is called the bearing edge. If you divide the bearing edge into five equal parts you will see that the center part is the toe area, two forward lateral parts are the side walls, and the two rear parts are the quarters. Above each quarter you will find the rounded soft extensions of the plantar cushion, which are called the heels.

The outer wall of hoof generally slopes a bit more than the inner; and the more the slope, the thicker the wall. The sole is jointed to the wall in the zone of the fleshy leaves—the *white line*. This white line is very important since nails should enter the hoof within its limits in as near a perpendicular course to the face of the shoe as possible, then curve outward, and ultimately surface on the outside of the horny wall about three-quarters inch above the bearing face of the shoe.

Good, healthy horn is fine-grained and tough. Unhealthy horn is coarse grained, and either readily crumbled or hard and brittle.

The hoof in operation is a fascinating structure. Essentially, when the horse puts weight on a foot, the whole back half expands laterally while the top front part contracts slightly. When the weight translates downward through the bones to the coffin bone, the plantar cushion expands laterally. The sole drops down slightly and the heels spread. The horny frog also widens, tending to force the back areas of the hoof wall apart. Obviously, these natural actions are somewhat inhibited by shoeing if the shoeing is not done properly. The nails should be placed in the front half of the foot to be sure the back half can slide out over the horseshoe surface when the weight comes down. This surface of the shoe should be just as wide and level and smooth as it can be made without interfering with the action of the inner parts of the bottom of the foot.

The Healthy Foot

A healthy foot should feel equally warm in all parts. It should not be tender to pressure from the hands or from moderate compression with hoof testers. The coronet should be soft and elastic and not protrude beyond the outer edge of the wall. The wall should be straight, whatever the slope, so that a straight edge placed perpendicular to the bottom edge of the wall and touching the coronet should touch the wall for its full length. The periople, the outer covering of the wall, should be left natural, unrasped, and there should be no cracks or irregularities in the wall.

Most hoofs will have rings of one kind or another more or less parallel to the coronet band. They should not be strongly marked and should be parallel to the coronet. Heavy rings suggest a weak hoof, but if limited in scope may tell the story of separation of the hoof wall from the laminae due to a recent injury or feeding problem. The bulbs should be well rounded and of equal size. The sole should be well hollowed out and not flat. The white line should be narrow and solid, not flaky. The frog should be flexible and well developed, while the bars should be straight.

Slope of Pastern

The slope of the pasterns on a natural horse running in the country at his own free will, such as a ranch horse in the West, will be somewhere between 42 and 48 degrees, depending on the conformation of the individual. If you take these natural angles as guides you will not be far off in doing the conventional shoeing job. This will give you an adequately strong lower leg and a good ride with some comfort, combined with suitable flexibility for the horse to cover all kinds of ground with speed and safety.

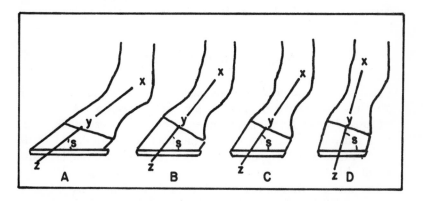

Fig. 5. Side view of foot showing range of slope of the pastern.

A. Represents an angle of about 38°, which would have been considered a "comfortable angle" for a lady's traveling horse during Civil War times. Low angles like this are often associated with long pasterns.

B. The classical foot today with an angle of about 52°. Forty years ago the classical angle was thought to be about 45°.

C. The modern endurance ride foot with an angle of 55°.

D. With an angle of more than 65° we have a very inflexible fetlock, making for too much shock for both horse and rider. The steeper the pastern, the shorter as a rule. A short pastern with very hard structure in the range of 55°–60° is ideal for endurance riding.

In all cases we have indicated the foot-axis line x-y-z to be properly straight to indicate that these are conformational types and not problems of crookedness in any way.

If you cut the angle down very much—say, to 35 degrees, as they used to do for ladies in the Victorian Age—you will have amazing comfort but not much safety and not much ability to cover real miles. If you steepen the angle to 65 degrees you will create an artificial stump foot and have a horse that has the same muscular-skeletal problem as one that was severely over at the knees. The horse would stumble easily and have little ability to compensate for coming down too soon with a foot. We conclude that the endurance horse should probably have a slightly steeper angle than he would naturally carry, making him more like a short-springed Jeep than a long-springed Cadillac. In checking hundreds of feet and legs of successful horses in the Tevis Cup Ride during the summer of 1976, we discovered that the working slope in front was not less than 48 degrees nor more than 55 degrees with an almost equally steep sloping shoulder; in the back feet we found slopes up to 65 degrees.

Irregular Growth, Stance, Shape

All parts of the hoof grow downward and forward. The rate of growth is associated with blood supply, use, the season, and necessity because of wear. Exercise, grooming, exposure to reasonable moisture, and removing overgrowth of the hoof parts are conducive to building horn of good quality. Lack of exercise, dryness, and excessive length of hoof hinder growth.

Irregular growth can reflect diet, but in a working horse it is usually associated with uneven distribution of body weight over the hoof—that is, an unbalanced foot.

A newborn horse has surprisingly straight pasterns with tiny hoofs that remind one of a deer. As the young horse develops the ability to move around, he usually wears the foot rather evenly, and the pastern begins to slope more during the passing months. If the foot is not dressed from time to time, the hoof can grow long in the toe and cause undue stress on the tendons. The opposite condition, with continued high heels, is conducive to limited action of the fetlock. Therefore, a young horse should have his feet cared for from the start in order to help him develop the right angulation, not only in the first three bones in the straight column between the fetlock and the coffin bone, but also in the bones above, which may begin to reflect bad adjustments in lower portions. Lack of attention to anatomical detail of the feet and legs of a horse can bring on heavy strains that can affect any part of the horse almost up to his ears! In conversation with several riders on the cross-country ride from New York to California during the summer of 1976, a number told us they didn't have serious shoeing problems, just a lot of sore tendons. They did not understand that the sore tendons were almost certainly a direct result of inadequate shoeing.

If, in trimming a hoof, one side is shortened more than another so that the foot-axis line is broken and not straight, the long side of the hoof wall will strike the ground first and continue to bring on a slight twisting in the bone section of the pasterns until it wears down to a proper degree of evenness. In an unshod horse this is not a big problem, but when shoes prevent the wear, you have a very real problem. If this mistake is prolonged, the high side will grow rapidly thicker, while the short side, being anemic due to lack of use, will grow thinner and ultimately result in a crooked foot. The next time you see a crooked foot, think about this. And if you see a crooked foot or crooked legs, find another horse.

Again, without going deeply into conformational problems, let us consider two fundamental problems of *stance* in their extreme form to help you visualize a potential difficulty in endurance-ride horseshoeing: the splay-footed and pigeon-toed horses. In a properly constructed lower leg, the foot axis from the center of the cannon bone all the way to the toe should run right through the center of the toe when viewed from the front with no suggestion of twisting either outward, as in the splay-footed horse, or inward, as in the pigeon-toed horse.

With the *splay-footed* horse, whose feet toe out, the outer wall is more slanting, longer, and thicker than the inside wall. The outer quarter is more curved and there is more sole on the outside of the frog than on the inside, but the weight is carried on the thin-walled inside of the hoof just the same.

The *pigeon-toed* horse exhibits the opposite tendencies but not to such a marked degree. Since the weight falls more on the outside of this foot than on the inside, the motion requires a breaking over the outside of the toe, and the foot moves forward in a circular path in a motion called paddling. If a pigeon-toed horse is shod so his toes seem to point straight ahead, he will frequently interfere, while a naturally pigeon-toed horse who is left pigeon-toed will rarely interfere.

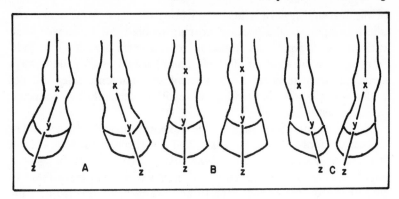

Fig. 6. Feet viewed from the front.

A illustrates the splay-footed position. The outer side of the hoof slopes less steeply than the inside. Consequently the outer wall is thicker; but the inner, lower side is bearing most of the weight.

B represents the ideal, balanced foot. The x-y-z foot-axis line centers on the cannon bone above and passes through the center of the hoof at the toe.

C illustrates the pigeon-toed position. The inner wall slants more than the outer and is consequently a bit thicker; but the outside is bearing most of the weight. The inner quarter is often more curved than the outer in this situation.

When a hoof slopes too steeply it is often called *stumpy*. This is when the foot axis is straight and slopes more than 60 degrees to the ground. The hoof is relatively short from toe to heel, which causes the weight to fall more toward the front part of the foot. This means that the heels do not have to expand as much as in the classical construction. An angle of 55 degrees (plus or minus 5 degrees) is desirable in an endurance horse, depending on overall conformation.

Now consider the slope of the hoof walls when viewed from the front. Classically, horsemen have wanted a "good-sized foot" with room enough for the action inside of the hoof capsule and a "bit of slope" so that the wall tends to grow with a good thickness. A wide hoof is almost circular, while a narrow hoof tends to have a distinctly longer-in-line axis than the transverse axis. The wide hoof has little concavity to the sole and a large frog; the quality of the horn tends to be coarse. The narrow hoof, on the other hand, has a strong, well-cupped sole, a small frog, nearly perpendicular side walls, and fine-grained, tough horn. We found that the most successful horses in the Tevis Cup Ride in 1976 were generally narrow-footed although their feet were not small. The slope of the outside and inside of the horny wall at the widest part of the foot tended to approximate 80 degrees.

While the front feet, on which we have mainly focused, seem to harbor most problems in endurance horses, the *hind feet* are influenced in the same general way by the orientation of the pastern bones relative to the coffin bone. The hoofs are not round like the front feet. The greatest width should be about two thirds of the way back. The soles tend to be more concave and the heels relatively wider than in front feet. The toe is often steeper on a hind foot by as much as 5 degrees.

Shoeing

There are four distinct phases in the process of shoeing a horse: (1) Examine the horse to see how to do the job. (2) Prepare the foot. (3) Make the shoe. (4) Put it on. We shall consider the subject of shoeing in terms of these four phases.

1). In *Examining the foot,* it is necessary to observe the horse at rest and in motion. At rest, the horse should stand with weight equally distributed, at least between the two fore feet at first. Look at them from the front and keep in mind the *foot-axis line.* This imaginary line should run from the center of the cannon bone down through the long pastern and seem to pass through the center of the toe. The horse may seem a bit base narrow or base wide. From the side the feet may give an impression of the heel being too low and the toe long or the foot too stumpy. Remember that *weight is carried on the lowest part* of the foot ordinarily, so if the heel seems low, the weight is carried toward the back of the shoe, and consequently this part of the shoe should show more wear than the toe. Similarly, if the horse is base wide, the inside will be low and the wear should be greatest on the inside branch of the shoe. Check the shoes to confirm your observations of the shape of the pastern relative to the cannon and the hoof itself.

Having done this, you should know what the *flight* of each foot should seem to be and how the foot breaks away from the ground and how it comes down. Move the horse at a trot and confirm the findings from the view at rest and the observation of the shoes themselves. If you find agreement, then you should know the essential way that the foot should be prepared and the shape that the new shoe should have. If your findings do not conform—that is, if there is disagreement between observations of the foot itself and the wear on the shoe—then look again or try to learn why this disagreement exists. Unless you can explain or re-evaluate any discrepancy between your observations, you are not ready to prescribe how to trim the foot or how to make the shoe.

Do the same thing with the back feet. Once you have the two fores and the two hinds well in mind, then watch the horse once more in motion at the trot to determine any tendency to seem to go short or to overreach or brush.

This is also a good time to make an elementary decision about the appropriate *weight of the shoe*. Many endurance riders are beginning to use slightly overweight shoes to help strengthen horses' legs. Then for contests they use lighter shoes. This practice requires some thought. First, the classical flight pattern of the moving foot past the fixed foot is thought to follow a more or less symmetrical, elliptical path, with the highest point opposite the fixed leg. The low-heeled, long-toed foot must be picked up earlier and then descend on a low-angle path to the ground. This uses considerable extra energy over a long distance. The short-toed, high-heeled foot, on the other hand, leaves the ground on a low-angle path and rises to its highest point in front of the fixed foot, and thus has to descend on a steep slope in contact with the ground. This action puts undue strain on the sole in hard contact with the ground. The balanced flight path uses the least energy and commits the individual foot to the least concussive strain in landing.

With a light shoe, the foot tends to follow a shallow path, sometimes called daisy cutting. In this case the flying foot may even pass the fixed leg at a height above the ground that is slightly less than the height of the fetlock. With a heavy shoe the horse tends to carry his feet higher in the air so that the flying foot crosses the line of the fixed leg considerably above the fetlock. In judging how heavy the shoes should be, you may observe your horse being led at the trot. Watch the front legs. Observe where the flying foot passes the fixed leg. If it is low, the horse can probably use a heavier shoe. If high, the shoe should probably be lighter, all other things being equal. At any rate, the weight and type of shoe should generally allow the passage of the flying foot at a point just slightly above the fetlock on the fixed leg.

When you examine *the old shoe* for wear you should remember that a shoe can show wear in a part for more than one reason. It can be the way the foot leaves the ground. For example, the toe will generally show a bit more wear because of the friction as the hoof turns forward and rolls over the ground in taking off. One branch of a shoe may be thinner than the other because more weight has been borne on the thin side or also because the shoe was not set squarely on the foot or was set too close on the inside of the thin side, causing more weight to be borne on that side than on the side farther out. All these things have to be taken into consideration. But going back to the fundamentals and watching for the foot axis on each foot both in the line of travel and transversely to be sure it is straight and not broken upward-forward or downward-backward is the most important single consideration. Then minor adjustments may be made to accommodate any tendency to overreach or brush and at the same time to trim the foot and position the shoe so that wear is as even as possible all over.

Experts have agreed for many years that no man is competent to shoe or to tell a shoer what he wants until he can make these observations and clearly understand what the fundamental observations mean.

2). In *Preparing the foot,* the clinches on the old shoe are carefully raised and the nails drawn one at a time. The idea of wrenching the shoe off as some shoers are prone to do is reflective of little skill. We cannot afford the risk of breaking off horn. The old shoe should be critically examined on the hoof face as well as on the ground for telltale signs of weight-bearing or excessive strain. Be certain that all parts of nails are removed from the hoof wall. Then clean dirt or partially detached horn away from the bottom of the foot.

In trimming—that is, cutting off excess growth on the walls and soles—one must be sure to take enough but not too much. In principle, the amount of old horn that would be taken would be about one-third inch per month. If the shoeing job is on a six-week schedule you would expect the average toe discard to be about one-half inch thick. But there is a more precise way of determining just what is the right amount for the average horse. When the foot is finally prepared for the shoe, the old horn should be cut back and leveled so that, as a rule, about one-eighth inch of sole will also come in contact with the new shoe. [See Fig. 8 side detail (c).] This, of course, is an observation that can be made after the rasping phase of preparation is completed. The wall is leveled with a rasp until the correct angles between the pasterns and the bottom of the foot are established, the full thickness of the wall is observable, the white line is observable, and one-eighth inch of the edge of the sole forms a flat plane. This area from the outside of the hoof to the inside of the one-eighth-inch sole area is called the bearing area of the foot, and comes in contact with the hoof face of the shoe.

The *frog* should not be touched except to remove parts almost falling off. The bars may be shortened if necessary but never pared from the sides. The natural flaking off of parts of the bottom of a horse's foot is called exfoliation. Whatever part of the sole, frog, or bars are pared or cleaned out, evidence of exfoliation should not be completely removed so that the part looks too clean and raw.

Corns are ordinarily caused by pressure on the sole in the quarters due to the old horn that has become thick and dry and very hard. Therefore, the branches of the sole in the area between the bars and the quarter walls should be so trimmed that there will be no sole pressure on the inside of the web of the shoe. With flat-soled feet the horseshoer often dresses the shoe itself by hammering a bevel on the inside of the web to assure that this will not happen. [See Fig. 8 side detail (d).]

There is a strong tendency for horseshoers today to rasp away minor irregularities on the outer surface of the hoof. Many books suggest that the shiny surface, which old-timers call "varnish," only grows down a short distance on the wall and therefore you can rasp the outer surface away to make a more regular-shaped hoof capsule. The theory is that in the long run a good hoof shape is more important than a "momentary" loss of possible fluid from the hoof capsule through an unprotected horny wall. The problem is that this absence of periople, if rasped away, can allow the development of a crack in the horny wall, which may be a serious detriment for a year or more.

It is not uncommon in the final rasping for some shoers to bevel the edge of the outside wall very slightly to be sure the horn will not break back. This is an acceptable practice, but any rasping for any reason above the line of the new nails is unforgivable, and rasping below this line should be sparing if done at all. Certainly the practice

of stubbing the front of the toe by rasping it back to fit the shoe is
the mark of a very low-class shoeing job!

3–4). Finally we come to *Making the shoe and putting it on.*
While "store-bought shoes" are quite satisfactory for the ordinary
riding horse, they are relatively inadequate for an endurance horse.
Many fine shoes for regular purposes are too hard or, in other
words, ring with a rather high tone when you hit them with a hammer. This high-vibration seismic wave (sound wave moving through a
solid material) can cause very slight but continuously aggravating
tensions in the horse's legs, something like being hit repeatedly on
the "crazy bone" of your elbow.

Endurance ride shoes are best made from scratch by the hot-shoe
method out of malleable material about of the consistency of cement
reinforcing rod. This is a *low-vibration iron,* which is very comfortable and has many advantages over ordinary shoes.

Before going into details of shape, we should note that classically
the branches of a shoe are narrower than the toe, and the width of
the toe area of the shoe is thought to be about twice the thickness
of the wall at the toe. Because of the heavy strains encountered in
endurance riding, this basic formula has proven somewhat inadequate.
The width of the shoe can be as much as three times the thickness
of the wall at the toe. Therefore, a wide *web* shoe is desirable. The
limiting dimensions, of course, is that the shoe should not in any case
interfere with the point of the natural frog or bear in any way on
the sole except for the one-eighth-inch part where the sole joins the
white-line zone of the wall. The branches of an endurance-ride shoe
may be kept wider than the conventionally accepted dimension,
especially for persons planning to use borium spots or lateral clips.

The *thickness* of a classical shoe is enough to take about four to
six weeks' wear under ordinary conditions. Since the endurance-ride
horse is probably going to put in at least three times the wear of an
ordinary horse, the thickness of the shoe must take this into account.

There are two schools of thought regarding endurance-ride shoes
in general. Some riders like to have shoes that will grip the ground
and rock ledges to avoid *slipping.* They sometimes use cleats and
often resort to the expensive practice of putting borium on the
ground face at the toes and heels and at spots between the nail holes.
The argument for this practice is that the horse must have sure footing in all situations to avoid falling or hurting himself.

Another school prefers a slippery shoe with the heels rounded off so if the horse does get on a ledge and his foot slips, there is, in their opinion, less strain on the leg bones and tendons than if the heavy body is on one end of the leg while it is locked securely at the other end by a cleat or borium contact. They feel the leg takes too much continuous strain if the foot is too securely placed, and that a bit of slippage reduces this strain. Both schools have proved successful in many kinds of rides. We tend to go along with the slippery-shoe school. We also note, in the accompanying photos of feet, that Nos. 59 and 11 had no pads, while No. 6, which came in fourth, did have pads on the front. All of them show the short, rounded heel with no borium or other shapes to give the horse extra-sure footing.

Classically, if the pastern slopes considerably—that is, approaching 45 degrees—the weight is borne toward the back of the bottom of the foot, and a good shoe will project backward from the end of the horn as much as a half inch in some cases to compensate for this. The *projection* makes it very difficult to keep these shoes intact in rough going at high speed. With a steeper angle, on the other hand, such as between 55 degrees and 60 degrees, the shoe can end within one-eighth inch of the end of the horn. This means that there is no projection to get caught on rocks and bring about a parting of the shoe from the foot.

Fundamentally, as we've indicated previously, the shoe must fit the foot, not the foot the shoe. Where minor corrections have to be made, the *shape* of the shoe should lean toward the way we want the hoof to grow in the future rather than fit the hoof as is at that particular moment.

If the shoe protrudes very slightly beyond the outline of the hoof wall all around by one-sixteenth inch and actually follows the contour of the outside of the foot, it is basically well shaped. There is an old saying that you should be able to roll a dime on the part of the shoe that is outside the hoof wall, especially in the front. Finally, the shoe must be absolutely flat on the bearing face.

Heel movement suggests a further reinforcement in shoeing. We have mentioned that the heels spread significantly each time the weight comes down on a foot. To realize the importance of very small movements to an endurance rider, let us consider that a horse's stride is about the same as a man's—say, nearly three feet. This means that each foot comes down about every six feet when traveling at a walk or a trot. A bit of arithmetic will tell you that in a hundred-mile ride this expanding and contracting, pumping action happens

85,000 times for each foot. If the inside of the shoe is really polished from the widest part back to the heels of each branch, the back half of the hoof can slide over it easily during that instant expanding process when the weight comes down, and it can make it much easier for this natural action to occur. We have learned that if the inside (bearing face) of the shoe is polished by a simple burnishing before nailing it on, you have a great trick for making life easier for those hard-working legs.

Nailing is very important in endurance riding. Remembering that the hoof expands in the back half, we would not put nails any farther back than the widest part of the foot—that is, about halfway back on the bearing surface in front and two thirds of the way back on the hind feet. Whereas in classical horseshoeing they say not to nail too fine or too high, we have to take into account that an endurance horse may have to be shod much more frequently than ordinary horses. Consequently, if a nail comes out about three-quarters inch above the bottom of the hoof, the hole will have descended about half an inch for the next shoeing and give a good, solid place for nails without creating an opportunity for parts of the hoof wall to break away. You have to plan the location of each nail hole to be sure you have solid nailing areas in the next shoeing job. Some people use four nails on a side and some three. Some like to see the back nail a bit higher than the others. Some like the nails to come out on a line parallel to the line of the base of the hoof. Some shoers can't tell exactly where the nail will come out! We favor the three-nail school with a parallel setting for practice and four nails for contests. If there is a tendency to loosen shoes through shearing action, we use toe clips and side clips, making sure they are not so tight that they bind the hoof in any way. The toe and side clips take much of the strain off the nails in the case of shearing.

Corrective shoeing is not properly a concern in connection with shoeing and foot situations of endurance horses, for if a horse needs any serious corrections in his feet he probably is not going to do well in endurance riding anyway.

Extras

We come to the subject of using *pads* or not using pads. Again we find two schools. One says, "They are excellent insurance." The other says, "They are a crutch." Many people practice without pads and then put pads on just before the big contest. A few use pads almost continuously. An equal number never use pads. Resorting again to the 1976 study of top riders in the Tevis Cup, Nos. 59 and 11, who shared the best time, had no pads. No. 11, as we have noted, also won the cup for best condition. No. 6, on the other hand, was padded in front, as was the fourth-place horse. We saw the top two horses before and after the ride, but were unable to observe the third- and fourth-place horses afterward because they were not available for examination. If one look at the top ten horses in the Tevis Cup Ride in 1976, the choice of pads or no pads was about evenly divided (pads used only on front feet in all cases). If you consider the top twenty horses, you find the choice favors the unpadded foot. Very few horses were shod with borium shoes.

A few special considerations for the person who chooses pads are:

1. Because there is the cushion between the shoe and the wall there is a strong possibility of shearing and losing a shoe. Consequently, toe and side clips would probably be a good idea.

2. Due to rolling motion, which rounds off the front of any shoe and foot in this type of riding, much care should be taken to be sure that fine grit does not accumulate in the crack that invariably develops between the pad and the sole in the front of the foot.

3. Because grit and foreign material of all kinds can enter and lodge between the sole and the pad, the interstitial area should be filled. Most people today agree that this material should be one of the new flexible types such as silicone rather than the older forms such as oakum, since the new materials stay in place better and do not fall out. In addition to filling the void between the pad and the natural sole, the lining material provides a cushion to help distribute the weight over a larger part of the foot. For this purpose modern silicone appears to be the most desirable material as well.

We have observed that a good foot with a good shoe and a healthy frog can negotiate very slippery surfaces and actually seem to clutch on a rock like a cat's paw. When you cover the frog with a pad you replace a critically irregular and rubbery sort of surface and frog with a smooth surface that has no capability to function like a cat's paw. On the other hand, there is absolutely no doubt that at high speed a horse could come down on a hard, sharp object and get a bruise that would cause him to be eliminated from the contest. Of course, there are some particular kinds of terrain that might demand pads. The reader is advised to take into account his own horse, realizing that the use of pads will probably tend to weaken his horse's feet, to watch to see how people and their horses fare in the type of contest he wishes to enter, and then decide accordingly.

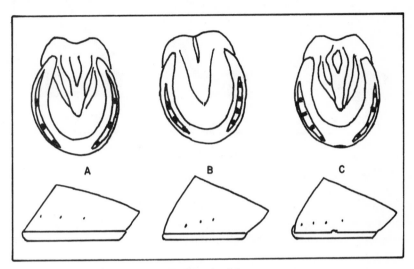

Fig. 7. The shod foot.

A represents the classical idea of a good shoeing job for general purpose on a left front foot. Three nails in each branch are evenly placed on a good substantial shoe. The hoof is not dubbed to make the hoof fit the shoe, but the shoe is rounded slightly at the toe to assist in breaking over when the foot leaves the ground. The shoe extends slightly beyond the hoof in front and in back.

B is an interpretive sketch based on the foot of Witezarif on the morning after the Tevis Cup Ride, 1976. Note that the foot is not balanced. There is more sole on the inside of the foot than the outside, and the frog does not aim precisely at the toe. The toe is dubbed. The shoe has four nails on the inside and three on the outside. The nails come out on the outside of the hoof in a line sloping upward to the rear. The shoe is standard with the regular fullered groove and is of rather light weight.

C represents an ideal endurance-ride shoe on an ideal foot. Note that the shoe is no thicker than Witezarif's but it is wider in front with four nails in each branch. The nails come out on a level, even line. The shoe has a toe and two side clips to take the shear strain off the nails. The shoe is slightly wider on the outside behind than on the inside, and the foot is balanced.

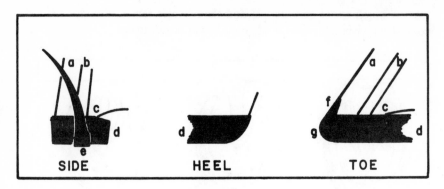

Fig. 8. Details of the shoe.

The side view shows the nail seated almost completely in the punched hole and entering the white-line area of the hoof. It curves gently, emerging out of the horny wall about three-quarters inch above the shoe-bearing face. The heel is shown rounded and flush with the rear of the hoof wall. The toe is rounded slightly and shows the toe clip.

In all drawings (a) represents the horny wall, (b) represents the white line, (c) represents the sole, (d) is the shoe, (e) is the nail, and (f) is the clip; (g) shows the ideal, slight upward curving of the shoe at the toe and the rounding to insure good break-over.

Nos. 18, 19, and 20 are views of the left front foot of Witezarif on the morning after the Tevis Cup Ride, 1976. Note in No. 18 the straightforward shoeing job. The hoof appears in good shape, but slightly out of balance. No. 19 also reveals a good foot, dubbed slightly at the toe. No. 20 shows a sound sole but a slightly unbalanced foot.

18.

19.

20.

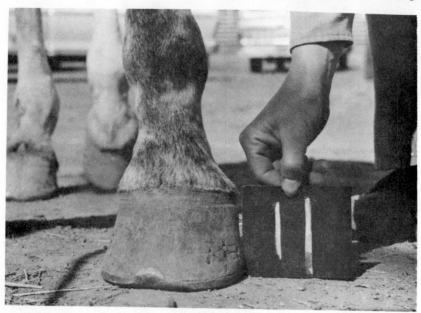

21.

Nos 21 through 23 are pictures of Champion, the Arab who tied Witezarif for first place and won the Haggin Cup for best condition. These pictures were made on the morning after the Tevis Cup, 1976. No. 21 shows a slightly crooked foot. The shoe has a toe clip. No. 22 shows several extra old nail holes, which are undesirable. There are no side clips. No. 23 shows a slightly wider web than Witezarif used.

22.

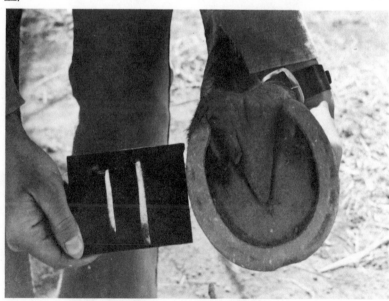

23.

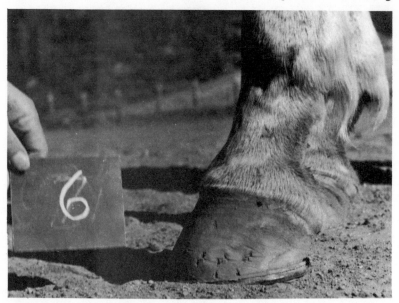

24.

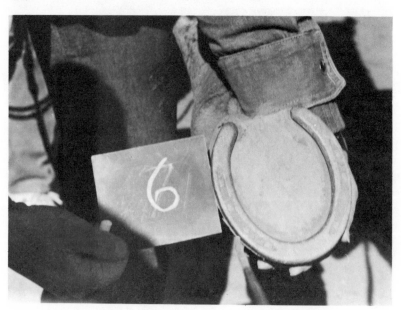

25.

Finally, if you look closely along a trail right after an endurance ride, you will see many objects that have dropped off for one reason or another, but the most common object is a shoe with a pad attached.

Easy boot is perhaps one of the most significant developments in recent years. It is a patented rubber overshoe that can be fastened to the horse's foot by a simple but ingenious tension-wire arrangement, which is supplemented, if desired, by a lateral-screw device to make it more secure. Easy Boots have been used successfully on a day-to-day basis in place of regular iron shoes. For example, at least four horses on the St. Joseph to Sacramento Pony Express Race, July 17 to September 14, 1976, used Easy Boots for most of the race, but in general they are used like a "spare tire." If you lose a shoe in practice or in a contest, you can put this boot on to prevent breaking up the horn or wearing down the face of the foot during the few miles there might be to cover before the regular shoe can be replaced. We are not of the school that would use these to replace shoes, but we do believe it is a good idea to carry one in order to make the best of a cast shoe on the trail a long way from home.

When we have the last set of shoes put on, about two weeks before a contest, we have a set of *extra shoes* made and marked to take with us. Should one come off during the contest, the crew can have a shoe ready for the emergency farrier at the next stop. This saves him much time when he might be loaded with work and at the same time ensures a good fit for our horse.

We feel that Illustration No. 26 tells the whole story, however, which boils down to the simple fact that while we live in an age capable of sending a man to the moon, we are still learning about horses' feet!

Nos. 24 and 25 are photos of the left front foot of Prince Koslaif, who placed fourth. These were taken on the day before the Tevis Cup Ride, 1976. The horse was not available for photos on the day after. No. 24 shows a great many extra nail holes. No. 25 reveals the pad held on with a four-nail job in each branch. There are no clips on toe or sides.

26. Bruce Branscomb, D.V.M., one of the most skillful judges in this sport, puzzles over Witezarif's right front foot. Should he go or should he stop? We feel this picture should make the point that it's not all that easy to decide about a horse's feet and shoes. Mother Nature will fool us all at least one more time. On this occasion Witezarif did go— and you should know what happened. He won again!

PART III

For Trainers, Crews, Riders

1

Physical Therapy for the Athletic Horse

Theories and Principles

Physical therapy is generally defined as the science of treating disability, injury, and disease by external physical means such as electricity, heat, light, massage, exercise, etc. Here we limit treatment to muscular disability and certain types of injury, and do not attempt to treat disease.

We further limit the conception in that we do not use electricity except in an indirect way to create heat or vibration.

Despite the risks involved in seeming to "oversimplify" nature, we will consider only three interrelated "systems" in the horse's body until we have progressed farther into the subject. These three are:

1. The skeletal system
2. The muscular system
3. The nervous system

It is self-evident that the muscles must be joined to the bones or they could not exert any influence on the bones. It is also self-evident that the nervous system must be integrated throughout the muscular system in order to perform its function of relating the whole animal to his environment and parts of the animal to each other.

Of course, the circulatory and glandular systems are involved, too, particularly in a tired or sick horse, but to grasp the subject of physical therapy we must at first limit ourselves to understanding certain fundamentals.

From the horseman's point of view, we have found it most helpful to think of the muscles in an animal's body as performing essentially two functions. One function involves precision movements requiring a complex association with the nervous system. In a human this is exemplified by any of the activities requiring manual dexterity, such as typing, playing a musical instrument, working with precision tools, etc. These muscles are relatively delicate, highly sensitive, and trainable to an amazing degree. The second function involves the grosser movements such as kicking or raising an arm or in other ways moving a part of the body against the pull of gravity. The muscles involved in these movements are large and relatively insensitive.

We call the large, lifting muscles the "antigravity" muscles. They must be relatively insensitive because they function in some degree almost continuously, even in sleep; if they were highly sensitive they would place an inordinate strain on the whole nervous system.

The small, precision muscles we call the "control" muscles. They can afford to be more sensitive because they are not in continuous use.

To demonstrate the two sets of muscles in use, lift your arm straight away from your side. In doing so, you are using large "antigravity" muscles primarily located in your back and particularly lying over the planes of your shoulders. There is no special feeling of sensitiveness in this maneuver. There is an old saying that we never feel the parts of ourselves until there is something the matter with them.

With your arm outstretched to the side, move your fingers and thumb as independently as you can. Let your index finger brush very lightly against your thumb and you will see that the sensory system is linked with the movement of your muscles in a very refined way. Without looking, you can touch your thumb with precision with any other finger in the same hand.

Now close your eyes and raise the other arm to the other side, keeping the first arm outstretched. Bring the two arms together (eyes closed) and attempt to touch the forefinger of one hand with the forefinger of the other. If you move slowly you will discover that the nervous system is not able to report with as much precision how close together your hands are until they touch. This illustrates the relative lack of refinement in the linkage between the nervous system and the big antigravity muscles.

In a horse, the simple movement of advancing his front legs at the trot falls in the class of using the big antigravity muscles that lie in the body of the horse, primarily in the shoulders and chest and along the spine. Should the horse wish to place his feet in a special way upon landing, because of obstacles or unevenness of the ground, he would bring smaller, more precise control muscles into play based on the use of his nervous system. This can involve the whole nervous system, not just the sensory nerves in the muscles themselves. It can involve the eyes or even the ears, the memory system, and, of course, the sense of touch.

Some horses have unusual movements in their front legs, such as winging, paddling, pointing their toes, or other extraneous movements associated with the simple act of moving their legs forward. These are evidences of involuntary, normally unnecessary, and undesirable linkages of control muscles to antigravity muscles. These involuntary and unnecessary linkages bring about fatigue, because they involve muscles that normally function only sporadically, rather than the large muscles designed for continuous use.

To demonstrate the relation of fatigue to the use of the two types of muscles, consider the human head. It is surprisingly heavy; it sits balanced at the top of the skeleton, where it is held in position by large antigravity muscles that function in a healthy person all day long without undue fatigue. But try holding your head cocked slightly to one side for a few minutes. This brings into play certain control muscles. Soon you will feel painful aches developing all the way down your back! Now relate this experience to that of a horse. The horse's head is also very heavy and placed, proportionately, even farther away from the main part of his body than yours. Consider, then, the possible aches and pains and consequent poor performance you may induce in the horse by requiring him to hold his head in an unnatural position for a long time by the application of of the wrong bit or the wrong application of the right bit!

Whenever unnecessary wear and tear on certain muscles is involved because of overuse or incorrect use, we should diagnose the nature of the ache or pain, contemplate the cause, and make long-range adjustments as necessary to avoid repeating this misuse. Immediately, however, we can, in many instances, through physical therapeutic techniques, do something to relieve pain and improve the situation.

Examination to Determine Therapy

It is unwise to attempt to render assistance until you are quite certain what the trouble is, and it may require years of experience to be able to know just how to go about rendering physical therapeutic assistance. But basically there are only a few ideas to master in order to be reasonably proficient.

First, one must have a good general idea about the relationship between the bones and the muscles in a horse's body. For this purpose we recommend any good book of anatomy. It is interesting, however, how much can be ascertained from a careful examination of a healthy athletic horse's body itself.

Second, one should appreciate the general lay-out of a single antigravity-type muscle wherever it may lie in the body, and the general lay-out of a control muscle wherever it may lie. We present here schematic diagrams of these two types of muscles and a schematic diagram showing the principle of their joining together and the relationship of the nerve areas.

Third, the student should appreciate certain simple mechanical ideas to see how muscles can combine to achieve an indefinite number of effects in movement. These movements are illustrated by a simple vector diagram in one plane and a couple established between two vector planes to show how quickly and easily motions may be established in a muscle system.

Fourth, the student must appreciate how, by shearing relationships between certain muscles and severing connections between muscles or muscles and bones, we can encounter a gamut of trouble from a simple sprain to a torn muscle or a pulled tendon.

Fifth, we must appreciate that there may be not only mechanical breakdowns in the muscle system, but chemical breakdowns as well, resulting in swelling, accumulated worn or burned-out tissues, even accumulations of trapped blood under circumstances of bruising or direct blows of various types.

Sixth and last, we must consider situations in which the muscular-skeletal system has been asked to do more than it can or has been exposed to strains beyond its reasonable limits or has been put out of adjustment by traumatic stress of one kind or another.

The *range of diagnosis* spans situations from simple tired muscles to broken bones. Broken bones and completely torn muscle represent extreme conditions of maladjustment that often leave the horse crippled for life, if not in such condition that he must be destroyed.

A severely torn or pulled muscle is nearly as bad as a broken bone. Consider a bowed tendon, for example. This injury is almost always observed in a front leg on a horse that has suffered a severe strain on the heavy tendon at the back of the leg that joins to a large combination of antigravity and control muscles in the forearm (which are in turn linked to muscles lying in the shoulder). The very hard cordlike material called the tendon is pulled out to a length beyond its normal as the result of a severe stretch. The cause is frequently a digging in of a foot in accelerating at the beginning of a race or similarly straining the muscle system in a phase of jumping or dramatic change of direction, as in the case of a cutting horse leaping back and forth. Once the fibers of the tendon have been pulled with relation to each other (sheared), it is virtually impossible for nature to put them back into the smooth, tight arrangement they enjoyed before the strain.

As a matter of principle, wherever a tendon or tendon sheath has been stretched, the horse should be laid up for a long time. He should have his feet trimmed short in the toe and high in the heel.

The symptoms of a stretched tendon or tendon sheath are immediate and obvious pain accompanied by lameness, either continuous or incidental to work. When the tendon is "bowed," the stretching has been so great that the actual length is materially increased and the sheath actually does bow along the line of the bone. This is almost always the digital flexor tendon running along the back of the cannon bone and down over the pullylike structure on the back of the fetlock.

At the other end of the spectrum of muscular-skeletal difficulty, we encounter the very subtle sources of lameness. The examiner may say of the difficult case, "This must be a case of navicular disease," or "It seems to be in the shoulder," or he makes some other vague statement that, translated bluntly, simply means that he just does not know what the matter is.

If you are asked to examine a horse that is reported to be lame or sore, do not pay a great deal of attention to the statements of the rider other than that the horse is not moving right. Most riders are conscious from either the feel of the horse or the appearance of the horse that there is an irregularity in his motion, but when they start

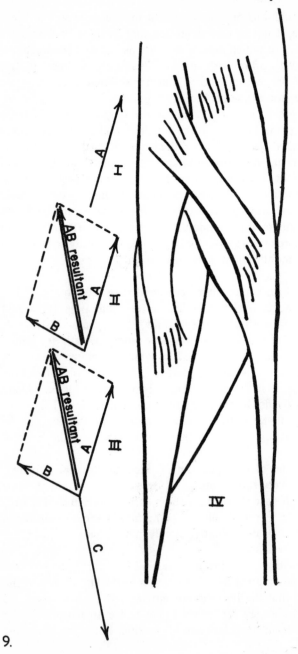

9.

Fig. 9. I, II, and III are vector diagrams illustrating the theoretical nature of force application in muscle. It suggests a simple muscle contraction in the direction of the arrow with a force indicated by the length A.

II shows the same arrow (A) with the additional effect of another muscle working the direction and degree of force indicated by B. The net result is called a resultant vector and is indicated by the double arrow A-B.

III shows this picture being counterpoised by the arrow C.

Here we see how a multitude of effects can be achieved by only two muscles working together.

IV is a schematic drawing of some hypothetical muscles that could contract and work together to produce the effects suggested in the vector diagrams.

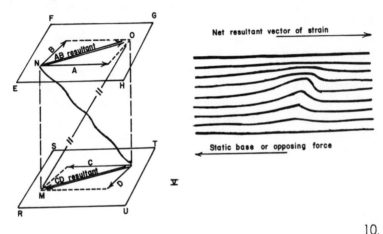

10.

Fig. 10. Planes EFGH and RSTU contain vector diagrams like the one in 11 in Fig. 9. The forces are applied generally toward the right in the upper plane and toward the left in the lower plane. This situation can result in a "couple" with either a compression resultant suggested by the wavy line NP or a shearing resultant suggested by the split line MO. Such forces between layers of muscles can manifest themselves in a "nappe," as indicated in the next diagram to the right. These nappes compare to ripple marks in the sandy bottom of a river when the current has dragged particles of sand.

A nappe in a muscle can be very painful, and very limiting to any animal.

to go into details to describe the problem, in most instances their words only serve to confuse the examiner. Therefore we recommend you do your own observing and do your own thinking following a set procedure.

Upon approaching the horse for examination, take time to see the whole animal to form an overall impression. Too many examiners go straight to the point or assumed point of difficulty and attempt to make a decision on the basis of what the informing person says and a local examination of the horse's body.

As soon as you have established a general frame of reference for the horse by looking at the whole horse in one sweeping view, look closely at his head, noting any signs of pain such as stiff ears, hard eyes, or other attitudes, including the attitude of the head in relation to the rest of the animal.

Use your hands and particularly your fingertips, being sure to use the flats of the fingers, not the tips. It is useful to practice feeling of horses as well as looking at them when they are in good condition and have nothing wrong with them. This experience will give you a basis for making decisions about disabilities. It is much easier to see something wrong if you are first acquainted with what is right.

Bear in mind that an apparent unevenness of motion can result from a compensatory requirement in the horse's body. A person, for example, may have a kink in his back and consequently step with a short stride on one side and place his foot lightly. An inexperienced examiner might think there was something wrong with the person's foot, when, in fact, it is a problem with his back. Similarly, but complicated by the fact that a horse has four legs, we may find a case in which the right front foot seems to be sore when, in fact, it is the left hind or the back.

No matter what the apparent problem is, it is very worthwhile to follow a set procedure in examining the horse. After examining the head you might note the neck and shoulders briefly. We commonly manipulate the spine lightly to see if there is any flinching before addressing our attention to the horse's legs. Assuming the right hind appears to be sore, we do not go to the right hind. We always begin with the right front, then go to the right hind, then the left hind, then the left front. In this way we are able to maintain a stable frame of reference for making observations. We follow this order beginning with the right front and working around the horse ending with the left front no matter where the apparent lameness is.

27. Kathy Tellington demonstrates taking TPRs simultaneously. Thermometer in rectum, pulse with left hand on root of tail, and respiration by eye watching flank.

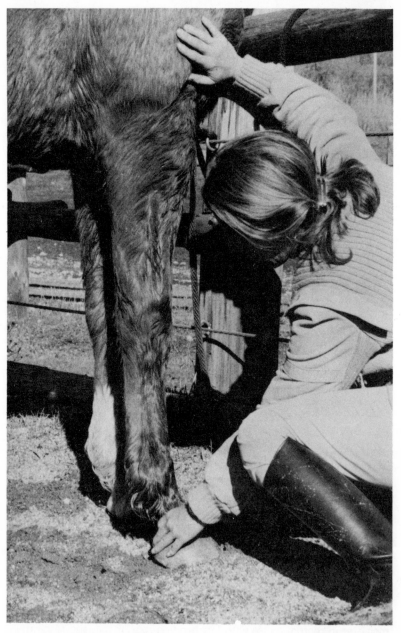

28. Kathy taking digital pulse between bulbs on front foot.

We are feeling for several possible *symptoms* of difficulty with the muscular-skeletal system. They are:

1. Localized spots are warmer to the touch than surrounding areas. We call this "heat in the part."

2. Localized soft spots that have an abnormal tactile character. We call these puffs or swellings, and they may range from very soft and flabby types to firm, rubbery types or hard swellings. The flabby soft types, which may actually move under the touch of the finger, are often called wind puffs.

3. Sore spots that are revealed by the horse's reluctance to have them touched at all or are revealed only when the horse adopts a certain specific stance. Subtle soreness is often more easily detected in a leg when it is not supporting weight. When it is supporting weight there is sufficient tightness throughout the whole leg to conceal light soreness in many instances. In general, if the soreness is revealed only with the leg in a nonsupport position, we associate this with recent injury. If the soreness is revealed only when the leg is in a support position, we associate this with an old injury.

4. Digital pulse differentials. It is possible to take a pulse near the bottom of the leg in most horses. This is felt at the back of the foot just over the bulbs in the hollow part under the fetlock. In the case of a healthy horse at rest, this digital pulse is often difficult to feel. But after a horse has exercised hard it is usually easy enough to find because of the excessive pumping of blood under these conditions. Once you have developed some feel for this, you can use this diagnostic technique to very good advantage. If a horse has sustained a strain beyond reasonable capability in any one foot, he will usually reveal a strong-feeling digital pulse within a minute or two after the injury when compared to the opposite leg. For example, if a horse strains a left front foot in jumping or sudden turning or in any other way, you can find a strong throbbing pulse in that foot that will not appear in the right front foot. This is what we call a differential digital pulse. It will reveal itself as a rule some time before the horse takes a lame step, except in the most severe cases. And the digital pulse will maintain the differential character for several hours after the injury.

Injuries to Feet or Legs

With relation to most injuries to horses' feet or legs, the order or experience would be:

1. The injury. As a rule a competent rider will know that the horse might have been injured because of the nature of the circumstance, or because of the horse's immediate reaction to the moment of injury.

2. Development of a digital pulse. This is sometimes accompanied by momentary severe limping. It compares to your hitting your thumb with a hammer. Almost instantly you jump around and shake with pain. A digital pulse immediately follows in your thumb, but a few minutes later it does not feel quite so bad. The real pain will settle in perhaps 30 minutes later. Similarly with the horse, there is the immediate nervous reaction to the initial injury, followed by the digital pulse. At that moment there has obviously been no time to develop swelling or any other sign of trouble.

3. 2 to 15 minutes after the digital pulse has developed, swelling may begin to reveal itself along with growing tenderness.

4. About 10 minutes after the injury the horse will begin to favor the injured leg by limping in such a way that the sore leg carries little or none of his weight as it moves through its cycle with relation to the other three legs. Because of the four-legged motion of the horse, the diagonal legs work more or less together, and an injury in a given leg may be confused with a possible injury in its diagonal counterpart—for example, the left front with the right rear, or the right front with the left rear. Where the injury is subtle (showing no swelling or localized tenderness), it is often possible to make a positive identification of the true sore leg by careful analysis of the apparent heat in the part of the leg or by noting differences in the pulse. The rate of the pulse will be the same, but the apparent strength of the pulse will be greater in the true sore leg.

5. Notable overall reaction to the injury. The horse may begin to sweat with pain a few minutes after the injury and keep it up until he experiences some relief. This is only in the case of relatively severe injuries, and the sweat is different from working sweat. It has a cold, clammy character, and is usually developed in the antigravity muscles most closely associated with the injured part. This, of course, is the primary glandular reaction to injury. The heartbeat may go up in response to the injury. The respiration also often rises or remains up in a range well above 40 breaths per minute.

6. The horse will often appear to crave something to chew on. This parallels a person's desire to have something to clench in a fist to help overcome pain. Until the examination is completed it is unwise to let the horse chew on hay or anything else, because the chewing motion itself disturbs the horse sufficiently to obscure certain subtle actions and motions that would be very useful to the examiner. For example, it is nearly impossible to get a good pulse reading with a stethoscope on a horse while it is eating.

Beware of assuming that the first injury identified is the only one, especially if the injury was sustained in jumping. The horse could easily have injured more than one leg. If it happens to be the two fronts or the two back legs, immediate observation of difficulty may not be easy. In this case digital-pulse observations may be impossible, unless one leg is injured more severely than the other. The prime sources of information about the injury in this situation would be careful feeling for localized soreness in each leg, which requires a great deal of experience.

The value of sensing out localized injuries during their early stages cannot be overemphasized. The skillful horseman should develop the ability to detect correctly and very early the advent of trouble. For example, if an injured leg can be diagnosed by the horseman within one minute of the time of the injury, he has many critical minutes in which to do things of a physical therapeutic nature that can cut the "down time" from as much as 6 months to as little as 2 days! Good horsemen should therefore be as well versed in these arts as possible, because no one can hope to have a veterinarian available even on an hour's notice in many situations.

29. Ernie Sanchez, Navajo Indian, trainer, and movie stunt rider who was on the staff of the Research Farm, demonstrates the original gypsy system for manipulating a horse's back. Note the extreme variance in slope of croup under the trained touch of his hands.

Treatments

The treatment to apply depends, of course, on the *nature and condition of the injury:* whether it is severe or light, new or old, an open wound or under the surface. But equally important, we must take into consideration the horse's environment: climate; season; stable size. Even the presence or absence of flies may affect the therapist's choice of treatment. For example, using water on a cold, windy night is much different from using it on a warm, sunny day. And whether the water itself is chemically conditioned city water or clear, unadulterated country water is a significant factor in therapy.

As in all aspects of the subject of physical therapy, a knowledge of the fundamentals is our first consideration.

The basic *tools* of the therapist are cloths, water, simple manipulations such as rubbing, elementary chemical compounds such as leg braces and liniments, bandages of various types, and, finally, specific manipulations of the injured parts. Again, a few elementary physical principles govern our choice of tools.

Hot and cold, Wet or dry—are among basic considerations in treatment. If we compare a damp to a dry medium—water to air, for example—we learn that damp materials have a more penetrating effect than dry ones. You can stand for a while in air at a temperature of 125° F without too much discomfort. But try immersing yourself in water at 125°! Or, more dramatically, imagine yourself walking around in clothes in air at a temperature of 40° F, but try remaining in the same clothes in a tub of water at 40°! Each medium has a place in our system of treatment, but they are *rarely* interchangeable. There is a great difference between a heat lamp and a hot compress.

Heat and cold themselves, however applied, have positive effects on the physiological system. Heat applied to a part tends to act as a crutch to the blood in that it relieves the blood of the problem of keeping that part warm—one of the primary functions of blood being to maintain even temperatures in given parts of the body. Correct warm temperatures applied for correct periods of time will bring about a decrease in the volume of blood flowing to and from that part. Cold temperatures affect the flow of blood in the opposite way. When a part starts to cool, blood immediately flows into that part with more vigor.

When tissues have been damaged in a part, there is a tendency at first to clog the avenues of traffic with the damaged materials. Heat applied will help to loosen up the damaged materials (which is beneficial), but at the same time it will slow down the flow of blood (which is not desirable). Cold applied to the part tends to solidify the damaged materials and make them hard to move (which is not desirable), but it tends to make the blood flow with more vigor (which is beneficial). It may be useful to imagine the body is like a big city and a point in the leg is like a street intersection near a freeway where the on-ramp traffic can be affected by the condition of traffic at the street intersection. If a traffic accident occurs at the intersection it is common to have the general flow of traffic interrupted by cars mildly involved, pinned into lines of traffic, or casually slowing down to see what happened. This is not unlike the condition of blood particles and tissue particles in an injured part of the body.

The solution is for a traffic officer to come along and reroute traffic as well as he can, hurrying people past the scene of the accident. In the body this is best done by applying cold water and making the blood hurry along through the nearby "streets" (the veins and arteries) until the "wrecker" can get to the scene of the accident.

As traffic clears up slowly, the wrecker finally arrives and the "dead tissue" is removed from the scene of the accident. Finally normal traffic is resumed.

The wrecker is in the form of applied heat to the part of the body. The heat can break up the old tissue and help the blood to pick it up.

Thus we see a clear reason for alternating cold and hot applications. These are usually best if they are damp because of the extra penetrating quality of damp media compared to dry media. We must remember that in inclement conditions damp media may be too traumatic for the body as a whole, and chill, cold, or shock can set in.

In summary, for a "traffic accident" in a part of the body (an injury involving damaged tissue and blocked flow of blood), we apply a cold compress to keep the traffic moving and get the blood coming into and out of the area rapidly. Then we apply a hot compress and erode away some of the clogged blood near the seat of the damage. We then shift back to cold water to get that much moved out and, after a few minutes, change again to heat until we have the swelling (the blocked traffic in the localized area) under control.

In almost all cases, the sequence is to apply cold then heat to damaged parts.

Certain *chemicals,* simple penetrants and salts, such as common salt, Epsom salt, bicarbonate of soda, alcohol, iodine, glycerine, and certain oils like camphor or eucalyptus, may be useful in therapy.

Epsom salt, for example, is a purgative or cleanser with considerable potency. It has the ability to irritate tissue in such a way that the glands are induced to pour out a greater amount of secretion. It is through the action of cleansing in this way that a certain amount of the source of swelling in a localized part may be "drawn out" of the area directly through the skin.

Bicarbonate of soda, because it is an antacid, has very soothing qualities whether taken internally or applied to delicate membranes or to skin as a whole. Often it has a very good effect if applied to a damaged area with the object of soothing the part so the overall system works with less strain. It is like keeping the crowd calm around the scene of the accident. The officials and ambulances and wreckers can work more efficiently in a serene atmosphere than in a tense one. So we associate bicarbonate of soda with maintaining a certain physical serenity and Epsom salt with removing certain kinds of material that contribute to the swelling.

Alcohol is a very interesting substance. Made basically by yeasts working on sugars (as in simple wine making), it may be distilled to a high level of purity and consequent potency. When mixed with wood naphtha it forms the ordinary rubbing alcohol that we refer to here. This is poisonous if administered internally; but it has many characteristics that make it very useful in treating wounds and injuries. Because it freezes at a low temperature, it is an excellent coolant and may be used to cool a part in place of cold water, thus causing blood to flow with more vigor. Alcohol is also a drying agent. It can dry skin, as we all know. This means that it draws water from the upper parts of the skin, then it coagulates the protoplasm in the local area and thus hardens it, so that micro-organisms are imprisoned in the outer layers and consequently cannot contaminate the wound. Continuing our analogy with a traffic accident, we might see the alcohol acting as a person with flares keeping other cars from crashing into the scene of the accident and compounding the situation. It would also compare to taking general precautions around the scene of the accident to prevent fires or explosions, etc. Alcohol seals off and halts the movement of micro-organisms that might contaminate the area in its moment of weakness. Alcohol also dissolves fats. This means it can take away fatty materials in the skin that are natural places where the potentially dangerous micro-organisms normally live. The micro-organisms, a necessary part of the healthy ecological system, are to be controlled around a weakened part if possible.

Iodine is a nonmetallic element found largely in seaweed or kelp. In concentrated form it is a powerful irritant and will act on glands in a very interesting way. Painted on skin, it first stains, then causes the skin to flake off. Used in combination with rubbing alcohol it seems to have a beneficial effect on the growth of hair, but it must not be used in too strong a solution.

Glycerine is a heavy, clear liquid which, although mildly irritating in some ways, has the overall effect of a soothant to the skin. It works well in softening the skin surface to allow the absorption of other drugs. When combined with alcohol and iodine it helps them to penetrate deeper.

Camphor is an oily substance that acts first as a mild stimulant to the nerve endings in the skin and then has the long-range effect of a sedative. Oil of eucalyptus also dulls pain and is called an antispasmodic. Thus we see that alcohol mixed with the oils is effective in clearing away debris after an accident to a part in the body.

Most of the rubbing compounds, liniments, etc., are combinations of the ingredients discussed here, often blended with more esoteric drugs in mild forms. In general, using regular preparations is appropriate, but for certain kinds of injury a mixture of one-sixteenth cup oil of eucalyptus, three-sixteenths cup glycerine, one-quarter cup tincture of iodine, and one-half cup ordinary rubbing alcohol makes a clear fluid for application to injured parts. We shall refer to this as the iodine mix.

Epsom salts poured into hot water make a marvelous solution for soaking sore or tired parts. A normal salt solution is described as that condition of salts in water in which the water has absorbed all that it can. Epsom salts in normal solution make an excellent conditioner for tired flesh. Bicarbonate of soda in warm water is also very good for tired flesh.

Simple fatigue differs from localized injury only in degree of damage and extent. The injury usually involves much more damage per unit part, while fatigue involves a general or wide distribution of light damage. Alcohol rubs and hot baths are good for fatigue but not sufficient for injuries, whereas iodine mixes and potent solutions are good for injured parts but much too stimulating for simple cases of fatigue.

Cloths and bandages vary considerably in character and use. Cloths, as we think of them for therapeutic use, range from a roll of cotton

30. Kathy Tellington demonstrates watering a leg with use of gunny sack and ordinary garden hose.

batten to a burlap sack, and bandages run the gamut from loose coverings to hard supports and elastic restricters.

Because of its lightness, easy manipulation, and absorbent qualities, soft cotton (called absorbent cotton) is extremely useful in a variety of ways, from a vehicle for a liquid solution to a mechanical cushion around a tender part. It should be in the therapist's kit at all times. Standard bandage material, on the other hand, has little use around horses because it is difficult to keep in place. For covering parts, it is simpler to use material such as gauze, or absorbent cotton covered with gauze, wrapped with a standard horse bandage or horse wrap that has elastic qualities. Bandage materials that have mild adhesive characteristics are very useful, but one must be aware that these bandages inhibit circulation of air to the skin and can, if too tight, inhibit the flow of blood under the skin.

Although it is possible for a medical doctor or surgeon to use antiseptics and various physical measures to control contamination around wounds and injuries of people, it is virtually impossible to create or sustain such conditions for horses. One cannot say to a horse, "Now lie down and take it easy." Nor can he say, "Keep this clean" as he wraps up the wound. The nearest the horseman can get to the pure conditions necessary for good healing of open wounds is to put the horse in a nice big green-grass pasture where there is ample room and he is not standing in his own bedding, as in the case of a stall, or in his well-trodden and manure-laden environment, as in the case of a small paddock. It is much more difficult to heal a wound in a stall or small paddock than it is in a big green pasture.

Water alone is probably the therapist's best friend, if used properly, but, in general, water applied to an open wound may do more damage than good. It has been our experience that this will be followed by occurrences of proud flesh in varying degrees, poor heals in the form of heavy, unsightly ridges around the original wound area, and exposure to secondary infections.

If an injury involves both an *open wound and internal damage* we must make a decision to favor the open wound or the general damage. If the wound is small and clear while the general damage is rather extensive, as in the case of a horse that has crashed into a jump and is developing a large swelling although the broken skin amounts only to light superficial bruises and a few minor lacerations, we would go ahead with water treatments and finish off with a cool application of our iodine mix. We would almost certainly not use bandages of any kind.

If, on the other hand, the wound is paramount, being an open cut several inches long, we know the swelling will not amount to much since the damaged tissues have a direct avenue of escape out the wound itself and do not need to be "carted off" a long distance by the blood in order to be dissipated. Therefore we give our attention to the wound and let the problem of swelling go. In this case we would not use water. In a city environment we would feel some obligation to disinfect, but we would not use soap and water, nor would we use wire brushes or other major irritants. We would probably prepare our simple iodine mix (as much as two quarts) for a sizable wound. Then we would flush the wound by squirting the mix out of a bulb-type applicator, making sure not to touch the wound in any way with anything but the iodine mix itself. *We would not scrub or dab or touch—* even if there was obvious dirt or other foreign particles, even sticks and stones, in the wound. This is an instance of gypsy theory superseding modern medicine.

We followed this method in healing a heavy wound that penetrated to the bone in the forearm of a young stallion. In the illustrations, you can see that the wound healed very well. We could fill this book with pictures of good results. We have also tried following the procedures of using strong antiseptics, antibiotics, and plastic surgery. In almost all cases, the treatment that involved sewing up the wound has resulted in relatively unsightly scars and obvious misconnection of certain muscles on opposite sides of the wound.

We would in general not cover a wound. Just let it gape open. The only exception would be during a period of fly infestation. In that case, we would wrap the wound with a light gauze cover and remove this bandage daily to be sure no part of it became involved in the healing scab.

There is a certain kind of a wound that is difficult for horsemen to deal with in an objective way. This is a wound made by a foreign object of good size that breaks off and is found sticking into the horse's flesh. The packers in wilderness areas often call this "a stick," or "the horse stuck himself." It is common in coniferous tree country where the horse catches himself on an old log or on the side of a tree and punctures himself with a stub of a pine or spruce bow that breaks off from the tree. We have seen sticks an inch or more in diameter and ten or twelve inches long broken off in this way after being caught inside a horse's leg or in the stomach itself. The penetration would range from half an inch to three or four inches. For many years we followed our instinct to "suffer for the horse" and we pulled the stick out, then probed into the hole with various devices to disinfect the wound. The results were invariably the same: a serious problem of infection, followed by from two weeks to two months of daily care, and finally a closed wound with a large knot in the flesh where the stick had been. After learning the gypsy technique, we simply left the stick in the flesh until it came out of its own accord. We discovered that the flesh soon formed a pussy material that completely surrounded the stick, protecting the flesh from contamination. It also provided a lubricant for the stick to slide out without disrupting the skin. And miracle of all miracles, with no medicine, no rubbing, no attention of any kind, the wound healed without a trace of a scar within two weeks!

To conclude the observations regarding open wounds we would say:

1. Let nature do the job for the most part.
   a. In the event of clean wounds, regardless of size or location, leave them alone.
   b. If the environment is basically natural, leave the wound alone.
2. When necessary, use medication.
   a. With punctures where anarobic activities may take place, it is wise to protect the horse from tetanus by appropriate medication.
   b. In circumstances where even the air is not clean, as in most city situations, following normal medical procedures is probably the only thing to do.

With injuries to muscles where no breach of skin cover is involved, the normal procedure would be:

1. Survey the extent of damage, being sure that there is not more than one locus of injury.
2. In warm circumstances make an early application of cold water. This may be done by wrapping the part with a burlap sack and wetting the sack, since a certain cooling, or even supercooling, action can take place by air moving through the wet sack near the wound. This is the action of a simple evaporating water cooler such as the type used commonly in the Southwest. This cool-water treatment would normally require about fifteen minutes.

3. Follow instantly with a hot compress composed of very hot water soaked into a soft bandage. The hot water would be a normal solution of Epsom or simple table salt. This hot treatment would require two repetitions about five minutes apart.
4. Repeat the alternation of cold and hot at least four complete cycles or until the affected part shows no sign of stabilizing itself in a hard, swollen condition.
5. End the treatment on a cold-water application followed by a rub-down of the part and a final application of the iodine mix.
6. After about six hours, repeat the process as necessary. If there is heat in the part, start with cold water. If the part is not hot, start with a hot compress.
7. Depending on the injury, start exercising the horse within six hours of the time of the accident. If the injury causes a basic conformational change, such as a bowed tendon, do not exercise. If the injury involves only swelling, no matter how much, the horse should be exercised within six hours. If the swelling is very large and you are sure there is no bone involvement (for example, injury to the bone cover, periostium, or the bone itself), exercise should be commenced within an hour of the accident.

There is a specific kind of injury that requires a different treatment. Whenever moving bones meet, there are little covers over the *joints* called joint capsules. Inside these capsules the body provides a certain correct amount of lubricating fluid called synovia. Injuries involving the joint capsule are often very touchy. A capped hock is this kind of an injury, as are certain kinds of "popped" knees.

In cases involving joint capsules we have never found hot water or heavy drugs to be of any value. Cold water is preferred.

Some persons advocate draining the excess fluid that is secreted to alleviate the pain in the joint. But our experience leads us to conclude that any unnecessary penetration of this capsule should be avoided. We do not favor draining joints. Nor do we favor injections of any kind, particularly of cortisones.

For injuries to joint capsules we recommend complete rest in a large open pasture, a light diet involving very little if any grain, cold-water treatment once a day for about half an hour, and a good dose of patience. We have had excellent results following this procedure, even in one case where a very expensive Thoroughbred was down in a van and was kicked viciously, injuring his face almost beyond definition and his front legs, with joint capsule involvement in both knees. This horse was declared by competent veterinarians to be totally unsound and unlikely to ever walk again. After four months of the treatment prescribed here, the horse was working regularly in horseshows and won an amateur hunt club flat race by a handy sixteen lengths—within a year of the injury!

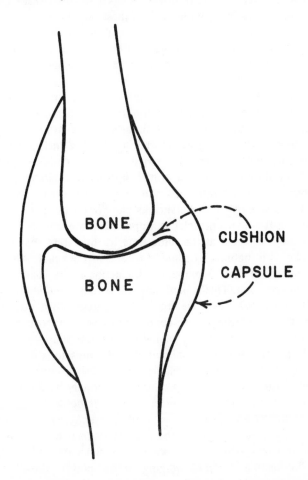

Fig. 11. This schematic drawing shows how bone ends meet inside a capsule. This simple but mystifying mechanical linkage should rarely if ever be tampered with except by the external application of cold water.

Rubbing and Manipulation

Two aspects of treatment, perhaps the most significant and least understood of all, involve manipulation and rubdowns.

How much movement and what kind of movement are good for a sore muscle or a bruised bone or an injured-joint capsule or even an open wound? Before getting down to cases, let us consider certain physical principles involved in each of these situations.

A truth of physics is that any movement requires an application of energy. Furthermore, an application of energy manifesting itself in a movement involves a change, or to be more specific, an exchange, which in turn involves the development of heat.

This means that a muscle in a healthy horse is a mechanism capable of converting a chemical into a motion. The chemical is activated, apparently, by a nerve signal and changes as necessary to cause the muscle to shrink in size, thus shortening itself in such a way that it pulls together whatever may be joined to its two ends. For example, a muscle on the inside of your arm shrinks as you fold your forearm up toward your upper arm. That muscle relaxes and a muscle running along the outside of your arm shrinks and your arm opens out again. By working these two muscles in opposition to each other, you can exercise both of them at the same time to the extent that your arm will shake with inability to respond to one or the other. An interesting phenomenon that accompanies this action is the instant creation of heat in your arm. This is how simple it is to make one arm warmer than the other. Whenever we are cold we shiver. This is an involuntary act resulting from setting control muscles in opposition to each other, and it is nature's way of helping us warm up.

When a little bit of material stored in the muscle is used to make the muscle work, there is a residue that we might compare to ashes left after a fire. This residue is removed routinely by the blood as it comes by. A new batch of a kind of sugar is delivered and the old material picked up more or less continuously. When the muscle is damaged by a physical blow, the blood has an overload of work in bringing up fresh tissue and taking away the damaged tissue. If it has to do this in addition to bringing up the "power juices," or sugar, which are needed to make the muscle move, the blood is carrying a very heavy load and the process breaks down. This is why swellings generally are larger if we work an injured part than if we rest it. On the other hand, the very movement of the muscle helps jar loose the dead tissue so the blood can pick it up easier. Therefore a judicious amount of movement (enough to physically loosen the old tissue without requiring too much in the form of "power juices") is beneficial. Experience has taught us that, as a rule, mild exercise is helpful in relieving pain and reducing swelling in injured parts. It was to meet the requirements of this condition that various electrical massaging devices have been developed.

This, of course, brings us directly to the subject of manipulation and rubdowns. If, instead of requiring the horse to use his "power juices" and exercise himself, we simply move his muscles in a skillful way by manipulating them for him, we accomplish the desired loosening of dead tissue while holding down the horse's level of requirement of power juice. Furthermore, if as a result of understanding how the muscles work and relate to each other, we can move the skeletal parts with relation to each other, we can hope to accomplish therapeutic adjustments of the muscles one to another, in addition to jarring loose dead tissue.

Everyone knows how good it feels to stretch. Everyone knows how good it feels to relax. Stretching and relaxing involve the biggest muscles in the part that stretches or relaxes. With stretching there is a tautness that brings about an almost tingly feeling as the nerves in the control muscles are compressed by the big antigravity muscles on either side of them. Relaxing, on the other hand, reduces feeling to as little as possible, as the big antigravity muscles achieve the ultimate in softness in their contact with the control muscle and consequently reduce the intermuscular pressure on the nerves.

A hot-water application—a deep hot bath, for example—brings about a general slowing down of flow of blood for a short time and a general easing off of the activity of the whole system, thus resulting in an overall feeling of relaxedness. A cold shower brings about an instant springing to action of the circulatory system, thus resulting in an overall feeling of exhilaration.

A dry-heat application, such as a heat lamp, or an afternoon on the beach in the sun can slow your blood flow down so much that you have a hard time remaining awake.

A good massage followed by a soothing rubdown has equally salutary effects. In this case the relaxedness takes a slightly different form, and if the massager combines his efforts with skillful applications of hot water, very cold water, and dry heat, as in the case of Turkish and sauna baths, you can feel so relaxed for a long period afterward that you might think you are coming apart at the joints.

Skillful uses of heat and cold, dry and wet, and rubdowns have again and again made the difference between winning and losing for baseball pitchers, boxers, fencers, swimmers, and divers—just about every person who has ever been engaged in athletics. But the rubdown for the horse is not, as a general rule, thoroughly understood or applied as it is for human athletes. With their knowledgeability in this area, gypsies in Europe were for many centuries able to do marvelous things with horses.

Rubbing has three effects: first, the simple creation of heat through friction, which in itself is beneficial; second, the working of parts of a muscle with relation to other parts of the same muscle, thus bringing about an improvement in local circulation. This aids in working dead tissue out of the muscle and thus restores a feeling of well-being. Finally, through a combination of rubbing and manipulating, the massager is able to move one muscle with relation to another, even slightly, thus bringing about the smoothest possible structural relationship between muscles. This is essentially what a trainer is doing in giving a baseball pitcher a rubdown. As a matter of fact, this structural smoothing out is essentially what is happening under the skin of any athlete when he is warming up.

Muscles in slight misadjustment are said to be tight. We have all heard the expression "having a Charley horse" or "getting a cramp" or "getting a knot" in a muscle. A very slight nappe in a control muscle brought about by an inadvertent couple set up between two large antigravity muscles can bring on sudden pain and near total immobilization of the part where this condition occurs.

The intergravity-muscle nappe (a precise physical term for a charley horse) is usually relieved by sudden and dramatic movement of the whole affected part or by very positive massage in a direction transverse to the antigravity muscle nearest the surface in the local area.

Massaging and manipulation should be undertaken with the object, primarily, of finishing in such a way that the muscles are laid very smoothly one over the other from the bones to the skin with no irregularities and no misalignments. Where control muscles are highly developed, as in the case of piano players and baseball pitchers, there is, as a rule, little difficulty with knots in muscles. A long, slow warm-up time precludes the possibility of an imminent tie-up, such as occurs when the muscles are brought into full play too rapidly.

With horses this problem is slightly different. A dressage horse whose movements have been schooled to a point of high refinement requires a very slow and careful warm-up, while a polo horse or a race-horse can be expected to warm up relatively rapidly. Whereas the dressage horse may only be a bit stiff, the polo horse or the race-horse can get a tied muscle much more easily.

The actual technique of manipulating involves stretching the legs with relation to the body of the horse and manipulating the spine and the muscles along the spine ever so slightly to bring about the internal feeling of freshness that a deep but gentle, penetrating but sympathetic manipulation of flesh can do. The accompanying photographs illustrate the way of establishing differential pressures between the thumbs of the two hands and the fingers on either side of them in working on the horse's back. One should be careful as he approaches the wither area because the vertebrae have longer parts extending upward, and consequently give the massager greater leverage in working one bone with relation to its neighbor.

Having manipulated the back while standing on the near side, the massager moves to the off side of the horse and repeats the process, working from wither to tail bone with emphasis in the lumbar area between the lower rib and the pelvic area. He works slowly and with a patient firmness, waiting each time he exerts pressure to feel the horse relax under his grip. Then he releases his grip suddenly. A transverse strain is built up in a point of the spine by steady pressure with a sympathetic feel waiting for the horse to "give." When a maximum of local deviation has been established the pressure is rapidly released, thus allowing the horse's own muscles to do most of the actual relative manipulating. This compares to the principles of Japanese combat wrestling, in which the combatant attempts to use his opponent's weight and strength to his advantage. The massager can never apply enough pressure to do much good himself. He must work the parts into a good position with slow, steady, more or less intermittent but unrelenting force, then let go.

The front leg is then lifted in such a way that the cannon bone is held parallel to the ground. By holding the cannon bone parallel to the ground and swinging the forearm back and forth, a good check on any possible tie-up in that leg is possible. If the movement in the leg is restricted for any reason, the plane of the bottom of the foot will change its angle with the ground as the leg is moved back and forth. If the muscular-skeletal relationships are normal, the angle between the plane of the foot and the ground will not change.

The front leg is then pulled directly back until the foot is about

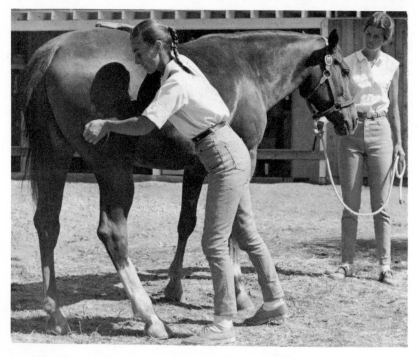

31. Linda demonstrates massaging.

even with the point of the hip but about a foot or more below that point. It is then coaxed gently to give as much as possible. With patience the massager will feel the horse finally give between two and five inches more than expected. Do not hold this position more than a second or two. Let the leg go back promptly but smoothly. Then, without allowing the leg to touch the ground, pull it forward and upward until the foot is even with the bottom of the chest at least, or a bit higher, and the leg is extended straight to the front. Then again, with a patient urging, get the horse to give you that extra two to five inches as he gains confidence that all is well. As in the case of pulling backward, hold this extended position only a second or so and let the horse draw the leg in swiftly but smoothly and put it down. This may be repeated two or three times, but no more. Too much of this is not good for a horse since it can disrupt the relation between his biggest antigravity muscles and the scapula itself.

The hind legs are manipulated in the same way, pulling them first to the front until the foot is even with the elbow; and again the patient, teasing pulling applied gently but firmly will result in the horse's giving you that extra two to five inches of stretch. Move the foot through an arc close to the ground without touching the ground and pull it straight to the rear until the bones in the back leg form a straight line. Again wait for that extra stretch and then let the horse put the leg down. Rest for a minute and repeat, but not more than a total of three times for each hind leg.

There are various signs the massager should look for in the horse during these maneuvers to observe pain or evidence of pleasant relief. Pain obviously is first registered by jerking the foot to a more normal position. Pleasure is registered by closing the eyes, laying the ears back, quivering the lower lip, and co-operating with the movements of the massager.

Naturally, these maneuvers are so strange to a horse the first time they are tried that you will get little more than resentful co-operation, but patient understanding and a few repetitions spaced by a week or more will soon bring the horse around to a very co-operative frame of mind. Horses educated to these manipulations learn to take big stretches themselves, extending one back leg out behind them as far as possible at times and doing a deep chest stretch involving setting the two front legs far out in front while sinking the chest to a position almost touching the ground, while the hind legs remain more or less in a normal position. In this maneuver the horse stretches his neck as far out as possible.

The actual technique of rubbing involves a highly developed sense of touch on the part of the massager. By exploring the horse's upper legs, shoulders and haunches, you can get the feel of the muscle pattern of the outermost antigravity muscles. Remember, there is a sensitive layer of control muscles between the skin and these larger muscular configurations. The upper extremities of any of the antigravity muscles are broad and become lost in the pattern of other muscles. As you feel your way downward and outward along the lines of these muscles, the contour of the individual muscle becomes more precisely defined and it finally cones out into a very sharply defined line, which is the tendon sheath in the lower leg. The clearest tendon sheath is the large digital flexor on the back of each leg forming a solid-feeling line about the size of a lead pencil directly behind the cannon bone in the front leg.

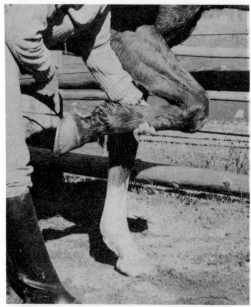

32.

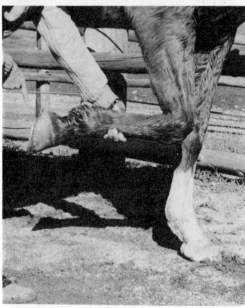

33.

Nos. 32 and 33. When the front leg is held with the cannon bone parallel to the ground, the knee may be moved forward or back without changing the angle between the plane of the bottom of the foot and the ground. If this angle changes, the horse has a serious conformation fault in his legs.

Massaging tendons as such is fruitless, except in the case of injured tendons when massage creates friction and encourages slight but very rewarding readjustments of individual fibers with relation to each other in tightening up and shortening the tendon and sheath. Naturally, a trim job on the feet involving a high heel and a short toe has a beneficial effect twenty-four hours a day on the shortening of the flexor tendon in the case of a bow. If the heels are let go long and the toes short, massaging the tendon has good results. Massaging without the proper foot trim is useless.

The first layer of control muscles under the skin may be counted upon to lay in every conceivable direction. Rotational massage is best for these muscles; and it need not be a harsh rubbing job. As a matter of fact, if overcoming tension is the prime objective of the massager, a gentle rubdown and a decent grooming are sufficient to accomplish the desired result.

If true athletic relaxation is desired, the massager must commence by vigorous transverse squeezing and rubbing of the biggest anti-gravity muscles he can identify by eye or with his hands. This is accompanied by local manipulation of the legs, with particular emphasis

34. There should be no hint of roughness.

on full flexion of all joints in all planes. The manipulation of one bone with relation to another should involve full flexing in the logical direction and also maximum allowable twisting of one bone with relation to the next above or near to the spine. The foot itself should be rotated in the plane of the bottom of the foot until a full stop is felt in the joint system farther up the leg. This has a very beneficial effect on the circulatory system as well as on the muscular system.

Having worked the deep muscles as much as possible back and forth across their natural axes, the massager then rubs them both up and down along the grain, moving more upward than downward to encourage the transfer of dead tissue toward the center of the body. The lower legs are massaged by cupping the hands and rubbing very firmly. As the massaging approaches its completion, a mild circular rubbing with a closed fist is very useful. There should be varying pressure in the circle with the maximum pressure in that part of the circle where the hand is moving toward the heart of the horse. Final massaging is characterized by very smooth gentle rubbing, following the natural planes of the outer surface of the horse's body.

To do a complete job in *overcoming tenseness,* it is well to begin with a general application of heat through laying hot towels or gunny sacks over the horse's back and holding warm cloths under the tail and between the back legs high in the dock area, for at least five minutes on the main parts of the body and a minute in each of the subparts. As an aside, this treatment sympathetically given to a mare in heat will often help her overcome a feeling of tenseness in the presence of a stallion. Try it about ten minutes or less before attempting a breeding. It is a very old trick. But we would not wet a horse except in warm circumstances and between one hour after sunrise and one hour before sunset.

It is inconvenient to have the horse eating or otherwise occupied while the therapeutic manipulation or massage is going on, at least until near the end of the treatment. Having a munch of warm, salty bran mash ready for the horse as the massager approaches the end of his work is more than worth the effort. This brings us to a few considerations of diet for the horse in physical therapy.

Diet, Medicines, Formulas, and Environment

There is no question that a good diet is essential for the athletic horse. It is also true that the quality and condition of the drinking

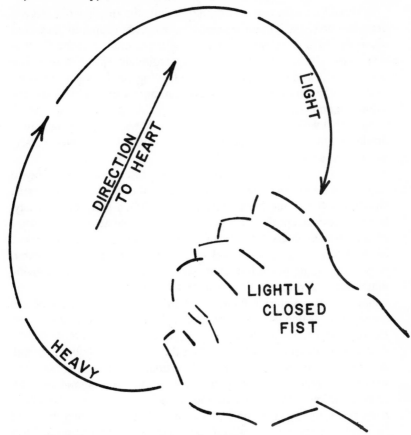

Fig. 12. The closed-fist massaging technique. Use pressure in that part of the circle where the fist is moving toward the heart.

water are important. But there is one interesting point about diet that nature continues to teach us but that we have been amazingly persistent in refusing to learn in connection with sick animals. Animals, when hurt, will go off by themselves. They will rest, and they will eat very sparingly if at all.

It should be automatic, in harmony with the therapeutics already discussed, to see to it that the animal has ample but carefully measured quantities of cool, clear water—spring type, not city water. For a sick horse in the city we would buy mountain spring water. The cost for a few days to get recoveries going in the right direction would not be over five dollars in any community in America, and the value is immeasurable.

Note that we say carefully measured quantities. The way an animal drinks is one of the key activities that should be observed closely by the therapist.

An animal will consume consistent quantities of water from day to day, varying somewhat with his activity and the weather. A horseman should know how much his horse drinks within a pint or so per day, but very few except the most professional appreciate the significance of this simple observation. If an animal is going to become sick—be a state of malaise—he will change his requirement for water, either consuming much less or much more than normal, thus giving many hours of warning. We recommend that horses drink from fixed containers that require refilling. With this system, any time a person comes in to water the horse he is immediately alerted if the water-bucket is still full or bone dry.

It is also automatic to cut back on the feed for an injured animal. The drastic cuts are made in the grain ration. For any serious skeletal-muscular problem, we would first wish to see the animal in tight, trim condition before we could hope to help it in any truly beneficial way. It is virtually impossible to manipulate muscle through layers of fat, and it is equally difficult for the horse's system to help itself if it is loaded down with "excess baggage."

Any horse in long-range therapy—that is, being treated for a bowed tendon or founder or a popped knee or any other physical problem requiring months to heal—should be fed so his ribs show clearly. His blood should be checked frequently and maintained at decent working levels and in good balance. The most common problem causing poor blood is worms. Therefore the horse's worm count should be checked every month during the lay-up period, and adequate worming performed as necessary.

After receiving the type of treatments recommended here, a horse will often not only show complete recovery from the original difficulty, but also a big dividend in a better working digestive system than he had since he was a foal!

If the horse's *blood* begins to show a low red-cell count or a lack of balance between red and white cells, the first thing many people think of is medicine. We are much more inclined to look for a good feed supplement, but we must remember that good foods work relatively slowly compared to medicines. We should beware of fast-operating materials, such as electrolytes, etc., that can be fed or injected into a horse's system.

The only time an injection would be in order, according to the therapeutic system advanced here, would be if the horse might die unless the injection were given.

Iron is very important to the recuperating horse and comes naturally in good digestible form in good-quality molasses. As in the case of spring water, we would buy health-food grades of molasses in place of agricultural grades, and we would probably mix a cup a day with part of his hay ration. We would also feed a quarter of a cup a day of unpreserved, pure apple-cider vinegar, probably mixed with the molasses before combining with a pound or so of hay or a small quantity of wet bran.

For the ailments we have considered, we would also want to feed a portion of combined powdered buttermilk and powdered skim milk. The buttermilk can be of an acid type or a sweet type, but the sweet type is preferable even though the acid shows a higher protein percentage as a rule. Many foods need catalysts to make them work to full advantage, and powdered milk (one-third buttermilk with a fat content of over 5 per cent and two-thirds skimmed milk) needs comfrey symphtum (sun dried). There may be other plants, but this one we do know about. Finally, we add a reasonable amount of good-quality sea kelp (Macrocystis pyrifera)—the giant type that grows in 50 to 300 feet of good clean ocean water, not in the shadow of oil wells or harbor flotsam.

Except in unusual situations, the recuperating horse should be kept in the largest available area within which it is easy to gather up the animal for examination (i.e., two to ten acres), in company with at least one other horse. Our experience indicates that horses in isolation from other horses do not fare as well as horses that have the advantage of some equine company. It is particularly beneficial if the sick horse can have a few very young horses for company or even a calf or a donkey or a goat.

Most athletic horses develop great capacity for association with other animals and are useful in animal husbandry as "babysitters" for young stock. They also reveal interesting aspects of their personality by the choice of "friends" in a barnyard. We have had great horses that chose the following "friends": ducks, chickens, sheep, goats, frogs, dogs, cats, wild birds, donkeys, and even people.

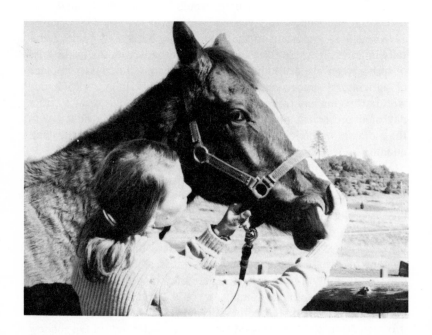

35.

Nos. 35 through 37. Salmon pink—Yes. Red, white, and blue—No.

36.

37.

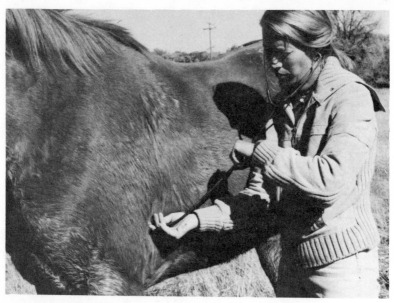

38. Relax and fill. Contract and expel. Strong hearts sound positive and unstrained.

2

Back Problems in Distance Horses

By Kerry Ridgway, D.V.M.

Back problems rank high as a major source of trouble in horses that are used for long distance as well as in horses used in other sports in which athletic ability is demanded over extended time periods and under stress conditions.

The sources of these problems may be broken down for discussion purposes as follows:

1. Rider-induced causes
   a. Balance and position
2. Inadequate training of the horse
   a. Balance
   b. Suppleness and flexibility
3. Conformation of the horse
4. Tack—type, fit, placement, and adjustment
   a. Saddles
   b. Padding
   c. Breast collars, plates, and crupper straps

For discussion purposes I wish to reverse the order of these sources. Though the key lies in the horse and rider, neither the rider nor the horse can do the job properly without adequate tack that fits properly.

Tack as a Cause of Sore Backs

Saddles and pads earn a high rating as sources of pain and problems for our four-footed friends.

The *saddle* should fit the horse's back naturally rather than being adapted by attempting to modify the back to fit the saddle with extra pads or cut-outs. This can be likened to trying to make a pair of ill-fitting shoes do. Wearing several pairs of socks, cutting out the toes, leaving the laces undone, etc., still leave them less than satisfactory.

Let's start with the pommel of the saddle as a source of trouble. The height and width are critical aspects, since the conformation of the withers can differ greatly from horse to horse. It is essential that one be able to get two fingers between the top of the withers and the pommel. The pads should be placed well forward and pushed up into the pommel groove before the cinch or girth is tightened. This will be discussed further under saddle pads and their associated problems.

The pommel clearance needs to be rechecked with the rider standing in the stirrups and forward in the saddle. This is of particular importance to the distance rider who spends a good deal of time in forward balance.

Pommel clearance can be a difficult problem in high-withered, narrow-shouldered horses, and one may have to go to a cutaway English saddle or to an older western saddle, most of which were made with a considerably deeper gullet than is found in contemporary western saddles.

It goes without saying that the rest of the tree must also conform to the horse's back. Common problems are trees that are too narrow, too wide, too long, or occasionally too short. The McClellan saddle is perhaps the best example of one that is often too narrow throughout the entire length of the tree. With the usage of so many Arabian or Arabian-type horses with their exeptionally short backs, there's the problem that many western saddles extend back too far, especially those with the square-cut skirting.

In discussing tree size and length, it should be recognized that though English saddles have one-half-inch gradations in seat size, there are actually only three tree sizes. It would sometimes behoove the rider to go one-half inch up or down in seat size to get the tree size best suited to the horse.

It is extremely important that the saddle construction ensures proper placement of the rider's weight. A frequently encountered problem is saddle construction that forces the rider's weight to the rear, thus causing excessive pressure over the loins. Many western saddles and some English saddles have the stirrups hung too far forward, which forces the rider's weight into the cantle and makes it difficult to stand in the stirrups and take forward balance. Stirrups hung too far back also occur and lead to insecurity as well as the possibility of being thrown forward, especially on descents.

It should be remembered that the tree on most English saddles ends ahead of the most distant point of the cantle. If one's weight is back, this drives the ends of the tree into the loins of the horse.

In order to ascertain the actual fit of a saddle, try it on the horse for which you intend to use it. Use a very minimum of clean padding under the saddle. Work the horse until he has developed a good sweat, remove the saddle, then check the sweat pattern and distribution. If there are specific dry areas (usually circular), they indicate points where there is an excess of pressure.

Saddles need to be carefully inspected to ensure that there are no worn spots or wrinkling in the sheepskin linings or leather coverings. Splinters and burrs have a propensity to find excellent hiding places in sheepskin linings and all types of saddle pads.

Since any discussion of types of *pads* draws on one's personal experience, there are bound to be areas of disagreement. Any particular pad may be fine for a specific animal or animals, but not for *all* animals. With this in mind, let's proceed.

In light of the fact that an English saddle is designed to be utilized with no pads at all, one can surmise that if the saddle fits well, a horse can be ridden long distances, as on endurance rides, without any pads and have no resulting back soreness. One can legitimately conclude that excess padding may add to problems rather than alleviate them.

Problems associated with pads:

1. Build-up of excessive heat
2. Wrinkling
3. Slippage
4. Irritation of the skin from the material itself
   a. Allergy
   b. Abrasiveness
5. Irritation from foreign material
   a. Dirt
   b. Detergent residues
   c. Slivers, burrs, etc.
6. Added weight, especially when wet
7. Cleaning problems

Cool back pads or hospital-type pads are perhaps the most praised or cursed distance riding pad. They are a synthetic material that is very light in weight. In my experience they have worked very well if certain considerations are observed. With the double-thickness form, some horses develop a tremendous heat build-up that results in scalded backs. When reduced to a single thickness, this problem usually disappears. In single thickness they allow good air circulation to the back. Other advantages are rapid drying of both the horse and the pad after removal of the saddle, machine washability, and general ease of care. In single thickness, cool back pads can present problems of wrinkling and slipping, especially after laundering.

Slipping pads bring to light another general problem that is associated with any pad. If a pad is placed on the horse's well-groomed back and then slid forward (or if it slips forward) to its proper position, the hair is bent backward. If held in this position, soreness often results. This can be likened to "sleeping wrong" on one's own hair and waking with a sore scalp.

Felt pads wear well, break in to fit the contours of the horse and saddle, and cause little irritation. They are, however, hard to clean and when sweat builds up they can increase in weight by ten pounds or more, thus adding to the weight load the horse must carry and also involving a very prolonged drying time.

Foam rubber or "egg crate" pads provide a lot of cushion, and some distance riders swear by them. I have found that they work well on some horses, but others tend to develop excess heat and skin irritation. Another disadvantage exists in that this pad places the rider farther from the horse. I will say more about this last point later. There are foam pads that come covered in denim or other materials. With wear and change in the shape of the foam, the covering material usually wrinkles and causes problems when in direct contact with the horse's skin.

Many who ride western prefer a *felt pad sandwiched between Navajo pads.* I have seen very few problems associated with this arrangement. The disadvantages, again, are weight when wet, slow drying, and some difficulty in cleaning.

Several other considerations are of importance when considering saddle pads.

In caring for all pads, it is imperative that they are kept clean. If they are cleaned with soap they must be rinsed thoroughly so that no detergent residue remains. The backs of most horses react readily to prolonged contact with a combination of soap, sweat, and heat.

If several pads are stacked up to prevent the saddle from creating uneven pressure, the saddle has more propensity to slip, twist, and create soreness. Multiple or thick padding also places the rider in a position of less contact with his horse. This is a distinct disadvantage in giving aids to and feeling and receiving communications from your horse. Many aids or cues are transmitted (wittingly or unwittingly) through your back, seat, and thighs. You also get feedback from your horse on his way of going through close contact with him.

As previously mentioned, regardless of the type of pads, they should be placed well forward and pushed up into the pommel groove or gullet before the cinch or girth is tightened. If this is not done, the padding can become stretched very tightly across the withers as the cinch is secured. The pressure created in this manner can very easily sore the withers.

There are many people who feel that if a horse is body clipped, the hair should never be clipped over the saddle or pad area. If it is, some horses will develop back soreness regardless of the type of pad used.

It should be noted that many of the back problems associated with pads result only in marked skin pain, rather than in deep pain in the musculature. This can be differentiated by observing the difference between applying flat-hand pressure for muscle soreness and light touching or rubbing motion for skin soreness.

Other items of tack worthy of discussion are proper-fitting *breast plates, breast collars, and cruppers.* The reason for their importance is twofold. First, when climbing an incline the horse's back shortens and on a descent it lengthens. This movement combined with the effect of gravity tend to make the saddle and padding slip. Second, most distance riders prefer a moderately loose girth. The shortening of the back and a loose girth combine to make an adequate-fitting breast collar or breast plate imperative for most horses in order to keep the saddle in place on steep climbs.

The importance of keeping the saddle in place is twofold with respect to the horse's back. First, if the saddle slips too far back, the weight load is significantly increased over the loins. Anatomically, the loins are the only area of the horse's back unsupported by bones other than the vertebrae. Therefore, as the weight load is increased in this area, the musculature and vertebral ligaments receive greatly increased stress. In addition, the skin becomes irritated from the hair on the back constantly "working" back and forth due to the saddle's forward and backward motion. This effect is much the same as that on your own legs from riding hard in new unwashed denim pants.

Proper adjustment of the breast collar or breast plate is important to ensure that pressure is not created on the thoracic inlet where the trachea passes into the chest.

Cruppers likewise function in keeping the saddle in place by preventing the saddle from riding up on the withers or, worse, onto the neck. This unfortunate occurrence takes place due to gravity and lengthening of the back during steep descents. Forward slippage is a problem particularly on mutton-withered horses since good withers are necessary to prevent the saddle from sliding forward.

There are occasional horses with good back and wither conformation combined with well-fitting saddles that can hold the saddle in place without the necessity of these additional pieces of tack.

A word of discussion is warranted regarding a moderately loose girth. Too tight a cinch or girth impairs deep breathing and becomes uncomfortable in the same manner as a belt that is too tight affects a person. It interferes with movement and makes one tense.

The Rider as a Contributory Cause

Perhaps the most significant source of sore backs lies in the faults of the rider. The most obvious rider fault involves rider balance, or the lack of it. It would seem that few people agree on the ideal balance or type of seat for riding distance horses. It must also be recognized that no good rider sits any two horses in exactly the same manner. He must adjust himself to the horse's variations in movement, his strengths, his weaknesses, and his infirmities. However, some general statements and the reasoning behind them certainly need to be presented.

Most basically, the saddle and the rider should be over the horse's center of gravity at all times. One recognizable similarity in all equine events requiring speed, from Pony Express riders to endurance riders to gymkhana riders to cross-country riders to jockeys racing on the track, is that as speed increases, the center of gravity moves forward and the rider shifts his position forward accordingly.

This phenomenon can be likened to the change in your center of gravity while skiing. As you start down the slope you lean farther and farther forward as you pick up speed—that is to say, your center of gravity shifts forward.

It is noteworthy that it is comfortable to the rider to sit back at the canter and in many western saddles to do so at even higher rates of speed. My concern here, however, is not for the rider's comfort but for relieving as much stress on the horse's back as possible.

Since the nature of distance riding requires considerable uphill and downhill work, discussion of rider position in these facets is critical to the health and welfare of the horse's back.

There is general acceptance of the premise that the rider must place more weight in the stirrups and take forward balance to take his weight off the horse's loins when the horse is climbing. When climbing, the horse *must* have the loins and hips free of encumbrance in order to climb.

In order to take forward balance going uphill the rider must bend at the hips. The common fault encountered is pushing the buttocks backward and simply laying the torso over the horse's neck by bending at the waist, instead of bringing the hips forward and bending from the hip. Though the torso is forward, the weight is still back.

The same problems exist for the horse going downhill. However, downhill position of the rider invariably sparks disagreement. Therefore the author can only present his point of view.

Anatomically and functionally the hindquarters act as both the propulsion and the brakes while descending. Propulsion is, of course, assisted by gravity. If the rider is leaning back or in any way interferes with loin freedom, he is impairing the mobility of the hips, stifles, and hocks. This results in stiff action in the back and joints, and the horse tends to slide or ski down steep descents.

Moreover, as previously stated, the loins, unlike the rest of the back, are structurally unsupported except by the vertebrae and the muscles of the loin. Weight on the loins when going downhill readily creates muscle and ligamentous strain.

As with the example of skiing, the rider's weight must come forward to stay over the center of gravity. The easiest way to determine if you are in true balance with your horse is to stand slightly in the stirrups, gripping with your knees, but without holding onto the mane or saddle in any manner. If you tend to fall backward, your weight is too far back. Conversely, if you fall forward, your weight is too far forward. This system works equally well for determining the point of balance on uphill terrain.

The rider's balance can readily be affected by the stirrup length. If the stirrups are too long, the rider's legs tend to be unsteady and to swing. Each time they move, the rider's balance point changes. He also inadvertently uses or gives a leg aid that can keep the horse confused and rapidly make him indifferent to leg aids. Also, the rider tends to post entirely off of the stirrups instead of utilizing his knees. This is fatiguing and the rider tends to land on the saddle with more force.

If the stirrups are too short, the rider's weight tends to be pushed toward the cantle and increases the load on the loins. Having the stirrups too short also tends to unduly fatigue the rider.

Another common rider fault is posting on only one diagonal. This puts more strain on one loin than the other and results in unilateral back pain. Most horses tend to favor the left shoulder back diagonal and try to keep the rider on that diagonal. The rider must make a point of developing the opposite diagonal.

Rider fatigue can readily contribute to the horse's back fatigue as well. Many riders as they tire tend to sit with a "cocked hip" or sag to one side, which places all their weight on one side of the back. Therefore, needless to say, the rider must also be well conditioned.

A great deal of muscle strain can be induced by overwork just as it is when we approach any sport too vigorously. It is said that the backache is modern man's most common affliction. It occurs because we sit all week long without utilizing our back muscles and then overdo at golf, tennis, riding, backpacking, etc., on the weekends.

We often force the same strain on our horse's back by an inconsistent or overzealous approach to training. Strain of this nature is also aggravated in this day of haste and lack of time by failure to cool our mounts out properly after working them.

Muscle strain received in this manner will often last through an entire ride season and is not likely to be cured until the horse is allowed as long as two or three months of rest.

This type of strain occurs most frequently in animals that have never been previously conditioned for distance riding and for the same reason is prevalent in young and first-year horses.

Incorrect use of hands is another rider-induced cause of difficulty for the horse. There is a term called "rein lame." It is a beautifully descriptive term that means that if the rider has heavy hands and abuses the horse's mouth, the horse will respond by being rigid and inflexible throughout all his musculature. This causes both him and the rider to experience a great deal of concussion in joints, tendons, and ligaments. The result of chronic hard hands is an unresponsive and/or lame horse.

The Athletic Ability of the Horse in Relation to Back Problems

The most significant sources of sore backs attributable to the horse himself are lack of suppleness, flexibility, and conformation.

Let us first discuss *lack of suppleness and flexibility* in the horse without discussing rider knowledge of how to produce it or correct problems, since that would rapidly get beyond the scope of this presentation.

Suppleness may be defined as ability of the horse to lengthen and shorten himself as illustrated by collection and extension. Flexibility refers to ability to bend laterally as required in circular movements.

Suppleness and flexibility are as necessary for the horse as for any human athlete if he is to be able to perform without producing muscle soreness and strain.

These abilities can be developed naturally by most horses through a lot of trail riding. It can, however, usually be learned much more rapidly with simple basic dressage training and ringwork combined with trailwork. Hillwork helps to develop the strength so essential in combination with suppleness and flexibility.

Typical cases of inflexibility or lack of suppleness occur in the horse that is *above the bit* (as most of our overanxious mounts tend to get). The reins are taut; the jaw, the head, and the neck are elevated and rigid. This rigidity is transmitted to the back, and the horse becomes hollow-backed and lacks support. He is unable to collect his movements or extend naturally. The result is muscle strain since the loin muscles are required to support the spine without being in the proper position to do so.

When collected, the horse's back actually rises slightly and gives better muscular support, much as when one sits erect rather than slumping.

The horse that is *behind the bit* also lacks suppleness. He is unable to extend well, lacks back support, and often tends to become rubber-necked when asked for lateral flexion.

In all fairness to the horse, remember that if he is often above or behind the bit, it is because of hard or abusive hands and bits or improper rider balance and position, or he may simply lack experience.

Effects of Conformation

Any conformation that fails to adequately absorb and reduce concussion will transmit that concussion to the horse's back and subsequently to the rider.

Examples of conformation problems leading to concussion transfer include steep pasterns and steep and/or short shoulders (the average shoulder angle is 57 degrees). Hind-leg problems include steep pasterns, straightness in the hocks, stifle, or hips.

It follows that a rider subjected to many hours of lack of "comfort factor" is usually less able to help the horse due to his own fatigue.

The conformation of the back itself is worthy of examination. Factors to consider are length of back and type and evenness of withers.

Too long a back tends to be a weaker back and therefore increases strain, for it implies a longer lever arm vs. muscular support. When going downhill, long-backed horses seem to develop a lateral swinging movement that interferes with both the horse's and the rider's optimum balance.

If the horse lacks withers, saddle movement in all directions is facilitated. The associated problems have been discussed. If the withers are too high, especially if accompanied by narrowness, saddle-fitting problems will be encountered.

When purchasing a horse, view the withers and shoulder from directly behind the animal. Stand on a box if necessary. Horses occasionally have one shoulder slightly lower than the other. This gives the appearance of asymmetrical withers. It is impossible to make a saddle properly fit this type of horse if even a small difference exists. When the horse moves, an uneven, twisting action is transmitted to the saddle. The saddle then creates uneven pressure on the back and transmits the twisting motion to the rider.

When selecting a mount, conformation that will promote long-range soundness and has a high "rider-comfort factor" cannot be overemphasized.

May I summarize by simply stating that back problems can be minimized if the rider:

1. Selects and trains an athletic mount (possessing suppleness and flexibility) to properly extend and collect.

2. Selects a mount with as few conformation faults as possible.

3. Works diligently at developing proper balance and seat.

4. Pays particular attention to the fit and adjustment of saddles, girths, breast collars, and cruppers, and is conscientious about the condition and state of repair of these items.

5. Selects a pad that best fits the horse's individual requirements and keeps it clean and free of foreign material.

6. Establishes a structured conditioning program and thoroughly cools out his friend and partner after each ride.

3

Equipment

One of the fine things about endurance and competitive trail riding is that you don't have to invest in hundreds of dollars' worth of specialized clothing and equipment, as is required for many horse-show classes and other forms of equestrian activity. The fundamental rule is "whatever you feel comfortable with." That obviously goes for your horse as well.

Your equipment may be classified under the headings of tack, clothing, and operational gear. We would include the saddle, bridle, and saddle pad under tack; your own equipment, from boots to hat, under clothing; and everything from emergency medical supplies to the halter under operational gear.

Some eastern rides, by tradition, expect contestants to appear in neat and trim clothing, but for the most part we repeat the fundamental admonition: Be comfortable.

There is one significant difference between long-distance riding contests and other forms of horse activity. *The show goes on,* rain or shine, 110 degrees in the shade or hailstones. That is one of the interesting challenges of this sport. So be ready for any weather and almost any kind of conditions.

It is quite natural in making decisions about equipment to watch what people already involved in this sport do and wear and use. But one must give that a bit of thought before simply saying, "I saw so-and-so, the famous endurance rider, galloping along with no shoes at all on her own feet while others were traveling with regular English riding boots." She may have had her foot stepped on and was forced, if she hoped to continue, to ride with no boot on her foot. This, of course, is a gross exaggeration, but it does serve to illustrate a point.

Donna Fitzgerald is copied so much because of her amazing record in endurance riding. If she showed up with red moccasins on there is little doubt that at the very next ride you would see quite a few red moccasins! In a recent conversation with Donna, we asked her what her experience was with flat saddles as compared to McClellans or western saddles. In the course of the discussion, we observed that Donna had apparently decided on an English jumping saddle as the best thing all in all. Now, Donna has a disarmingly simple and straightforward way of thinking and answering a question. She said: "Well, to tell the truth, someone sold that to me for only a hundred dollars, so I used it."

There are just now beginning to appear certain items specially designed for endurance riders. Up to very recently we had to choose saddles, girths, pads, bridles, boots, every bit of equipment that had been essentially designed for another kind of riding. This Johnny-come-lately, more or less orphan sport had to borrow from the Army, polo riders, stock riders, jumping people, a bit from here, a head-stall from somewhere else. But we are sorting things out, and some fundamentals may be distilled out of the last two or three decades of experience.

First, your own weight may have a great deal to do with what you choose as a saddle, what you wear, and how you will carry things you need on the trail. If you weigh 190 or so, you will obviously be watching every pound, while at the same time you will have to take into consideration how to distribute your weight on the horse's back. It might be fine to use a racing saddle to compensate for your size, but you and the horse would find it very uncomfortable in a very short distance. Conversely, if you weigh 105 soaking wet, you may have to fasten lead weights to your saddle to qualify for the local weight requirement.

Then again you may be mostly interested in competitive trail rides at which you can size up the field on arrival and if you are just on a margin weight class, you may be able, by changing three or four pounds of gear, to "go for lightweight champion" in one contest and "middleweight" next week in another. Many riders choose their gear and equipment and clothing with such hairline circumstances as primary considerations. Finally, you will probably discover, as we have, that trial and error will be significant in your final decisions regarding every piece of leather, every undergarment for yourself, and every sponge and every pail that you use.

Perhaps the most important overall lesson that we can pass on to you with no exception that comes to mind is that you should not try something new on the ride. Everything should be well tested and used to be absolutely sure it is going to be comfortable. The magic word for you and your horse is *comfort*. Long rides are tough enough without having to put up with a big blister on a knee because that new underwear had a seam in the wrong place or your horse developed a sore back because you had to "ride funny" to make up for a new adjustment to your saddle.

Let us now consider the subject of equipment in the following order: clothing, tack, and gear, with a final suggestion of a check list you may find useful.

Clothing

We have mentioned that you must be ready for a great variety of weather conditions if you go to very many contests at all. One rather experienced contestant we remember from several years ago decided to go to a contest in the Northwest after having ridden in several in Southern California. Up in the Northwest it is not at all uncommon to have to ride in the rain, so our friend, anticipating this eventuality, bought a fine yellow slicker of the kind many cowboys use in scuddy weather. Sure enough, on the second day of this ride it rained and our friend showed up with the yellow slicker. His horse had never seen anything like that in his life, being from "sunny California"! You guessed it! The horse was all over the place while our friend tried to get on. Finally he had to take the raincoat off and ride soaking wet. Just another first-class example of not trying something new on a ride.

Your own comfort will begin with your *underclothing* and your footgear. An old cavalryman cannot remember riding on any occasion, even in the hottest weather, without some kind of "long johns." They had very light cotton long underwear, which came in very handy on long marches or simply when playing polo. That underwear was designed not to have any seams in any of the areas where there would be constant contact with the saddle or stirrup straps. Most modern long underwear has seams on the inside of the legs, which can be very uncomfortable for a horseman. One of the greatest contributions to endurance riding has been the development of women's pantyhose, used commonly today by men as well as women to avoid chafing. Although pantyhose were not invented for endurance riders, one could say that they are generally accepted as

39. Drucilla Barner, Tevis Cup Winner, on Naqiya at Cougar Rock, August 3, 1974. Dru has done this course many times in many different years, so it behooves us to watch closely. Note she has a simple mechanical hackamore and a halter on the horse. This is early in the morning. She is wearing a cap, and no doubt has several "necessities" in the saddle bags. Although it does not show well in this early-morning light, you can just make out a lightweight breast strap. She is wearing gloves and loose-fitting pants. Hardly conventional riding britches, but you may be sure she has found them comfortable for her. All in all it is obvious that she and her horse are "calm, cool, and collected" going over this notoriously dangerous stretch of the trail, on her way to her 1,000-mile buckle.

perfect for the sport. The only drawback is that they are a bit awkward when you have to relieve yourself on the trail.

Your *footgear* is next most important. In the old days you might find people wearing conventional English riding boots or cowboy boots. Today the most commonly observed footgear is a pair of reinforced running shoes. A few years ago it was light hiking boots. The primary considerations are: (1) whether you expect to ride all the way (many rides require this), or whether you expect to lead your horse in some places; (2) if you expect to lead or tail the horse, where will you be doing this and how much ground will you cover on foot? It is not difficult to decide that if you are going to make fast time on the ground, any kind of riding boot may be unsatisfactory, and a hiking boot, all things considered, may be your best choice, especially if the ground is rough and rocky. A great many riders, when watering their horses along the trail, get off and go right into the water themselves. In this case the reinforced running shoes may be the best choice. In recent years in endurance competition we have seen very few English riding boots. We have seen very few cowboy boots. We still see quite a few lightweight hiking boots, but mostly we see running shoes.

Along with footgear we should consider socks or stockings. Some people like long stockings that come right up to the knee. Others settle for socks. Trial and error will soon determine what you will prefer. Generally, even though it sounds hot, a bit of extra weight is preferable to light weight, especially in avoiding blisters on heels when making it on foot. Needless to say, the socks or stockings should be clean and dry when you put them on.

Some people used to wear regular English riding britches or jodhpurs. Few do today. Most people have settled for good *jeans* without too tight a fit. To keep the legs from crawling up on you— "Indian britches," as they used to say—many people sew elastic straps to the bottoms of the legs, which pass under the foot inside the shoe and keep the jeans straight and wrinkle-free on your legs. We have seen some people riding with nothing more than leotards. An attractive girl in this get-up has a profound impact on the average judge!

A few people sew knee liners (like those on conventional riding britches) to their jeans. This decision should involve consideration of the shape of your saddle and what exactly your knees will be contacting.

The *belt* that holds your pants up may be more significant than you would at first surmise. With the right belt you can easily carry such a thing as a standard Army canteen. With the wrong one, the fastening may not fit or at least be impossible to get off when you want it. If you intend to carry a knife or anything else that might fasten to a belt, give this item some thought. There are many variations, including carrying all these things in some kind of little sack fastened to your saddle.

40. Mary Tiscornia wears a hat and conventional riding boots to go with her very proper-looking English saddle. She is one of those uniquely beautiful spirits you can find in this sport. We suspect even Mary won't do this with those fine boots many times! But it does look like a good way to "get it back together" in a hot canyon where the temperature is probably 110 degrees.

41. Eva Taylor on her wonderful mule, Hugo, on the same spot in the same year as Dru Barner. Hugo is wearing a very simple headstall with no bit. He has a breast harness to keep the saddle from slipping backward and a crupper strap to keep it from slipping forward.

Eva has no hat, not uncommon for this time of day; a very simple setup all in all, with riding britches anchored securely at the bottom by straps under her feet. She is wearing spurs, an uncommon sight in this kind of contest.

Eva piloted Hugo to win the Haggin Cup for best condition on this occasion, and that's something!

You can change your *shirt* during the day at rest stops, so choose what feels good for the time of day. Again the basic notion is that what feels good is the primary key.

You may need a *jacket*. The new very lightweight jackets used by hikers are very good in cold weather. Don't overlook the old Levi's jacket if you expect brush and rough bushes along the trail. *Sweaters* are very useful in many situations. The primary idea is to be able to be flexible with this item more than any other as the day goes on.

Gloves, hat, scarf—suit yourself. Almost everyone riding in hot sun wears a hat. Few people wear gloves except to have them along in case of unexpected cold snaps.

The cavalry used to wear fine big scarfs, which served many purposes. You could wrap a leg with one. You could scoop up water. You could cover your neck and keep dust out, which otherwise could be very irritating. You could wet the scarf and put a lot of water on your horse, then wrap the thing around your waist, keeping yourself cool all the way to the next water hole. Today some people use a terry-cloth towel in the same way.

Again, we point out that in some rides you may have to face snow or driving rains or alternatively a cruel, hot sun with no wind or water for miles.

There is one final, subtle, but significant consideration: *weight of small items.* What will you have in your pockets? What may be fastened to your clothes? It is vitally important, right down to the ounce, that you take these things into account. This consideration may cause you to rethink a few things such as whether you should have a string tie, a button, or a zipper here and there. Again we repeat: *whatever is comfortable.*

Tack

There is little doubt that the most significant part of your tack is the *saddle*, yet we are obliged to do with saddles invariably designed for other purposes than our sport. There are some efforts on the part of some saddlemakers to meet the needs of modern long-distance riders, but so far they still fall short of the mark.

The most common saddle in America is the western saddle. Consequently, a great many people start out endurance riding on one kind or another of these fine, romantic links with our past. There are, broadly speaking, two types of western saddle. There is one on which you wish to ride comfortably and with great flexibility for a short time without needing to rope a cow. A good example of this saddle is a cutting saddle. The basic alternative is a roping saddle. If you are going to "set down" on a thousand-pound steer you'd better be on a stout saddle, which of necessity must weigh a good deal. A cutting saddle, on the other hand, will generally be lighter. Obviously, for endurance riding we would immediately choose the lightest western saddle we could as long as it is built on a sound tree.

With all but a few western saddles there are some fundamental drawbacks in addition to the simple fact of unnecessary weight. The endurance rider needs a free-swinging *stirrup,* one that will move easily with no resistance to the location of his leg. The average western stirrup is wide and cumbersome in this respect. Furthermore, one thing we like to be able to do to relieve strain on the legs over long distances is change the stirrup length up or down a hole or two, like stretching your legs or pulling them up a bit, for the change of pace. It can be very restful compared to making the whole hundred miles with your legs in the same place all day and into the night. Most western saddles do not allow an easy change.

There are some good features about western saddles. First, as a rule, it is easy enough to carry little things on them. There are several places where you can tie on a sponge and other important items necessary along the trail. Then, too, they do present a good-sized surface to the horse's back, which is important if the rider is a big person.

If you want to use a western saddle for the comfort the seat gives you or the sense of security that the high pommel and cantle give you or for whatever reason, try to pick the smallest one you can be comfortable in and that covers the horse's back as little as possible.

The famous Army saddle—the McClellan, as it is called—comes nearer to the ideal endurance saddle than any other in most respects, but it too falls short of the ideal.

Perhaps this is a good time to consider what the ideals are as this sport has evolved since World War II. First, the saddle should be as light and rugged as possible, and be easy to clean. In these respects the McClellan meets the standards well. Second, the saddle should have good-sized bars so weight is distributed over the back in an even and substantial way. Again the McClellan meets the test, but not as well as we might wish. This great old saddle was made for good-sized Army horses who might have to continue in combat while having lost a good deal of weight in a campaign. The Arabian horse has emerged as the ideal horse for endurance riding, and if not a pure breed, he does represent the "type." These horses are considerably smaller than Army horses, and fine as it is in many ways, the McClellan just simply does not fit as well as it should. This saddle was designed to carry considerable weight on the pommel and as a consequence the bars run forward an extra inch or more. On short-backed Arabian types this digs in behind the scapula, particularly when going downhill, and is very uncomfortable.

The high pommel and cantle of the McClellan were designed to help the rider keep his seat in combat, and for many miles in endurance riding they serve a similar useful purpose. But in any high pommel-high cantle saddle, you cannot shift your weight forward far enough going uphill to be useful, even if you wish only to adopt a more classically accepted forward position.

Thus we arrive at the third ideal in construction of an endurance saddle: a relatively low pommel with a modest cutback so you can easily get forward going uphill and have no interference with the horse's back going downhill.

A fourth ideal in an endurance saddle is to have a long channel down the entire length of the saddle over the spine to allow a maximum of ventilation. The McClellan meets this requirement very well; however, the channel we are thinking of does not need to be open like a McClellan: The slot may be padded over.

A fifth ideal is to have the fastenings at appropriate places on the saddle so you can tie on a small banana bag or other items such as a towel. The McClellan meets this requirement as do most western saddles. English or flat saddles often do not meet this requirement.

This brings us to an evaluation of flat saddles for endurance riding. They have become the choice of most knowledgeable riders, even though they are far from the ultimate in desirability. They are light. They have, in most cases, adequate bars (they could be a bit larger for our sport). They have free-swinging stirrups and a minimum of leather covering the horse's back. All good features. But they simply were not designed for riding a hundred miles. Furthermore, they are finished with appearance as a high-priority factor since they are almost exclusively used for show purposes. Consequently they can be scuffed rather easily when placed out on the ground as an endurance saddle often, of necessity, is. Finally, most flat saddles are insufficient when it comes to fastening things to them.

It is fascinating to see how names stick sometimes. We all use the word "English" saddle to refer to a flat saddle even though today almost all of our good flat saddles are actually made in Germany. Among modern flat saddles, significant differences can be achieved by very slight lengthening or shortening of the bars and the degree of stuffing or padding of the panels. With thick panels the rider is pushed forward in the saddle, thought to be desirable in jumping. Some people try to compensate for this lack of fit in a saddle by placing an extra pad on the horse's back. This allows an excess of movement of the saddle relative to the back, and over a long ride this can be devastating to the horse's back muscles. The constant minor adjustment to compensate for this slack between the horse's back and the saddle can make both horse and rider very weary indeed.

Among saddlemakers who have attempted to address the problem of an endurance-ride saddle, we note an American and a German maker. The American, Porter Company, uses a western style in essence, which reflects Quarter Horse influence and consequently does not fit the endurance-horse back as well as it might. However, in many other respects the saddle represents a move in the right direction and should be encouraged. Sommar of Germany, a saddle company famous for its handmade dressage saddles, has developed an English-type saddle especially for riding long distances that combines the features of the military saddles of the past two centuries with modern technology. This saddle has an adequately deep seat, but with a low enough pommel to allow an easy uphill stance. It has good long panels, giving it the security and weight-bearing characteristics of a western saddle. With waterproof leather over a Fiberglas tree, it weighs in at eleven pounds stripped. The feature that makes it comfortable for long distances is a narrow throat so your legs do not feel spread apart as much as in an ordinary saddle.

In case you skipped, we urge you to read the previous chapter, "Back Problems in Distance Horses," in which Kerry Ridgway, D.V.M., has many excellent comments on saddles, padding, breast collars and plates, and crupper straps.

Among the various *girths* available, elastic and otherwise, the preponderance of successful endurance riders we see prefer a type of string girth. It seems to have less tendency to cause galls and swellings. Additionally, it is easy to clean in a washing machine. This easy-to-clean feature is also a high consideration in pads.

There are many choices of *saddle pads* on the market: horse hair; foam-rubber-covered and uncovered; felt; wool; sheepskin; artificial sheepskin; even folded Army blankets for the traditionalist. Each person develops his own preference, but we have found in addition to the very important factor already referred to—washability—that size is also very important. The pad should be just big enough to support the saddle without covering any more of the horse than necessary. This allows the maximum dissipation of heat, which is peculiar to this type of contest. Pad manufacturers take note: This could be a very good market if this one-dimensional aspect is addressed thoughtfully and called to the attention of people in this sport. It might even be a good idea for many other kinds of riding as well.

Having some thickness with a cushion function protects the sensitive spine and back area of a horse that has all the fat (which provides natural padding) worked off for endurance conditions. Since the spine houses the nerves and sensitive spinal cord, it is important for the comfort and confidence of the horse to give this area as much protection as possible. Although there are many suitable saddle pads on the market, we have found over the years that the Eagle Brand Wash-a-pad made in Dalton, Pennsylvania, gives excellent protection to the back, can be washed and dried in a machine, and has good wearing qualities. *Washing the pad regularly is one of the easiest ways to prevent back trouble.*

Some riders elect to use two thick pads on a horse with a sensitive back. This has the disadvantage of allowing movement of the saddle relative to the horse and putting the rider a long way from the horse. Any extra movement of the saddle causes the horse to use unnecessary control muscles in his entire back to compensate for the imbalance of the rider.

Although Dr. Ridgway goes into the fit of saddles and how to determine a good or a bad fit, we feel it might be useful here to point out that a poorly fitting saddle will cause *small* pressure points on the back where a good fit makes a broad, even distribution of weight—that is, pressure. A good way to determine how the shape of the saddle fits the shape of the back is to place talcum powder either on the back or on the underside of the panels of the saddle and place the saddle directly on the horse's back with no pad at all. Ride at the walk and slow trot, simply sitting in the saddle for about five minutes. With the direct contact between leather and skin there is no way for sweat to dissipate. Consequently, when you take the saddle off carefully you will see in the talcum powder clear *confir*mation patterns of the *confor*mational compatibility of saddle and back. The marks should be large and regular, not small and irregular.

The question of preparing a horse's back comes up. A pad that allows rubbing can cause a sensitivity that can become chronic, resulting in sore, sensitive spots, usually in the loin area. Although we might expect these to reveal themselves in the form of uneven sweat marks, they sometimes do not. If you feel lightly but evenly with your fingertips in exploring the area of saddle contact, you can find these little spots by a difference in heat. They will feel hot or warmer than areas around them. This soreness is also frequently indicated by the horse squatting under the rider when he gets on.

Considering *stirrups and stirrup leathers,* it is obvious that the emphasis in terms of comfort is now almost exclusively on the rider. We have well in mind the old adage, "a tired rider makes a tired horse," which is only too true. A safety point also comes up immediately. It is unwise to have stirrups that fit the foot too closely. You could get hung up in them. A good rule of thumb is to have the bottom of the stirrup about an inch wider than the sole of your shoe. This accomplishes two important things: (1) safety and ease of getting your foot out in a hurry; and (2) allowing you to ride with your foot on the inside of the stirrup, giving you maximum security and maximum comfort.

The stirrups should hang on very flexible leathers that do not chafe the leg in any way. If the leathers are pliable it is possible that chafing can be avoided simply by wearing pantyhose or heavy cotton long underwear or leotard-type garments. If a chafing problem still exists, there is a way to attach a movable fender to the stirrup leather. If you use western stirrup leathers, try to soften them as much as possible and be sure they are shaped so that there is no rotational vector of pressure, which tends to point your toe into the horse's side. This is not only potentially annoying to the horse, it is also a very tiring stance for a long-distance rider.

A fine point of riding comes up as we think about stirrups and leathers. A wide stirrup (to be preferred) encourages the rider to put more weight under the center of his foot (more toward the big toe) rather than on the outside of his foot (over the little toe). This may seem like a very technical point for an endurance rider, but in fact it is essential to riding with as little fatigue and effort as possible.

42. Linda Tellington-Jones and Ernie Sanchez finish ninth and tenth, respectively, in the Tevis Cup Ride. Ernie's grim expression reflects severe pain due to old wounds suffered in Korea as a Marine, but like many endurance riders, he comes through anyway.

Note the very light and simple gear they use toward the end of the ride. Linda's mount, Hungarian Brado, is a big stallion doing fine with a light noseband and no kind of bridle at all. Linda's saddle is a McClellan. Ernie's is a light western.

It is conceivable that you would use a variety of *bridles and bits* in the process of training, and perhaps two or three during a contest. Ideally the simplest arrangement possible, giving the horse the least encumbrance and maximum comfort, would be the thing to use. You could have trained with the usual starting bits and graduated to riding with no bit at all. Yet you might have the experience of seeing your horse going with no bit, safe, sane, and under control while training at home or with other "friends" but suddenly very difficult to control, peaked out and ready to go at 5:00 A.M. with two hundred horses milling around just as excited as he is.

Many riders choose mechanical hackamores since the horse can eat and drink readily and is not encumbered by a bit in his mouth. The only disadvantage comes from an ill-fitting hackamore, which can irritate the sides of the horse's face from the constant swinging of the long shanks. This irritation is something important to watch for and avoid. There are many horses accustomed to the excitement of endurance rides that may start out with a mechanical hackamore or a curb or a snaffle and then settle down during a competition and continue during the hot part of the day just wearing a halter with reins attached to the cheek rings. This is certainly comfortable for the horse and convenient for crews at rest stops, and is highly satisfactory for a well-balanced horse. Donna Fitzgerald rides Witezarif with a halter in most contests. However, for a horse that is not well balanced, or well conditioned, or that has a tendency to stumble, it is probably safer to have a light grazing curb so if he does stumble he can be pulled up quickly and helped to regain his balance. It is wise to avoid any curb bit that could damage a horse's mouth if he were to step on the reins.

Some people place a light grooming halter or a narrow cavesson under the bridle to act as a halter and save time at the vet checks. Naturally one needs some sort of lead rope that can be tied around the horse's neck or onto the saddle, but it is simpler to send it ahead with the crew. Some use the reins as a lead strap by simply attaching small, sturdy snaps to hook onto the bit.

A headstall that is made of narrow, strong material, whether leather or nylon, limits the source of irritation. Western bridles can serve this purpose well and cost about half as much as a similar narrow English bridle. There are also excellent nylon bridles on the market that have the advantage of being easily washable in a bucket and save money and labor in cleaning. On most competitive trail rides, tack is closely examined for cleanliness and condition, and the rider receives a score for horsemastership. This does not happen on endurance rides, but it is still of high-priority importance. *Keep all your equipment in good shape.* It is a shame to spend countless hours preparing for an endurance ride and then lose valuable time because of a broken piece of leather or a broken girth.

Dr. Ridgway has done such a fine job in his chapter on breast plates and other pieces of auxiliary saddle equipment that we shall not cover the subject here.

Gear

The last items to consider are under the general heading of gear. Some is customarily carried with the rider. The balance is carried by his support crew from stop to stop. One must always modify the ideas we set forth here in taking into account that some rides do not allow assistance. Naturally, the actual list you need will depend on the location, length of ride, time of year, and several other factors. Your own good judgment will be your guide.

During hot weather, especially in dry areas, it is wise to carry a canteen. Routinely we would carry a pocket knife, extra latigo string for needed repairs, hoof pick, sponge or towel for wetting down the horse at water holes along the trail, and an Easy Boot in case a shoe comes off. Some riders like to carry a stethoscope to check the horse's pulse at spot checks before presenting the horse to the veterinarian. An easy alternative to using the stethoscope for checking pulse is to take the pulse under the tail, four to six inches below the root. This is amply illustrated in the chapter entitled "Physical Therapy for the Athletic Horse."

If you have a saddle that allows a suitable place for a narrow *banana bag* (without touching the horse's back directly), by all means carry it with a few emergency supplies such as an extra lead rope, stirrup leather, rain-gear where necessary, and extra sponge or towel. *Have anything you intend to carry so attached that it does not drop off.* On many endurance rides there can be found sponges, sweaters, and other very useful items strewn along the trail, often items that the rider is hard pressed to do without.

Among stories about the very early days of the Tevis Cup Ride when only men were allowed because it was "too tough" for women, there is the one about Nick Mansfield on the very first ride feeling he had to bring along almost 100 pounds of horseshoeing equipment. They just didn't believe you could make it over those rocks without a whole lot of repair work on the shoes. Today women are not only beating the men a good deal of the time, but also the foot problem, if not handled by horseshoers at each stop, can be solved in between stops by the use of an Easy Boot. While we might laugh today at the idea of carrying 100 pounds of horseshoeing equipment, we have to remember that they didn't have a good shoer ready to meet them at the 40-, 65-, and 85-mile marks the way we do today.

Before and immediately after a contest you will need many items of equipment about which experience alone will serve to firm up your ideas concerning importance and type or even sizes or numbers. When you know what you need for your own kind of riding, we urge you to make a *check list,* which can be photocopied and used fresh for each contest. It should include the most obvious things, such as your running shoes or boots and the saddle, believe it or not. In the excitement of getting ready to go it is unbelievable what experienced contestants can leave behind! We will confess to having everything we needed for *seven* riders on one occasion in the early days only to realize we had arrived at the contest without a single girth! We had just had them specially cleaned. *We always use a check list now.* A check list, in addition to including all personal items and equipment for the rider, might also include the following:

Check List

Extra girth
Saddle
Bridle
Extra bridle
Two saddle pads
Extra set of horseshoes made specially for your horse
Extra lead rope
Water buckets
Buckets for grain and for cooling out
Containers to carry water
Enough feed to avoid sudden changes in diet

Bran mash for after the ride
Bandages
Liniments
Alcohol
Cooler
Warm blanket
Waterproof blankets or covers
Gunny sacks for cooling out
Electrolytes
Vet wrap and cottons in case of tendon problems
Grooming equipment
Scissors
Knife
A deep nonbreakable bucket that can be used to soak a horse's leg almost up to the knee if necessary (a five-gallon plastic bucket can serve this purpose and is available at any plastic supply house)
Flashlight
Outdoor eating utensils
Sponges
Paper plates
Cups
Thermos
Sleeping bag

An item that some people who participate in this sport frequently find very useful is a pair of whirlpool therapy boots. This brings to mind Epsom salt and other innocent chemicals, which are discussed in the chapter "Physical Therapy for the Athletic Horse."

We suggested to contest managers that they "try it on for size" and think ahead of every step in the process, step by step. As a contestant you should do the same thing. Good luck, and don't forget. . . .

4

Traveling with Horses

Here we have a fascinating subject primarily because it has two distinct sides: a theoretical, ideal side, and a practical side. We feel a clear obligation to record much theory and much idealism to reflect our research experience over more than ten years; but we must bow to facts of life and deal essentially with this subject as things are from day to day.

An example of idealism and practice comes up immediately when you talk about loading a horse into a trailer. Ideally it would be very good if every young horse, aged two or three months, could be encouraged to go into a good trailer with its mother and have time enough to relax. No one would actually be going anywhere, just practicing. After being placed inside the moving unit, a driver would start the car or tractor that is going to haul the trailer. Let the engine run a minute or so and let the little one have time to assimilate the vibrations and lower its level of fear. Then very gently move ahead a few feet and stop. Pet the little one. Get in with mother and foal and visit a bit. Again move ahead slowly and make a very slow, even turn. After not more than fifteen minutes' total elapsed time, let mother and foal out with a nice little "reward." Let them look the unit over from the outside and then leave to go about their daily life in the pasture.

More often than not you are faced with purchasing a horse that has little if any systematic training or experience in traveling. The animal may even have had one or more unhappy experiences and consequently be quite difficult to load. We shall, therefore, consider loading horses generally, ranging from innocent animals with no experience to horses that have come to resent any kind of hauling. We cannot go into this subject here as thoroughly as one would in a general training book, but we can point out a few principles.

Loading

There are five basic rules for loading a horse.

First, never attempt to load any horse unless you have a decent hauling unit that is fundamentally safe and reasonably comfortable.

Second, do not attempt to load any horse unless you have the basic equipment necessary, in good condition. This should include a properly fitting halter (not a rope halter), a good sound lead rope (at least eight feet long) that you would ordinarily tie a horse up with, an additional shank with a twenty-four-inch stud chain, a stiff buggy or training whip, and a long rope (about fifty feet) to use as a figure-eight loop over the back if you encounter early resistance. Wear gloves and a pair of stout shoes. With any green horse it is useful to have two people who can work together and be very calm, but in most instances the "crowd" around a horse is more disadvantageous than not.

Third, pick a decent location for the first training session.

Fourth, take your time, but do not dally.

Fifth, decide beforehand that, one way or another, your horse *is* going in the trailer. If you think there is a question about it, the horse will immediately know it.

Some people use long, drawn-out procedures involving "letting the horse go in the trailer on his own to discover feed in the manger" or otherwise using up days and days. We do not believe in this approach. We prefer to have this experience be a quietly systematic, disciplined, relatively brief moment in the horse's life like any other good training period.

There are certain preliminaries to be observed. Park the trailer in a good solid way with no obstacles nearby. Before approaching the trailer with your horse, get the stud chain over his nose as shown in Fig. 13. The psychological effect of the weight of the stud chain on a horse's nose prevents him from pulling away or arguing before the idea crosses his mind. The whip is not used to punish the horse but rather as a signaling device to have him step forward. Lead him about the area in a quiet, businesslike manner, standing on his left side with the stud chain *and* lead rope in the *left* hand (not looped around the hand) and the stiff whip in the right hand. Walk forward a few steps and halt with the command "Whoa" with a light, short pull on the stud chain. Stand still a few seconds and then move forward with the command "Walk," at the same time touching him lightly on the thigh with the whip. In a few minutes

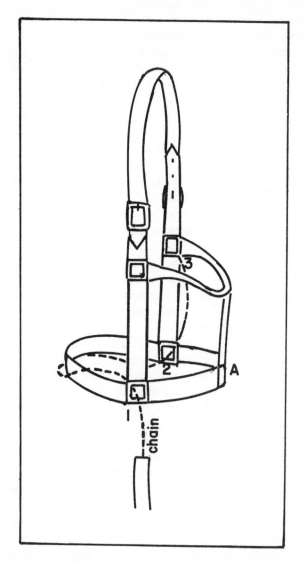

Fig. 13. This diagram shows the proper way to thread a stud chain through a standard halter, entering at 1, passing over the noseband, and going out at 2. The chain is then fastened at 3.

The rope with which you would tie the horse would be fastened in the usual way at A. At that time, the stud chain would be removed.

your horse will be paying attention to you with the signals from stud chain and whip combined with your choice. *One of the most important principles in loading a difficult horse is to have his attention and to keep him calm and unafraid.*

After only a few minutes of this exercise, pet the horse and then lead him up to the trailer and stop him. Let him sniff the floor, and then give him the signal to move forward. In teaching a young or difficult horse the first few times, go in the trailer with him and have feed in the manger waiting. Have an assistant shut the door and put up the butt chain, and then you go out the escape door, being sure the horse doesn't attempt to follow you out. It has happened more than once that a horse gets stuck halfway out the escape door. Never tie the horse with the stud chain, but rather with the normal lead rope that is already attached.

If you are dealing with a horse that has learned to fight a whip or will not move forward with the signal from the whip, then use the stud chain as we have already indicated and have an assistant pick up the horse's feet one at a time to move him forward, rewarding him as you go and preventing him from going backward from the effect of the stud chain. Be very quiet and calm and do not pull on the chain. A few minutes of patience and quiet handling are worth thirty minutes of whipping and yelling or trying to force him into the trailer.

There are times when it is helpful to have an assistant "encourage" a horse with a whip from behind by snapping the whip smartly on the ground right behind his feet or making small sharp moves in the direction of the point of the buttocks. When the person standing at the horse's head has the stud chain in hand, this method generally works with mature horses, but when you only have a lead rope attached to the halter, the normal reaction of the horse is to rear or run to the side of the trailer. We have found over the years in loading hundreds of problem horses that the less "fight" we instigate the more quickly and quietly the horse is loaded. Remember, each time you load a horse you should do it in such a way that the next time will be easier.

If a horse has been really spoiled or won't move forward from the touch of a whip or is badly frightened from a bad experience such as a trailer accident, we resort to a method demonstrated in photograph 43. Make the *figure-eight loop,* using a fifty-foot long rope, as shown in Fig. 14. The loops should be of such a size that the central knot is over the middle of the back, while the rear loop falls about halfway between the root of the tail and the hocks. When you take the slack out of the rope it should press on the horse's rump about eight inches below the root of the tail. The front loop should fit with reasonable snugness around the chest. The balance of the rope is run forward so that a "halter loop" about a foot long or slightly less fastens to the halter in such a way that when the rope is tight the horse's head still can move so he does not feel "pinned down." With this arrangement, instead of pulling the horse by the head you are able, when pulling on the rope, to "push" from behind.

43. Kathy Tellington holds the conventional lead rope in her right hand. This will ultimately be used to tie the horse. The loop over the horse's back and under the chest, with secondary loop to halter, is held in Kathy's left hand. A stud chain would also be fastened as shown in Fig. 13 for a difficult horse.

Take a double loop around something solid in the front of the trailer (the divider post, possibly), and after taking the slack out of the rope, with the horse usually only a foot from the ramp, bring him in inch by inch. It usually takes an assistant moving the horse's feet one by one, as he will normally lean a little on the rope. Keep his head toward the front with only a suggestion of pressure on the stud chain. Never pull steadily on a stud chain, as it is too severe and will cause the horse to fight. However, without the stud chain your horse will quickly learn that he can turn his head back from an ordinary lead rope and have his mind set on resisting rather than loading.

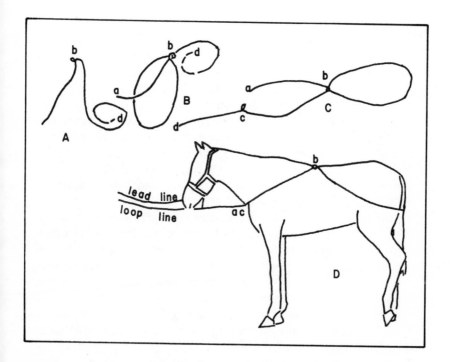

Fig. 14. This diagram shows in some detail the dimensions and method of arranging the loop rope for an average-sized horse.

Although this method has never failed us, it is always the last method that we use since there is almost certain to be a point when the horse will test the strength of the rope by sitting back against it. Discovering the true situation, he will with about equal certainty jump forward. If the handlers are not very careful, it is possible to get hurt, and it is a little unnerving the first time a horse sits back hard against that rope for a few seconds, possibly squirming like a giant fish on a line before he makes up his mind that there is no alternative but to jump in.

Once the horse is in the trailer, reward him with kind words and a few "goodies." A tasty tidbit in addition to hay to munch on helps the horse associate loading with a reward for his stomach in addition to verbal encouragement.

Types of Trailers

The trailer itself can make loading, traveling, and running good distances between stops much easier if it is built right. Again we have the ideal type and the very common type of trailer. Ideally a horse rides much better if he is facing backward. A brief for this position includes the following simple facts: (1) The most rapid and unexpected change in speed that the horse can experience is in a sudden stop, an unavoidable situation as far as the driver is concerned, but an experience that can keep a horse tensely expectant for long periods of time. If a horse is facing forward, during sudden stops he is thrown against the breast plate, and if he happens to be eating, he bumps his nose. Facing backward in the same situation, his strong hindquarters come up against the trailer with no strain on the horse at all. If he happens to be eating, the rapid deceleration lifts his nose up out of the manger instead of bumping it. He can take tremendous shock with his back legs that is impossible to take with his front legs. (2) With a trailer constructed so a horse enters from the front side and exits out the back, he never has to back up a step. He can see through, and consequently feels much more secure than if he is going into a tunnel with a dark, solid end, which makes early experiences difficult.

We transported horses, five at a time, for a distance accumulating slightly over 300,000 miles. One could face forward while another would face backward. We had stethoscopes fastened to each of them by anchoring them to a surcingle and using a somewhat longer tube between the listening unit and the earpieces. We could "plug in" any horse we wished without the horse realizing we were listening to his heart. Again and again we observed that in the same horse we would record a pulse of X when he faced forward and X-2 or X-3 when he faced backward. We believe this invariably slower pulse represented positive evidence that the horse much preferred to ride backward.

There are many small things about trailers that make life better for horses. It is more or less customary to paint the inside with a kind of dark spackle paint to cover up ugly-looking welds. We painted trailers a simple white inside and increased the sense of light with a consequent feeling of having more room, which the horses obviously appreciated. We found that in almost all cases keeping the horse from seeing out was beneficial (a bit like blinker hoods for a racehorse); and it was also useful to block light from passing cars at night so it did not disturb the horses. Finally, we discovered that an even, draft-free flow of air was very useful in keeping horses feeling good while traveling in hot or cold weather.

The fact is that most people will be loading a horse into a trailer from the back. If there is an escape door for the person leading the horse in, it should be quite small so the horse has no idea of trying to "escape" too. More and more trailers are made with swinging tail gates so the horse has to step up. We prefer this arrangement to a ramp-style tail gate. When the horse lifts his leg to take that step up he has to lower his head. When he puts his foot on a ramp, his head goes up. With the low head carriage he is much more likely to feel all right about it, and go in. With the high head carriage he is already in a stance, ready to rear if necessary to get away from the trailer. In closing the tail gate, while you are safe with a swinging door, you have to get too close in line with a flying foot to pick up the ramp.

In Motion

When you start to move the trailer, even with an experienced horse, it is well worth the extra five seconds to accelerate slowly. In turning, slow down carefully going into the turn, and do not accelerate until the trailer is completely through the turn.

If you are running at night, leave the lights on in the trailer. This reduces the effect of bright headlights shining into the trailer and creating fast-moving shadows, which at the very least annoy the horse.

With your horse traveling backward in a good van, you can go 1,000 miles without stopping for more than gas and a drink of water. He does not have to get out. Traveling forward in the average trailer, 400 miles is about all you can hope to go without a good rest. If a person is going to quite a few contests over a period of three or four years, he will save hundreds of dollars in motel costs and much hassle trying to find good spots to put the horse out. The savings in time, money, and energy can make it well worthwhile to buy a good trailer in the first place; and if you are going to do that, why not get one built so the horses can ride backward? It might cost an extra thousand dollars, but you will save it in much less time than you think if you go to many competitions. You will probably win more, too, because your horse will be in so much better shape.

Feeding and Watering

Feeding and watering horses on trips can be problems, especially with inexperienced animals. Great military commanders in past years made sure their horses were accustomed to eat at any time, anywhere, whenever they had a chance. We are given to understand that the conquistadors bringing horses to the New World often resorted to feeding hemp rope in place of ordinary hay if the sea voyage were longer than expected. There is one principle upon which most horsemen seem to agree: Feed lightly. Do not give a horse in transit much if any grain. Let him have as much hay as he wants because simple chewing can relieve much tension and apprehensiveness in the horse's mind as he rides along. Watering can be a problem, but there are a few simple steps one can take to minimize this. First, even months before taking your horse on a trip, get him accustomed to the taste of a little apple-cider vinegar in his water. If you encounter different-tasting water on your trip, the addition of a tablespoonful of vinegar in ten quarts of water can make it seem "just like home." Adding a bit of salt to slightly dampened hay is another time-honored way of "encouraging" your horse to drink. It pays, however, not to let yourself fret over your horse in any case, because this can bring on a very undesirable atmosphere, which can easily reinforce the horse's already high state of uneasiness.

The occasion may arise, because of a vehicle breakdown or a simple flat tire, that you see yourself stopped by the side of the road for a while. You may be tempted to take the horse out and let him drink out of that little pond of water or eat that lush-looking grass by the side of the road. But beware of possible road oils or gas floating on the water close to the highway, and beware of the possibility that the county agricultural people have just come by spraying the grass to kill weeds or keep fire hazards down near the road.

Temporary Enclosures

Some endurance riders have developed an interesting temporary corral device that attaches to their trailers. This is especially useful where there are no facilities and the alternative is to leave your horse tied up all night. This temporary corral is made up of a few panels, each separate from the other and connected by a variety of ingenious methods.

Each panel is made for 1¼-inch PVC plastic tubing as shown in photographs 44 and 45. On the back or side of the trailer there is welded a piece of pipe or steel tubing that will accept the plastic with a reasonably snug fit. Then the panels are joined in a six- seven- or eight-sided figure to enclose the horse. This is very light and sufficiently strong for almost all situations.

We have also seen some horsemen use portable electric fences, but in very dry country they are sometimes not too effective because of the lack of good grounding. This, of course, could be rectified by using a wire ground rather than depending on the ground itself. But all in all we favor the plastic tube corral since it is stiff, easily erected, and seems more like a real fence.

44. Here is a plastic-pipe portable corral in use.

45. A detail of the upper fastening used in a plastic-pipe corral.

For a Pleasant Trip

Whenever we stop for gas or water or for any human need we also check the horses, watching particularly for strange forms of sweat in unusual places such as on the shoulders or the belly. These could warn of an oncoming stiffening up or developing colic. In the event of such an observation, we would try to take the horse out for a good walk around the block and a bit of seeing what's new to take his mind off his problems. Early attention pays off in this situation.

Some people cover their horses with *blankets* when they travel. We rarely do even in winter if the trailer is well ventilated and not drafty. Nevertheless, it is a good idea to have a blanket just in case of sickness when keeping the horse warm is very important. If you suspect some problem developing because of any unusual observation, you might listen for bowel sounds with your ear firmly placed low on the horse's side a short distance ahead of the back leg. As a rule you will hear a healthy gurgle every few seconds on each side of the horse. Failing to hear these sounds is reinforcing evidence that your horse is getting sick. Simple leading around for a little while is excellent first-echelon therapy for a traveling horse. Taking a few minutes to do a bit of gentle grooming is also very useful in helping your horse relax and "get it back together."

Don't be surprised if your horse does not drink for the first day of a trip. It won't hurt him. Most horses will excrete shortly after getting into a trailer, a rather annoying habit when you have just gotten things ship shape for the trip! But urinating may be another thing. It has been known to be effective to place some fresh straw bedding under the horse to encourage him to urinate. We believe traveling horses should ordinarily have good, fresh bedding in their trailer stalls, and in the location where they stop. Fresh bedding is very encouraging and well worth the cost in keeping your horse fit and happy during a trip.

The *company of other animals* is very useful. If you can take your horse's pet dog or cat along in the trailer without it being too much trouble, do so.

Interstate travel can involve the great bureaucracy. If you plan an interstate trip, a consultation with your veterinarian can be very useful in avoiding unnecessary hold-ups along the way for the lack of traveling papers or other documentation. Recently Coggins tests have been required, which involve several days before the results can be verified, and many states require health and/or brand certificates. You should also check to find out if there is a specific warning out for a given area related to sleeping sickness or some other problem that has been covered in bulletins published by the USDA or state or county authorities. But, generally, taking horses most anywhere in the United States is an easy experience, especially since many horsemen do it, and you can find friendly assistance almost anywhere you wish to go.

Endurance and competitive trail riders soon develop established routes and stops on their way to and from their favorite contests. If you get involved at all, you will soon find friends who will be happy to give you the benefit of their experience going to and staying at any particular event. Often the management of the ride you want to try is helpful with information about the area and where to stay.

Traveling with horses is actually a rather pleasant experience once you and your horse have a trip or two under your belts.

PART IV

Time to Go

1

Riding the Contest

Degrees of Difficulty: Three Kinds of Rides

Endurance and competitive trail riding offer a very broad spectrum of degree of difficulty—surely broad enough to satisfy the requirements of any horseman when you consider that the distances can range from about 20 miles to over 100, the terrain can vary from almost perfectly flat to very mountainous, the weather conditions can vary from very hot to very cool if not downright cold, and, finally, the rules can vary from very strict and complicated to practically no rules at all. In some rides you are not allowed to have any assistance of any kind; in others you may have a bit of assistance on the trail and none at the stable; in others the rules are about the other way around. In such simple situations as getting a leg up to help you mount, most rides do not have rules, but some have clear specifications in this matter. We shall, therefore, select three levels of contest and go over them in some detail to give you an idea of actually riding in a contest. In some levels you may not have a "crew." In others it would seem virtually impossible to get through the ride without assistance. So we will introduce into the narrative the functions of the crew as well as the rider in the three basic situations.

There are many simple one-day competitive trail rides under the sponsorship of the NATRC each year in various parts of the country. There are probably an equal number put on by various riding groups across the land without sponsorship of anything other than a local organization. Consequently the rules will vary considerably. In general you will have a friend, a husband or wife, son or father, someone who will want to go along with you, not to ride but to

help when desirable and watch you have a good time. This casual assistance is your "crew."

Let's assume that the ride you select is 25 miles long in pleasant country with mostly back roads, perhaps 3 or 4 miles of pavement, a 10-mile stretch along a river that is a bit sandy, and one place where you have a choice of fording the river or going up over a regular bridge with quite a bit of vehicular traffic. There is a vet check with a one-hour lunch stop at the 15-mile mark near this bridge, and you have a choice of having as much assistance as you want or of going for the "Horsemanship Award," which requires you to do everything yourself. You are not a junior in this case. In fact, let's assume you are a middle-aged woman with help from her slightly reluctant husband (who, by the way, will soon be stuck by the "bug" and be urging you to ride more and more!). Since you are going for the Horsemanship Award you should read the rules very carefully. It is quite possible that on this occasion all your crew can do to help you is park the trailer.

The rules indicate that this ride, taking place on a Saturday, will have a check-in period from 7:30 to 9.00 A.M. with a starting time of 10:00 A.M. The riders will go out 30 seconds apart between two flagpoles. You are expected to come to the ride secretary's booth, pay your fee, get your paper for the judge inspection, and present your horse with or without a saddle and bridle. If approved to start, you weigh in, get your number, final instructions, and are ready to go.

The rules stipulate that you have to arrive at the lunch stop not earlier than 1:00 P.M. nor later than 1:30 P.M. plus your starting differential due to the 30-second spacing. Finally, you must arrive at the finish line not earlier than 4:00 P.M. nor later than 4:30 P.M., again taking into account your starting differential. The final judging will be concluded in time for an award ceremony at 6:00 P.M. followed by a no-host banquet at the local motel.

You do a bit of calculating and see that this ride is going to require an average speed of 5 miles per hour. Doesn't sound too tough, but you will be surprised to find that you cannot waste time. Even in this seemingly simple contest you will have to pay considerable attention to business if you hope to do well. It is not too early to try to size up the other riders and horses. Watch to see who has ridden successfully before. You will discover, as in other sports, that there is no shortage of "authorities" ready to give you any amount of advice you can take. Beware. Listen, but weigh carefully every bit of information you receive. In this instance you have not gone over the trail, but you do know the country in a general way and have seen some of the flagging along the way as you drove to the starting point. In other words, you do know pretty well where you are going even though you have not seen the whole course as such.

46. Linda Tellington-Jones showing her horse to the judges. Practice and training even in these details are very helpful in making proper impressions on judges and giving your horse the best chance he can have to look good.

Almost always at about this point there is some unexpected reason to panic over some little thing, like "Where are my gloves? Did you put them in the glove compartment? Where are they?" This sort of trivia can set the stage for a surge of apprehension that can build very rapidly between you and your horse. Yes, indeed, horses can pick up on nervousness very rapidly and then act up in some little way that sets you up another notch. First thing you know, you are at the starting line waiting to be called and your horse "for the first time in his life" is absolutely impossible to hold still. He is backing unceremoniously into someone else's horse to your utter embarrassment. What looked like a simple little contest hasn't even started and there you are completely unglued! You are trying to keep out of people's way and watch the judge at the same time to be sure you go between those flagged poles when you are supposed to. Right then you see his assistant look straight at your number and then write something on a paper. *You just know* they are making a note of the bad behavior and you will never win a Horsemanship Award this day! In fact, all the assistant is probably doing at that point is making sure to note your actual starting time. *You're called!*

Let's recap a bit here, just to be sure a few basic lessons are clear as crystal. About those gloves. If you had a check list you could glance and see a check mark indicating that the gloves are at least with you. If you develop good habits you will know where they are or at least where you have schooled yourself to put them every time. This holds for every other item of equipment you take 'o these contests.

Second, even if you lost the gloves, keep your cool. The experienced horsemen in this world are just about unflappable. They always remain calm with low voices, no panic. To use the current vernacular, you are "laid back," so laid back that the total amount of energy appearing to come out of you wouldn't light the bulb in a pen light!

Here we see why the NATRC has declared that one basic purpose of their rides is to teach good horsemanship; and they do a superb job of exactly that. We assume the judge on this contest is experienced. He sees you, but he can also spot that you are not very experienced, and you will find he is not the steel-minded, unyielding, tough critic you think. He is, in fact, almost certain to be quite sympathetic as long as you are trying.

You finally go through those poles and you are on your way.

What a relief! Your horse wants to *go*. Here you are wise if you let it flow a bit. Don't fight the horse any more than you have to. He probably should walk out to impress the judge, but better a little trot for 100 feet or so and get him settled than fight him right from the start. Here we add one more maxim, if you will. We said, *Keep cool*. We now say, *Use your head*.

Three miles down the trail you stop to check your girth, and who shows up behind you but your old friend "so-and-so," who has been on several rides before. You swing back on and ride with her, visiting at a great rate. You are just telling her about the "terrible start" when the trail, which has been following an old railroad grade running along beside the river, takes a turn unbeknownst to you down between some big bushes on a narrow path toward the water. After about 5 minutes you remark that you haven't seen a flag. Your old friend agrees. So you begin to watch closely, and in the next half mile you see no flag at all. You must have missed a turn!

You both turn around and put the horses into a good working trot back down the trail and, sure enough, there is the place where you should have turned. You can't complain because it is as well marked as it possibly could be. There is even a white sign with an arrow with the big word TURN on it. How could you both have possibly missed that? Well, the fact is, you did. Another lesson. *Keep cool. Use your head. Pay attention.*

Now you are not sure how far you have come. You had a pretty good idea that you would trot in the good places and walk in any bad places in this pre-lunch stretch and just keep the other horses in mind. You figured this was a simple way to "get there on time." But now you and your old friend are quite alone. She has been on several of these rides and should know what to do. She had arrived late at the start this morning because of some trouble loading her horse, so she was the very last person across the starting line, some 22 minutes behind you. She says you should probably both keep moving until you at least catch up with someone.

Off you go at a slow canter over excellent territory along the river. You bend away from the river as the trail climbs up a pretty good little hill. When you get to the top of the hill you can see several horses about half a mile ahead and you think you can tell where you are. Relief! You and your friend compare notes and take into consideration the fact that you are 22 minutes ahead of her in the field. You decide you should probably push along smartly to get closer to your proper time position coming into the lunch stop. You estimate there are a good 4 miles to go.

She decides to keep up with you for a little while at least, so you are off again together down the hill trotting, only to be spied on by a judge behind a bush who *definitely* does not approve of trotting downhill. Out into the flat the horses ahead of you are all gone now and "must be miles ahead still," you think. Keep pouring on the coal. Whatever happened to that simple 5-mile-an-hour average anyway? Suddenly you and your friend are coming around a big bend back toward the river and there ahead of you are 30 or more horses moving about in slow circles waiting for the minimum time to cross the line into the lunch stop. Your horse has gone fast enough to have a good sweat up. You consult your watch. The rule says you have to stay mounted and keep moving for the last 2 miles. Nothing to do but go around in circles like the others. But you only have five minutes to wait before your turn comes to cross the line.

You near the two flagged poles indicating where the timers are and wait for permission to cross without penalty points. There is the signal! Your dutiful husband is waiting with the truck and trailer in the field. You wave to him as you present your horse to the judge. The horse is pretty sweaty and still breathing hard. His PR is up there. And all this you *know* was totally unnecessary. So does the judge.

You groom your horse, giving him a few sips of water and a little hay, then you grab a sandwich yourself. Time seems to fly! It is already time to go back to the judge for a check-out. This time your horse is just fine. He really is a good animal and you have done a pretty decent job of training, so his recoveries are actually excellent. Points for you. You are cleared to leave in 15 minutes. The rules for this ride require you to keep your saddle on for the rest stop, so you have simply loosened the girth and straightened the blanket. Now you tighten it up, get the bridle on, consult your watch again, get your judge card in your hand, and mount up ready for the last 10 miles. Actually you feel you are settling down now, and so is the horse. The next leg should go much better. You will watch the trail. And you definitely will try to be *smarter*.

Off you go again, this time away from the lunch stop toward the ford in the river. You can see the traffic up on the big bridge. There is a huge truck going over the bridge, and you feel you surely don't want to get up there with that kind of traffic. You head for the ford. The horse is moving nicely, but as he gets close to the water he finds himself among five other horses, all of them refusing in various ways. You wait humbly and patiently for a while, then finally decide you may as well push him through the milling group, which has now swelled to eight horses. But lo and behold, your horse, which has forded just as tough a place as this many times, now elects to go with the "majority." Inexperienced horses can do exactly this, you know. They will do things very nicely at home, but here surrounded with strangers they may very well perform quite differently. After several minutes of pure frustration you decide to lead the horse just to train him. You *have* done this before but then you remember the rule. No forward progress unless you are in the saddle.

You finally give up and head for the steep bank to the road and the bridge. You slip back a bit, but watching the traffic, you just scramble and watch for a good opportunity to enter the bridge. There is a light point in traffic and you scoot onto the bridge and hold a good brisk walk on the pavement. Before you know it you are over the bridge and safely moving back to the trail, which is now climbing up another good hill. You pass another judge, who is making some kind of note. You wonder. Then you look back only to notice that your blanket has slipped almost completely out from under your saddle. Must have been when you scrambled up to that bridge. Now here you are on a narrow spot in the trail still in sight of that d— judge and no place to stop. You have to go on about 50 feet more to a little wide spot where you can resaddle your horse. What a mess!

You have the saddle loose and off. You shake out your blanket and set it on the horse's back. And of course that is the time when all of those horses that were trying to cross the ford have decided to do what you did, and they all come up on you together. By now your horse recognizes them, and developing a sudden moment of herdboundness, he wants to go along with them.

After 10 good minutes of real difficulty you get your saddle back on and you mount up. Again you are "behind time." You push up the rest of the hill at a good hard driving walk, knowing you will have to trot quite a bit to keep up. Nevertheless, you are not going to make the mistake you did during the morning of hurrying and then having to wait. After all, you *do* have a 30-minute grace period with no penalty points at the end.

You consult your watch carefully. You pull out the map and feel quite sure that the top of the hill is only four miles from the finish line, which is back where you started. Now you have it together. So you move uneventfully along trying to spot some of the riders who started just before or after you, but by now most of you have taken off a jacket or done something so you simply cannot recognize people. You wish now you had noticed the numbers just before you. But you hardly remember your own, to say nothing of anyone else's.

You decide to push along a bit faster. Somehow you worry about the extra time back there at the ford and the long climb up the hill when you know you are far from making 5 miles an hour. So you push up the last part of the hill at a trot. After all, it isn't that steep. Right there at the top of the hill is the man with the stethoscope. You should have known! High PRs again. But he lets you go with a mild admonition. Now you move off down the hill, a really great place to trot your horse, but you know judges don't like trotting downhill in this ride. So it's more walking. You know you are definitely late by now, so at the bottom of the hill, you really put your horse in gear and move out! There is a big sign saying 2 miles to go. You check your watch and realize you have forty minutes in which to make that 2 miles! You blew it again. Now you're just stumbling along at a snail's pace trying to kill time and you still come within sight of the finish line with 15 minutes to kill. More milling around.

Finally you may cross the finish line. At least your horse is not hot this time. You begin grooming your horse and getting the tack off. Finally it is time for the second check. You go over and get the strange feeling that you are almost being ignored. The judge checks your horse and, with scarcely a glance, dismisses you. *You are being ignored.* He has seen enough of your horse to be absolutely satisfied that it is perfectly all right, but it is nowhere near the winner's circle.

You wait around for the awards. It seems there are awards for everything you can think of. But you come away with your scorecard. And it does not look good. Right there in black and white you discover that the judge saw just about every dumb thing you did, *including* when you got lost!

You and your husband decide not to wait around for the banquet, so you load Old Smoky in the trailer and head for home, wondering if you will ever try that again. It was supposed to be so simple. Only 25 miles. Only 5 miles an hour. What happened? ? ?

At least you learned two things: *It pays to know the trail. And you simply must be able to rate your horse.*

Well, a year has passed. Your husband has bought a horse and the two of you have had a good time at several competitive trail rides. You have a good stack of trophies in the living room and you even placed ninth and tenth riding together in a field of 74 riders in a 50-mile endurance ride. It was the first one in your part of the country, and you folks discovered yourselves the local "authorities." Feels pretty good.

At Christmas you receive a nice little letter with a card from your old friend "so-and-so" who has moved back East and is now inviting you to come to a big *100-mile, 3-day ride*. Wow! What fun. But can you both find that much time off? It really will be a big trip. It takes four days just for the three-day contest itself when you count the time to check in. It will take you several days of hard trailering for the round trip. But you decide to take your friend up on her invitation. After all, it isn't everybody who gets a chance to ride in one of those big rides.

You really work on your rating. You really work on manners. You really study the route as well as you possibly can from maps, and you study someone's *Endurance and Competitive Trail Ride Manual* until it is about worn out!

You have been forewarned, and you have very nice casual riding clothes and some nice things to wear to the hotel in the evening. No problems with all that. But the thing you are not prepared for is the sight of the *beautiful* horses. You see that gorgeous beast being led by a groom from the stable to a riding area where his owner is waiting to exercise him. You suddenly feel squeamish about getting Old Smoky out of the trailer! Fortunately, your husband's horse is a bit more stylish and bigger, but here you see fine big hunter types one after the other. And if not that, there are very elegant Arabians with their regal way of going, tails up and eyes so bright. Your old friend greets you. She has a new horse, which has only been on this ride the previous year, but she is ready to help you in every way. There is no problem about starting, since she has arranged for you "guests" from so far away to "ride with her," or at least near enough so "you won't get lost this time"!

Your horses are a bit stiff from trailering, but they pass the in-coming inspection all right and you are assigned a nice box stall for each. The two stalls are in the middle of a long row with straw waiting and many very nice, hospitable touches. Your horses are surprisingly calm. After all, they have been in several contests by now, so a big group of horses is no new thing to them. You get tacked up and go for a brief ride just to loosen the horses up and give them an appetite. Back to the barns in about an hour and your friend suggests you drive over the country just to see where the trail goes.

You can't believe it. The hills are so steep in places. Sure the trails are fine, but the hills. Where you live the biggest thing within 100 miles is less than half the size of these. And they are just one after the other!

The next morning everyone is ready, with much pleasant jocularity and a great feeling of anticipation. Some of these people are doing this, you learn, for the twentieth time!

The whole day passes *beautifully*. Your experience has indeed paid off handsomely, and this time you really did pay attention, you used your head, your friend really did know the trail, and you paid attention and still had time to have a good time. There was nothing grim about it at all. Really fine! Back that evening you know you have only a short time to work on your horses before a final inspection.

A pleasant dinner, pleasant after-dinner visiting, and everyone decides to bed down a bit early.

Next morning you and your husband both feel a bit stiff, but at your age you expect it. "Nothing a bit of riding won't cure," you old endurance riders always say! After an early breakfast you are off to the barns to get the horses ready. Shock! You thought *you* were stiff. Look at them. They can hardly move at all! Rub them down. Work on those legs, but you can't do much. The rules are very strict about requiring the horse to remain stabled until the judge can inspect. They know that this stiffness is one of the most common things to watch for, and they want to see it. You see several of those fine smooth horses walking quite well, in fact, not observably stiff at all. This morning things are pretty serious, not like the first morning. It seems almost everyone is nursing some kind of little "secret" problem he hopes others do not see. The judges are very businesslike. Your horses move stiffly, to say the least. The judges ponder a bit, then suggest you move them around a bit on the halter and come back. You are grateful for the reprieve, and sure enough after 15 minutes they have worked out of their difficulties pretty well. You *know* that stall was the problem. Your horses, back home, have always been able to get out in the big corral after a contest, where they can stretch. Here they are cooped up, you feel, and it is no wonder that they get stiff. But what about those other horses? Few of them show much stiffness. Better give this some thought.

The lessons here are just as plain as the simple ones you learned on your first ride, but they are much more subtle. It may not be that stall that should take full blame for the stiffness. Possibly there is some horsemanship involved here that you should know about.

Anyway, the second day goes pretty well. There was a whale of a big mountain to go over, and your horses both showed clear signs of being pretty tired. After all, the average speed here is just short of a full trotting speed for most horses for the full distance. Also there was some pavement that had to be negotiated at a good clip.

After this day an old guy comes by to look at your horses. He seems very nice. He tells you he noticed how stiff they were this morning and asks if you know that you *can* spend a little time with your horses *after* the judging in the evening. You say yes, but you hadn't thought there was much to do after they had been judged. He says many of the horses here work in these hills a good deal and also have the experience of working two good days in a row and standing in stalls and they all look good because they are thoroughly *groomed*. He points out that a good massage at that time and some good stretching might just help a whole lot. You say to yourself, "Of course I should have thought of that! And massaging was in that book I read, too!" So this time you do exactly what you did yesterday, except that after the judge dismisses you, in that hour or so when you can do some more for your horse, you do pull his front legs out in a big stretch and his back legs out and back and forward and to the side, then the fronts again. This time you also use the locked-hands technique and rub upward against the grain of the hair on all four cannon bones. Then you rub and groom not too hard but firmly on the rump and neck and shoulders and loins, and inside the legs. All this is happening while your horses get a nice warm bran mash with some talking going on just to fill the air with good sounds. Nice *low* talk, *slow* talk, *loving* talk. Your horses are doing all right.

Next morning, it's as though there was magic. No stiffness at all that you can see. One horse may have a bit of a sore back leg, but otherwise all right.

You have covered two 40-mile days. This last 20 are taken pretty fast! You really have to move it. Again no problems. You are at the finish line and these judges are viewing you with a quality of professionalism and stylish horsemanship you haven't seen before. It is very impressive. They are nice, friendly, but impeccably proper in every way. You are aware of much tradition here, much propriety. Things are expected to go according to the way they have always gone.

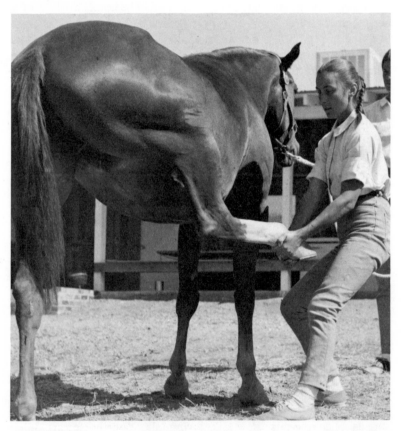

47. Linda demonstrates stretching of big muscles in hind leg. One might think this was very difficult and required much strength. On the contrary, one can pull these muscles too much. The idea is simply to get the leg up and then let the horse relax. When you might have gotten the foot to a given position, within a few seconds the horse will let his leg go out a bit farther. That's all there is to it.

After lunch the prizes come out and you do win a nice little award for coming the longest distance. Otherwise the prizes for lightweight, middleweight, and heavyweight, and all the others go to people who, like you, have a living room full of prizes. They just happen to have been doing it a lot longer and know much about this kind of riding that you simply do not know yet.

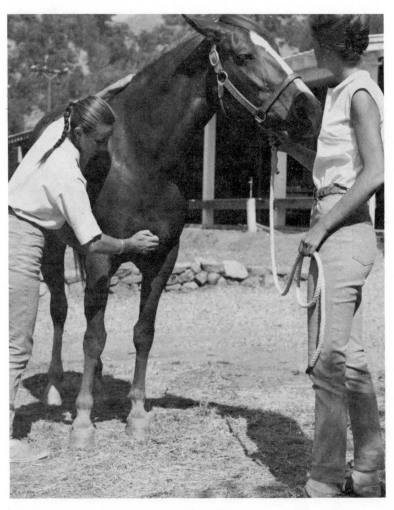

48. Bliss.

You have come a long way since you first started this sport. You don't make dumb mistakes anymore. You learned some fine points about caring for a horse that has to "go on" and you see the value of good experience. You know if you had the chance to do that ten more times you too might find the right horse and make all the right moves, and all in all you feel very good about the whole experience. It was an elegant time.

Here we are again at the end of another riding season. You and some equestrian friends are having dinner after a good ride in the country around home. All six of you get to talking about what it would be like to ride *100 miles in one day*. You don't feel Old Smoky is up to it. Oh he might make it, all right, but after all, he did just come from an ordinary backyard and never has had that quality of toughness you read about. And your husband's horse is definitely not one for that kind of ride. He never has been handy enough, for one thing. Your friends have Arabs and half Arabs that they think could do it if they had the chance to train.

You and your husband have talked about it before from time to time, but never really seriously. Now, it just seems the thing to do. You have recently read a piece by Dr. Ralph Paffenbarger extolling the value of stressful exercise. He has run the 100 miles over the Tevis Cup trail *on foot*. You realize you can't make that ride because it is the wrong time of year for you, but you could go to the Virginia City Ride in Nevada in the middle of September. You could even take two weeks off so you could ride over the trail beforehand in a series of 30 or so miles each day.

All six of you agree to begin working toward that end. Maybe even next September. But you have to find two new horses. You and your husband, after some letter writing, find what sounds like a good set of prospects out in Iowa or Nebraska on the open prairie country. The horses are old enough and have never been more than halter broke. The owner says he can start any one you choose so you can ride it with a reasonable degree of safety. So you take a long weekend and go out looking.

You have now ridden enough and you have seen enough horses in this sport so you really do know what you want. And there on a half snowy afternoon you ride in the rancher's pick-up out on the range and see horses that *have already seen you for some time*. Their heads are up. They come running. Maybe there's grain in that truck.

49. Matthew Mackay-Smith, D.V.M., keeps in good shape. He is one of the foremost practitioners of this sport, having placed high and/or won many times both East and West in a variety of contests. He is also the ideal judge because his actual experience in the saddle reinforces his skills as a veterinarian.

Every one of them looks bold. You have the feeling they can see for miles. They are as near to wild as they can be. You get out of the truck and find them really friendly. One takes your eye immediately. Nicely square-looking. Trim, but really strong. Very friendly, curious. Came right through the bunch to "find you." It's almost mystic! You know you shouldn't make up your mind so fast. But you did. Your husband has to look a bit more, but behind him there is a big horse that's just holding his nose about three inches from his neck, waiting. When your husband turns around, he says something like, "Well, where have you been?" He admires.

You have a veterinarian check them thoroughly to be sure they are sound. They are. Two weeks later you come back with your rig to pick up "two broke horses." They still don't look very well started to you, but they are basically gentle enough. So you are now off on an "experience." You realize this is becoming a way of life and you *do* really feel good.

Right through the winter you ride, really ride, whenever you can. The horses stand out in 30-below weather with no stable, no help at all except for a nice warm meal every now and then. They are getting an excellent combination grain mix and the best hay you can find. You are feeding natural foods almost entirely, with possibly a little vitamin and mineral supplement. "You just have to do that much," you say. You let them go barefooted enough to show you exactly how they wear their own feet, then you shoe them following this natural information. Spring comes and you put them into a couple of 50-mile endurance rides. You are now an experienced rider yourself. It's just that big 100 miles in one day that is out there in front of you waiting to add a dimension to your life. Your friends ride with you a good deal, counting on you because you do have much more experience than they have. All goes well. You have done everything you should and the day draws near when you all set out. Virginia City, here we come!

You have already written ahead and found people who are glad to show you the trail, and you decide to stay down in the valley and trailer up to various legs of the trail each of three days.

The very first day you get started comfortably about 8:00 A.M. in the valley and you plan to ride up the mountain to Virginia City, a distance of about 25 miles. You arrive in that crazy little town in the middle of the afternoon only to discover several "old-timers," some of them well-known endurance riders, who are having a beer in a local pub. They tell you they are waiting around for a few more people to show and they plan to have dinner, then ride down the mountain after dark to a big ranch about 25 miles away on the north side. Why don't you join them? Well, you have already ridden almost 30 miles. "So what else is new?" they say. It *would* be ideal experience to go down over that part of the trail in the dark in company with all these "pros." You have practiced in the dark at home, but usually on decent roads, and this country already looks very awe-inspiring. You talk it over with your friends and decide to do it to take advantage of the unusual opportunity. So you wait around, meet some more riders, and have a few beers. Finally you have a good dinner and mount up right after dark. It sure is cold!

To your alarm, these people trot down the road and hold this steady trot as they dive off over the shoulder through a very narrow little place and along the trail in single file—trot—trot—trot. As they near the top of a place like a pass they slow to a walk and pass some laughing comments around. Everyone stops to check their rigging. Then after a minute or two, everyone is back aboard again and trotting, trotting, trotting. About midnight you arrive at the big ranch and find a corral where you can turn your horses out. Someone is willing to drive around the valley to your trailers with you and drop you off. It turns out they live not too far from there anyway. You finally get your outfits to the big ranch about 3:00 in the morning, and pick up the horses. Back to where you are staying near Reno just before daylight, and you have covered the beginning and end of the trail and only have a center section to do. You sleep in until about 10:00 and then get saddled up after an early lunch. You do the center section in the valley in a short time, and come home, now able to rest an extra day thanks to crowding two days' riding into one.

Now, this is not the ideal thing to do. But it is the kind of thing that happens. You have to use your head. It might be very valuable to take advantage of that opportunity to ride with real "pros" in the dark over the actual trail. That is the point. But here you must learn to *weigh your priorities*.

You show up Friday afternoon for the vet check. A solid-looking man who looks as though he had just stepped out of a John Wayne movie beckons you and your horse to come over. You are looking at the head vet, a highly experienced individual with the western sun etched all over his face. He is every bit the professional you have met in other places, but he is very easy. His eye winks a bit as he hears how far you have come to make the ride. "Well, we can be bought pretty cheap," he jokes. All the time he is checking your horse with a speed and skill that is most impressive. You are asked to trot your horse out. "Look at that trot," he calls. "Not the horse —the rider!" "Okay, go get your number." You don't know whether to laugh or cry. It all seems so much easier than you thought it was going to be. One of your friend's horses almost didn't pass, you think. But you all are cleared to start in the morning.

It was really desert hot down in the valley during the day. Here up on the mountainside it is windy and very cold. Almost freezing. There is no good place for your horse. Just put up your portable corrals and put blankets on and hope for the best. The pre-ride meeting goes well. You get the feeling that this is a no-nonsense situation but it is still very loose somehow. Everyone is very friendly. The one overall feeling you have is that you must get in out of the cold. Your poor horse. A good dinner, then to your sleeping bag near the horse, ready for a night feeding and an early start. The start is actually at 4:00 A.M.

The first part of the ride is on pavement for a short distance. You follow a ride leader over this stretch at a good trot. Altogether, seventy or eighty contestants go down that crazy little path you took a few nights before. You are *very* glad you took advantage of that opportunity to ride when you did. It seems impossible, still, that you and your horse can do that at that speed with so much dirt and dust. But there you are doing it. Various riders, including you, have flashlights that come on every now and then for various reasons. Figures in the dark hunched in the cold, wrapped up moving fast into the dawn. The day finally begins after what seems like a long time. It is red and very colorful, even on the ground around you. Steam seems to rise up off the rocks. It reminds you of something in *Star Wars*. Finally you are at the first one-hour vet check only a short distance from the ranch you came to the other night.

You are very accustomed to the vet-stop routine by now. There are no new aspects. You have engaged the services of three local riding kids to help you at the stops. They have done it all before and come well recommended. You feel, every now and then, as though you are being treated a bit like a "dude," but they do just what you want them to do, so you can't complain.

By the time you get to the next one-hour check, you feel violently bad in the back, the legs, your stomach. You just can't go on. No way! You find your friends have been feeling that way for the past ten miles! It was horrible! Yet this was supposed to be the easiest part of the ride. It certainly was flatter, the trail was not bad, and the day was hot but not too hot. By the end of the hour you resolve to try to make it. After all, it is only 25 or 30 miles more and you have been over the trail. It makes so much difference to have been over the trail.

You and your friends are now separated by about an hour. But that is to be expected. You are out in front. It is interesting how the day has gone so far. You just held a good pace and let some people race past you in the dark and even on the center leg only to find them dropped out by this vet check. You were about fiftieth, you thought. Now after passing only about five riders, you are told you are fourteenth. How about that! Where you had hoped to just get through, you now get that sneaky feeling "You just might make it in the top ten."... And if *that,* there is the Best Condition Award." Wow, it blows your mind. Race fever they call this, and you're getting it!

It is late in the day, should be dark in a little while. Your horse feels good. You begin to feel better. That hot soup was just what the doctor ordered. You head up into the canyon on your last big climb back up to Virginia City. You see two riders ahead of you. They have stopped to sit on a cliff and watch the sun go down for a minute. You come along. Your horse still feels good, so you just wave and pass them. *Now you are No. 11.* Just one more to pass and you *will* be in the top 10. You wonder how your husband is doing behind you, and about your friends. You hope they are all right. But you must really pay attention now. No time to get lost when you are that close to the top 10!

Suddenly your horse slows down. He stops. Unexplainably. He will not take a step forward. You get off and try to lead. But no way. He is just not going another step. You look him over. Respiration not bad. The pulse might be a little high, but certainly not too bad. He isn't blowing hard or trying to have thumps. He just won't go. *You use your head,* and sit down with the reins in your hand and wait quietly as though there was *no place to go.* Do not fret. Do not panic.

You may have passable "readings" but your horse is "out of gas" just the same. You might listen for gut sounds in his side. *None.* Is he going to colic? What can you do? You're supposed to lead him

50. Mike Fitzgerald, shown here on the Nugget 50-mile ride followed closely by his dad, big Pat, has finished several big endurance rides in style. He finished the Virginia City 100 when he was not quite six years old.

around as a cure for colic, but he just won't lead. Still you do not
panic. You try massaging his belly. The two kids you passed are now
passing you. Quite a lot of time passes, and who should show up but
your husband.

He tells you he felt pretty bad a few miles before the last check
point so he got off and jogged with his horse maybe a mile or so.
Then he did it again shortly after the last check point. Now he feels
nice and loose. You think maybe you should have gotten off and
done a bit of that yourself. You both consult for a while, and finally
conclude he may as well go along and you will get in when you can.
After all, you still have your four friends behind you. He takes off
into the night. Then only minutes later two of your friends come by
and stop for a bit, but finally go on into the blackness. You try to
move your horse again. Finally! A step, then another. You decide to
lead him along the trail, at least make a little forward progress.
Your two other friends catch up and pass you. Alone again. Finally
your horse seems to be gathering strength again. You have lost an
hour and a half. The dream of top ten is far gone by now. But you
do get on and nurse your horse ahead gently. To your surprise, you
pass one of your friends who just has to get off and rest a minute.
This darkness gets to you after a while. On and on. You had forgotten how many steep places there were and how many ridges to go
over. The lights below are beautiful and weird at the same time. Now
you are going right along. The trail becomes good. You are trotting.
You sense people and horses ahead of you. You pass a group. Still
your husband is out in front. Where are your friends? You have
somehow lost touch. But you push on.

Finally there is the finish line, and a fire with people standing
around it. You ask about your husband and learn he placed *eighth*
and has gone to put his horse away so he can come back and help
you. Wow, *eighth*. Your friends came in all right and are just ahead
of you. After you clear the last vet check you swing back into the
saddle wearily and begin the slow walk over the pavement into town
to the technical finish line in front of the Delta Saloon. There you
see your husband coming in the pick-up. You are all together.

It was really something!

Tips for Rider and Crew

Let's stop dreaming just long enough to cover some *specifics* about dealing with big endurance rides, with some emphasis on the crew.

It is important to *keep records.* We kept logs on all our horses' daily experience in training and competing conditions, including problems and methods that worked well, as well as methods that didn't work. This book is largely derived from those old notes, and there is no reason why you, if you really take advantage of the rest stops, cannot train yourself to the highest level of achievement you desire.

Whenever you have a chance, *watch other contestants* and other crews to see how they do things and what equipment they feel is worthwhile. What a person may tell you about riding or doing things could be quite different from what you actually observe him doing or using during the contest. It is not only good to watch, but it is even better to try to evaluate whether the technique or tool in question seems to be doing some good.

We have learned that the rider and crew should attempt to develop some real co-ordinated way of doing things. *Good organization and relaxed discipline for you and your crew is the name of the game in endurance riding.* Many a big ride has been won or lost at the rest stops.

Having arrived at the check station well ahead of the expected arrival time of the rider, the crew should find an appropriate spot to set up. If the weather is hot and sunny, find some shade, or create it. Get close to the water but keep in mind that other people have to get to water, too. A secluded spot where horse and rider can get some rest, not in the immediate vicinity of the vetting area, is very desirable. Park the vehicle so it is possible to get out easily. With as many as two hundred contestants it can be pretty congested at times, and you don't want to be trapped in behind several vehicles and not be able to get to the next check point in time.

It is usually worthwhile to have several five-gallon containers to carry *water.* These are quite heavy, and some people prefer the two-gallon size even though it will obviously require more containers.

If you know the water at a rest stop is going to be very cold, be sure to have some hot water to mix with it for both bathing and drinking.

Keep your water buckets separate from each other. That is to say, do not let your horse drink out of the bucket that has the sponges you have just used to get mud off his legs. Make sure he drinks clean water out of a clean bucket.

Have a small pile of hay out with, perhaps, a handful of salt on it, or a bucket with a little grain in it. Have sponges and towels ready to care for the horse immediately upon arrival. Have a box of brushes and a hoofpick nearby.

On most endurance rides the horses are examined immediately upon arrival. After this, bring the house to your spot and pull the bridle and saddle off immediately. If the weather is very hot, let him have eight or ten swallows of water and then a bit of hay or grass while you quickly but systematically wash him all over, starting with his head, neck, all four legs, then his shoulders and croup, and finally the back and belly. This order gets the job done as fast as possible without possible shock. Wetting the back and belly first while the head and legs are still hot would be a mistake.

We just noted that you *pull the saddle* immediately after the incoming vet check. Riders whose experience has been with NATRC-type rides may question the idea of pulling off a saddle immediately, since this is something you would be penalized for in most competitive trail rides. This rule came into effect since some judges felt that heat bumps were caused by removing the saddle too quickly. The interesting fact is that while we have seen heat bumps on competitive trail-ride horses occasionally in the old days, we have never seen a heat bump on an *endurance* horse. It most likely comes from the fact that endurance horses are ridden more and longer distances than competitive trail-ride horses and don't carry the same amount of soft fat on their backs.

The principal idea for *basic care* within the one-hour rest time allowed is to get the heavy work done on the horse as soon as possible, get him watered out if necessary, and after checking his feet, see to it that he has as much *quiet* resting time as possible before he goes out again.

On a hot day you may have to walk the horse a bit between waterings, but if the horse has been able to get most of his water along the trail, this process will not absorb too much of the rest-stop time.

The rider should try to turn as much of this responsibility over to the crew as he can, and, in general, contribute to developing an atmosphere of calm.

Blankets may be in order. If the weather is cool, we will keep the horse blanketed and moving a bit more so that he does not lose too much heat and stiffen up. The important thing to remember is that care depends upon the temperature, humidity, and time of day, plus the condition of horse and rider.

It is the crew's responsibility to *keep close track of time,* so you have a maximum amount of time to rest and get ready to go out, and are prompt for the outgoing inspection.

It is the crew's responsibility to *watch the competition,* to know where they are when they come into the rest stop before or after their own rider, and be able to advise not only the time relationship but also the apparent condition of the competition. After the horse is cared for and standing quietly near, the end of the hour is a good time to consult between rider and crew, to take the competition into account and plan how things will go in the next leg of the contest. Often the crew can meet the rider between rest stops for a brief bit of assistance, a bottle of Gatorade, a bit of water for the horse if it is scarce along the trail, and even some hay, especially just before or after some very difficult part of the trail.

The rider's *well-being* can be almost as crucial as the horse's. He should have a change of clothes ready, especially in the case of a soaking rain or a shift to colder weather. He should have food and drink available that is appealing to him. It is easy for a rider to become so considerate of his horse that he forgets himself. At times the crew may have to insist that a rider eat, particularly if it is a first ride and he is nervous. We have seen riders become totally exhausted and feel too tired to eat, but recover very quickly after having eaten. Often the start is too rushed for a good breakfast. Perhaps there seems to be only time enough to grab a doughnut and coffee offered by management with the best of intentions. We feel it would be wise to skip the doughnuts and eat something solid but not artificially sweet, and drink some fruit juice to provide the energy needed to get to the first stop, where food can be prepared and waiting.

Hot, thick soup in the case of cold weather or for a late-night vet stop is really welcome. Light consommé (even jellied in hot weather) is a good source of energy and easy to digest. Fruit is almost always welcome, and something to drink immediately upon arrival at a stop is wise. However, it is smart to avoid carbonated soft drinks. Fruit juices or Gatorade seem to be a rider favorite.

When we were gathering ideas for the revision of this book, one ride manager said she had, over the years, seen four different riders who failed to eat breakfast before the 6:00 A.M. start. When they reached the noon check they were so exhausted that they wanted to quit right there. When the manager prevailed on them to eat some good food, all four recovered and finished the ride.

In addition to food it is most helpful if a rider has a quiet place to lie down and *rest,* even if it is for only ten minutes. This can be in a camper or on a sleeping bag or foam pad under a tree.

Finally, it is critically important that the crew maintain a calm, relaxed, and deliberate attitude at all times. It is just too easy to "get up-tight," as we say these days. This is no help to horse or rider. *No matter what seems to have gone wrong, if you think about it, getting excited and letting your emotions run away with you is not going to do a bit of good.*

This sport is tough for the best and most experienced competitors —*not just you.*

Coping with Problems

Now we'll reveal some *tricks of the trade* that can be helpful during the contest.

Problems can develop from the moment you decide you want to try one of these contests—anytime during the training stage and even while you are transporting your horse to the contest. But we shall address here only some of the common situations and conditions that have to be faced, and attempt to give some idea of how to deal with them immediately before, during, and after the contest. All situations are purely hypothetical; and to varying degrees, the tactics may be modified to match similar situations in either competitive trail rides or endurance rides. These situations may have to be handled without assistance. If, however, reasonable recovery is not effected in reasonable time, you should consult a veterinarian promptly.

Situation 1: Despite the best of care, your horse has arrived and fails to urinate or has dark, cloudy urine.

The judge doesn't know about your problem, but you know it is vital. What to do? First, check to be sure your observation is correct. *You do not panic.* Having satisfied yourself that this is the true situation, you dig out two tablespoonsful of bucu leaves, which you mix with a bit of grain. You add to this four crushed aspirin tablets and two tablespoonsful of bicarbonate of soda, which you feed directly. You relax for half an hour or so, keeping an eye on your horse. Then you lead him quietly around, perhaps a quarter of a mile, to some spot away from the crowd. You could even ride him bareback, but it is very important that you do not transmit your concern to the horse. Gently massage the loin area almost the way you might rub a cat's back. Do not make a big issue of this massaging. The easy walk, the relaxing, quiet away from the gathering crowd, and/or the mild medication are very likely to bring this kidney problem into focus. Any more treatment could put the horse so far off that he probably could not make the contest anyway.

Situation 2: Your horse won't drink.

The answer is that this simply should not happen if you have practiced good horsemastership before you ever arrived at the contest. You avoid this by having cut back on the water by 20 per cent to 30 per cent for two days prior to traveling and increasing the salt very slightly by introducing a teaspoonful in the feed. We are assuming your horse is accustomed to the taste of vinegar.

Take the ordinary water away from the horse immediately if he won't drink. Wait a little while, perhaps an hour. Put a bit of water, not less than a cupful or more than a quart, with a bit of vinegar added (one-quarter teaspoonful per quart) in a clean bucket. Set it where the horse can get at it comfortably and go away a short distance. Do not let the horse feel you are the least bit apprehensive. As in Situation 1, *relax*. Keep an eye on the horse without bugging him in any way. The trick is to behave as though the tiny bit of water is all there is! Before long, your horse will drink all right, and will have, as it were, broken the ice in the new environment. This will almost always solve the water problem before it arises and solve the urine problem too if when you arrive in a new place you offer just a bit of water first, not a whole bucketful. Once he decides to drink, you can increase the amount of water until he has his fill.

Situation 3: The contest is on. *Your horse is so excited that he simply won't go quietly. He is fighting the bit every inch of the way.*

What to do? Perhaps you should have trained more carefully by practicing with groups of riders before the contest. But then again, a horse on his first time out might well behave this way. Do not fight him constantly. Do not cling to the reins with a steady pressure. Either stop and let everyone go ahead, or, alternatively, let him get out front, whichever tactic will use up the least energy. But *do not fight him.* If you are shooting for the top ten, it is often better to go faster than you planned for a bit rather than wasting energy fighting him. If you are out in front, give him his head and *relax.* Very shortly he will behave much better. If you are behind, wait until the field is well out of sight, then mount up deliberately, holding him in the old "statue" pose you practiced when you first started to train. Now, away from the other horses, slow him down with intermittent bit pressure (kept to a minimum), sitting lightly and slightly off his back until he settles slowly. When a horse is eager to catch up he has a tendency to get his head up, which in turn lowers the back, causing him pain over the spine if the rider sits heavily in the saddle. As a consequence, while sitting down on a dressage horse might be the thing to do, it is not the best method here. When the horse, already tending to be excited, has his head up and back low, the heavy ·seat, bringing on unnecessary pain, will cause the horse to want to go faster to escape the pain, as well as to catch up with the other horses.

Situation 4: An annoying person on a very undisciplined horse rides up uncomfortably near you.

It makes your horse excited. Then someone else gets near you in essentially the same way. You cannot see that these people are necessarily trying to do this on purpose, but it is happening, nevertheless.

Smile. Make a sportsmanlike effort to get away. Stop and wait, or get ahead, or just excuse yourself and say you'd like to ride alone. Failing this, ride in such a way that the other horse is on poorer footing than your horse or faces more obstacles such as trees along the side of the trail, ditch edges—anything. Just be sure your horse has better footing than the other rider's horse as long as he persists in being bothersome. If a horse won't "ride off" in this trail-ride counterpart to a polo game, the rider might have picked a bolder horse in the first place. *Keep your cool.*

Situation 5: You had to ride harder than you expected and your horse came in to a check point with a high respiration.

You have 30 minutes to bring it down considerably. Except in the case of cold and windy weather, get just as much water as you can on the horse, following the normal routine, but faster and with more water. Walk the horse in rhythm with his present breathing rate. Then slow down carefully and tentatively just a bit. His breathing rate will be strongly inclined to follow the rate of movement as you slow down. This is what we call a "rate of the rate" problem, so do not slow down too abruptly. Often, if you do this skillfully, you can get the horse to take a few very deep breaths suddenly and cut his respiration rate as much as 25 per cent or more in less than 5 minutes! It is possible, with skill and practice, to change the respiration from 100 per minute to 25 per minute in 15 minutes' time.

Situation 6: You are surprised to discover that your horse's pulse is higher than you planned by a significant but not alarming amount.

For example, you thought it would be about 65 and it turned out to be 95. You have half an hour to do something about it.

Again, use as much water externally as possible. You begin strenuous massage on the hips and forearms, using a circular motion with the heavy part of the stroke during the part of the circle when your hand is moving in the direction of the heart. You massage the legs in the cannon areas by locking your fingers together behind the tendons and with the heels of the hands pressing hard against the side of the bone and rubbing upward (not downward) with the firmest grip the horse will permit. Follow this treatment with 10 minutes of tranquillity before the 30-minute vet check. There are more details of this in the chapter on physical therapy. In a surprisingly short time, you should have gained control of the pulse, and can, with some practice, set it at whatever rate you desire as long as your horse is not sick or lame.

Situation 7: Your horse's temperature turns out to be significantly but not alarmingly higher than you planned.

It is 104.5° F, and you hoped it would be 103.0° at this particular check. Again you have an hour to work.

First, under any conditions, be sure you have command of pulse and respiration. With a slow, even pulse, temperature is very unlikely to remain high in a healthy horse.

If it is very hot and dry, wet the horse all over with gunny sacks soaked in cold water. Make sure you get a good bit of water directly over the head in the poll area. Let the horse suck on a wet sponge, but be careful about letting him drink. Sponge his legs with liberal amounts of water. Let him drink not more than 10 swallows between short walking sessions until he is watered out. This process should not normally require more than 10 to 15 minutes. Then with mild walking with the wet gunny sacks over his back, shoulders, and hips, and a quiet opportunity to eat a bit of grass or hay apart from the crowd in the most relaxing environment you can find, you will bring the temperature down. This is so effective that you must be careful not to bring it down too much!

If it is warm and humid, use essentially the same technique, but with warm water. The idea is to promote as much evaporation as possible.

If it is cool and dry, cover the horse with a light cooler. If he is healthy, his temperature is almost certain to go down surprisingly fast. The main trick in this situation is not to let him sink into a state of shock. This situation is very common at the first check point in the Tevis Cup Ride, and many inexperienced people pour cold water on the horse and into the horse only to see him tie up almost instantly. If he drinks cold water without adequate moving, he can colic in a hurry.

If it is cool and wet, wipe the horse dry as well as you can, working under a waterproof blanket. Raise the blanket in parts, first over the shoulders and then over the hips as required to let heat escape, but keep the horse covered. Do not use cold water.

Situation 8: 15 or 20 minutes after arriving at a rest stop, you observe your horse beginning to move stiffly with his hind legs.

You have made some mistake in caring for him and you have only ten minutes before the judge is going to look at him.

In this situation, move the horse about very smartly. If necessary, sacrifice a good respiration recovery picture to be sure he is moving freely. This treatment is also appropriate in case your horse gets too much water too fast. Sacrifice a good respiration rate, but keep him moving until the judge allows him to go on.

Situation 9: You lift the saddle off only to find a raised place the size of a silver dollar—heat bumps. You have half an hour.

Ideally, alternate applications of ice and then hot Epsom salt water, but since most competitive trail rides don't allow this (and most heat bumps occur on competitive trail rides), you are limited. Practically speaking, you would alternate firm massaging with applications of a cool, damp cloth, gently pressed. The cool, damp cloth would probably have to come first to begin to relieve pain before any significant massaging can be done.

Situation 10: The most serious condition, acute shock.

The horse's temperature has dropped to a subnormal range (for example, 99.5°), the respiration is so shallow that the horse is panting, and the heart is thumping so hard you can see the vibration from ten feet away.

Blanket him immediately. When a veterinarian is available, call him immediately. If not, give the horse a cup of cool ale of the strongest vintage you can find. If he needs walking because he appears to be tieing up, move him very gently. Pat him occasionally, because there is nothing more soothing to an animal so highly oriented to human emotion than a little love. But, by all means, do not bug him with care. Essentially let him know he is not alone—but leave him alone. After half an hour, let him have another sip of the good ale. And whatever you did to get him in that condition, *don't do it again.*

Finally, as with all athletes, a good clean-up is invaluable after workouts, during training, and in contests.

1. *Time spent grooming pays off.*

2. *Under no circumstances allow yourself or your crew to get tense.*

3. *Keep loose. Resolve to compete with your best self and simply try to do as well as the day will allow.* Yes, endurance riding is a strange kind of racing, *but do not let it become a race between you and someone else.*

4. *Remember that the people who race by rarely even finish.*

5. *Plan ahead and follow your plan as closely as you can. Do not change your plan without an overwhelmingly important reason for doing so.*

6. *Presumably you are in this for a good time. Do not get grim.* The horse, when fit, will really enjoy this experience over and over again. But if the joy goes out of the experience, your horse can become weary, sour, totally disinterested, and require months of recuperation for his mind even if he is in top physical condition.

2

"Let's Go!"

We couldn't resist the temptation to title this last chapter after our column in *Western Horseman* that we wrote for so many years and in which we were able to promote so much of the early competitive trail-ride and endurance-ride experience.

Trying to tell you about a specific ride is actually more difficult than you might at first imagine. For some strange reason it brings to mind some of that very odd experience of the early days of automobiling. Back in New England shortly after World War I, about the time the Army was conducting the very first endurance rides in Vermont, it was not uncommon to see a considerable number of automobiles touring up through the mountains. We had several difficult places called "notches." There were Franconia, Dixville, and Pinckham notches, to name a few. It was quite easy to get turned around up in those mountains and not be sure which way to go. The local police officers standing near the center of the town squares delighted in being a bit devilish about the way they gave "those folks from the city" a hard time about directions. Two common bits of local advice came on about so: "You drove from Boston all the way up here, and don't know where you're going? No wonder you're lost. . . ." or "Hmmm, Lancaster? Yeh, I know where it's at, but you just can't get there from here." Naturally, in the due course of time, the poor, lost stranger would get some decent advice, but not until he had put up with a bit of this "New England humor."

We have picked a few rides to describe in as much detail as we can to give you an idea of what they are like, but we say again, you just have to write to the ride you want, get an entry blank, make an effort to try the trail if possible before the contest, and then put your horse in the trailer and "do your thing."

American River Ride

The biggest and one of the oldest "50-mile, 1-day" endurance rides is the American River Ride from Sacramento to Auburn, California. It actually begins at the Cal Expo Fair Grounds and ends at the Auburn Fair Grounds.

All of the old, established rides of all kinds throughout America from Florida to California happen each year on dates you can count on like Labor Day weekend, or in this case, the third Saturday in April. Most people arrive for the American River Ride on Friday afternoon, have their horses examined by the veterinary committee, go to the preride meeting in the horse-show stands in the evening, and get to bed early, usually in sleeping bags near the horses. The accommodations here, by the way, are very good, since this is a big fair grounds. You find a nice batch of straw in your stall when you arrive, and the people are, as in all of these events, very friendly and easy to get along with in every way.

We picked this ride to describe largely because it is the biggest 50-mile, 1-day contest we know of anywhere, but also because between 250 and 300 riders start off *together* at the gallop to travel on the top of a dike that is only about 20 feet wide for a considerable distance. The first few miles are so dusty that you literally cannot see below your knees for long stretches, and in many places for hundreds of yards at a time the dust completely enshrouds you, so you simply have to depend on your horse and go with the mass of horseflesh like riding on a wave.

Many people try this ride in California for their first time out. Many more enter this ride because it happens rather early in the year and is a good opportunity to school their horses in preparation for other, tougher rides later. This business of fighting all the dust is really not too much of a problem. If you don't like the sound of that, simply dismount and hold your horse for only 4 or 5 minutes, remount, and follow along in perfectly clear conditions. There is lots of time to catch up with the herd. You will be surprised how many people you will pass if you take a bit of time in the first 15 or 20 minutes and then get into your pace "after the dust settles."

All in all, the terrain is not difficult. You have to ford the American River at a very good and safe place shortly after the ride starts. Then you come to places with fascinating names like Rattlesnake Bar as you follow the river and the north shore of Folsom Lake.

51. The start of the American River Ride. Two hundred horses at the gallop require over a mile to "get things sorted out."

It is easy for your crew to get to the service areas, and there is considerable room at each place to maneuver. The management provides you with a map and a description of the trail, which you can use to find the rest stops and other significant parts of the trail. As with any of these rides, it really is worthwhile to have ridden over the trail and had a good look at the stops.

Statistics: Vet inspection between 1:00 P.M. and 7:00 P.M., followed by ride briefing on Friday, at Cal Expo Fair Grounds, Sacramento, California. Start at 6:00 A.M. on the third Saturday in April; entry fee, $50. Two rest stops of one hour each; additional brief pulse checks as required. Good footing, no big hills, altitude range 50 feet to 1,300 feet above sea level, pleasant trail, pleasant weather as a rule. No minimum time; maximum time 10½ hours, including all stops. Approximately 275 start and 150 finish. Awards for best time and best condition; various other awards for breeds of horse and age of rider. A reasonably well-conditioned horse can make this ride with little difficulty, but you have to figure on 10 miles per hour average speed to place high. The high-placing horses gallop most of the way, but the great majority trot and walk. We imagine there may be as many as 500 starters in the next few years with no insurmountable problems.

Address:

> American River Endurance Ride
> P. O. Box 1593
> Auburn, Calif. 95603

Bitterroot Competitive Trail Ride

This is a very well-managed ride of midrange difficulty in beautiful country around Hamilton, Montana. It has, in recent years, become affiliated with several other rides in Montana, Idaho, and Wyoming, and now has an association with several rides in the province of Alberta, Canada, with dates throughout the summer and an International Cup offered.

This ride has a declared purpose: to demonstrate sound methods of *conditioning* horses, and to encourage able and responsible *horsemanship*. After about ten years of continuously successful experience, the management spent nearly a year in serious self-assessment in an effort to make this a model ride in every respect. From this "appraisal of its philosophy, procedures, function, and purposes . . . is emerging an assessment procedure . . . to comprehensively and continuously judge the performance of the animal from the initial check-in, through performance on the trail, and on to the final check-out upon ride completion." These quotations from their rule book should serve notice that this is an entirely different kind of contest from the American River Ride, whose only declared purpose is to see if you and your horse can do it without hurting the horse.

It's the middle of August. We have been in touch with the secretary of the Bitterroot Ride and we're on our way to Hamilton, Montana. You will see on a map of the country that this little town nestles in between some very large mountains in some gorgeous wilderness country on the very westerly edge of Montana. This is real western ranch territory, where the Nez Percé Indians put up such a skillful struggle against the U. S. Army in the days before barbed wire. Highway 93 on the way to Hamilton follows the path of flight of these old Indians whose name, in French, is believed to derive from their custom of piercing their noses and wearing seashells. Yes indeed, we are really in the Wild West, with people who take their horsemanship seriously. But that doesn't dampen their hospitality!

This is a 60-mile ride, 40 on Friday and 20 on Saturday. If you just want to try the 20, you can do that. There are weight divisions: heavyweight—185 pounds or over; lightweight—up to 185 pounds. These weights include you and all your tack. Then there is a junior division for ages 10 through 17. Riding time may change due to weather, but as a rule we will be doing the 40 miles in a riding time of 6½ to 7 hours, and the 20 the next day in 2½ to 3 hours of riding time. There may be some surprise checks along the way in compliance with that policy of continuous surveillance. The 40-mile route, following orange-red paint markers, leaves the Ravalli County Fair Grounds and goes up through rolling hills to the rugged areas of the Sapphire Mountains east of Hamilton. There are good mileage markers every two miles. The Saturday 20-mile route is not so strenuous generally, getting into slightly climbing hillsides but otherwise following ditch banks. The trail is very good all the way both days. The first day there are some very steep pitches of considerable length, such as the climb up to Calypso Hill, with a 10-minute vet check at the top. There is a 1-hour vet check and rest station on the first day at the 27½-mile mark, and it is easy enough for helpers to get there with whatever things you feel you will need. Generally there are few rules, but you have to be well acquainted with them. One rule we run into here is that while you may lead your horse anywhere you wish, you must be mounted for the last 2 miles.

Statistics: Check-in is on Thursday between 1:00 P.M. and 6:00 P.M. followed by briefing Thursday evening. Entry fee, $20. Entries must be received by about a week before the ride starts. Excellent stables and facilities, with several motels available. Altitude range is 3,500 to 6,500 feet above sea level. The temperature is usually between 90° and 100° F. The average number of entries is about 50; finishers about 38. There is one interesting admonition: "Watch for gopher holes." Many trophies, prizes, and awards, with ribbons to sixth place.

Address:

> Bitterroot Competitive Trail Ride
> Secretary, Dorothy Robinson
> 2122 NE Willow Creek Road
> Corvallis, Mont. 59828

Florida Horsemen's Association 100-Mile Competitive Trail Ride

Now, just to see how much variety there can be in this sport, let's take our magic carpet to Florida. We just left Montana with that big old Calypso Hill, and here we are in Umatilla, Florida, with no elevation more than a few feet above sea level. But don't let that fool you! The heat and sand can make this as tough a situation as you may wish to try for some time. This ride happens in the spring and draws many contestants from farther north, where the weather is still very cool. Coming down to Florida, the horses and riders often have difficulty coping with the heat. Then when you realize that mile after mile is made in the heavy going of sand, you can see that this can be a pretty tough ride.

The town of Umatilla is on the south side of the Ocala National Forest in north-central Florida, and the ride is composed of three big loops in the area of the forest south of Highway 40 and west of 19, skirting the edge of a U. S. Navy bombing range, which is closed to public use. The country is very beautiful, with many lovely lakes. The ride is a total of 100 miles with two 40-mile days followed by a 20. The first day's trail has red markers; the second, white; and the third, blue, and to the initiate it could seem that the trail markers go every which way for the first few miles going out of and coming back into the Sewell Ranch 2 miles west of Umatilla (the headquarters). There are limited motel accommodations but good camping. This ride is the first each year of a series on the East Coast of the United States ranging from Florida to Maine. The date is always in mid-March followed by the Virginia Ride in April, New Jersey in May, New York in July, Vermont in late August, Ohio in September, and North California in October. There is an Eastern United States 100-Mile Challenge Trophy presented annually by the Florida Horsemen's Association to the rider who has completed and accumulated the most points in any three 100-mile rides in any single calendar year with the same horse, and the trophy may be retired after being won three times by the same combination of horse and rider.

52. Two big winners in the eastern circuit. Diane Dickhut on A M Lord Plushbottom has done well in Vermont, North Carolina, and Florida, and has won numerous one-day rides. The gray Arab, Ibn Aahdin, owned and ridden by Harvey Amster, president of the Florida ride, has won more ribbons and trophies in a single ride than any horse in the history of these contests. This photo taken on the Florida Ride in 1972 gives us an idea of that sand they talk about. (Photo by Sykes, Lakeland, Florida)

Having been organized for almost 30 years, this ride is well run, with many traditions and long-established ceremonies. Since it is very representative of the 100-mile-3-day eastern rides, we shall quote fully from the General Information section of the program and the Schedule of Events, which are received by each contestant.

General Information

This ride is judged on 100 per cent for perfect condition of the horse, with point penalty for being late. All categories are judged on a point system. Mileage markers are placed every 5 miles and every mile the last 5.

Time allowed is as follows: 7 hours with a minimum of 6½ hours each on the first 2 days for the 40 miles. 7½ allowed for maximum, and no horse is "out of the Ride" until he has taken MORE than 7½ hours. The third day's ride is 3 hours, with 15 minutes early allowed, and 3½ hours allowed as a maximum for the 20 miles.

REMEMBER TO ADJUST YOUR TIME SCHEDULE FOR THE FREE HOLD TIME ON THE TRAIL.

No medications, shots, liniments, rubs, sprays, or bandages are allowed at any time. No hoses may be used. Water at ordinary temperature, one bucket at a time, may be used for washing or standing in.

Weight carried is by the following rule:

Lightweight Division—MUST be at least 150 through 165 pounds.

Middleweight Division—166 pounds through 204 pounds.

Heavyweight Division—205 pounds and over.

Junior Division—No weight rule but age 11 through 15, as of date of ride.

Starting positions will be drawn each day and recorded by the starter. These cannot be exchanged.

Horses must NOT be removed from stalls in the mornings until called by the Official Starter to line up.

Horses may be cooled and walked anywhere within the Stable Grounds.

Horses must NOT be removed from stalls after cooling time is called. 5:00 P.M. is cut-off hour Thursday and Friday, 1:00 P.M. is cut-off hour for cooling on Saturday.

Stable limits for night-time will be marked and strictly observed by all riders. Stable closes at 9:00 P.M., open for feeding 5:00 A.M.

You may stop as long or as short a period for morning trail lunch as you wish. But if the Judges are there, they may want to check your horse, so it is best to find out.

The Official Veterinarian HAS THE AUTHORITY TO PULL YOUR HORSE if disaster to his well-being seems possible. This is to protect us all. AND our horses.

Riders are requested NOT to BUNCH UP when approaching the Judges on the Trail, as this makes it difficult for them, and unfair for your horse not to be well observed.

On the trail, only the rider can care for his own mount, except for such small aids as holding horse or assistance in mounting.

SCHEDULE OF EVENTS—19—
WEDNESDAY, MARCH 16

10:00 A.M.	Preliminary judging. Declarations. Riders to be ready when called.
3:00 P.M.	Riders draw starting positions for Thursday.
7:30 P.M.	"Get-acquainted Barbeque" for riders and officials at Stable Area.
10:00 P.M.	Stable closed.

THURSDAY, MARCH 17

5:00 A.M.	Stable open.
7:00 A.M.	Weighing of riders.
7:25 A.M.	Final instructions by Starter as horses are called.
7:30 A.M.	Horses leaving individually.
11:00 A.M.	Trail lunches for riders. Spectators may see riders and purchase lunch by turning left off Hwy. 19 onto Forest Rd. to Farles Lake.
2:00 P.M.	Horses begin returning. Judged during cool-out.
4:00 P.M.	Starting positions drawn for Friday.
7:00 P.M.	Stable check by Judges. Riders called by Starter.
9:00 P.M.	Stable closed.

FRIDAY, MARCH 18

5:00 A.M.	Stable open.
7:00 A.M.	Weighing of riders.
7:25 A.M.	Starter calls positions.
7:30 A.M.	Horses leave individually.
11:00 A.M.	Trail lunch at Forest Rd. 73 and powerline.
2:00 P.M.	Horses begin returning. Judged during cool-out.
4:00 P.M.	Starting positions drawn for Saturday.
7:00 P.M.	Stable check by Judges. Riders called by Starter.
9:00 P.M.	Stable closed.

SATURDAY, MARCH 19

5:00 A.M.	Stable open.
7:00 A.M.	Weighing of riders.
7:25 A.M.	Starter calls positions.
7:30 A.M.	Horses leave individually.
10:45 A.M.	Horses begin returning. Judged during cool-out.
2:30 P.M.	Stable closed.
3:00 P.M.	Final judging begins. Possible roadwork or other tests as called for by Judges for close finishing horses.
8:00 P.M.	Final ceremonies, award of trophies in show ring.

We eliminate the statistics section for this ride since the preceding direct quotes from their program cover the material amply.
Address:

> Florida Horsemen's Association
> 100-Mile Competitive Trail Ride
> Sewell Ranch
> Umatilla, Florida 32784

Before we continue further with this effort to touch upon the highlights of our sport in terms of the specific contests, it might be of use to recap a bit. Had you noticed that inadvertently we are turning out to be "alphabetical"? First the American River Ride, then the Bitterroot, the Florida, and now we move to the Mount Diablo and finally the Western States Trail Ride. The American River Ride is intimately associated with the American Endurance Ride Conference, an organization celebrating its sixth anniversary in 1978. This outfit has grown so fast that it now has six "Regions" covering the whole United States with an average of about 22 rides in each Region. The Northeast Region is the smallest at this time, but it contains both the Old Dominion and the Empire 100-Mile-1-Day Rides. These are all endurance rides—that is, open-ended, in which the fastest time in reasonable condition wins the prize.

The Bitterroot Ride was the nucleus of the Rocky Mountain Trail Ride Association, now composed of five rides in the Northwest not connected with either the the AERC or the NATRC. The Rocky Mountain group of five rides is now affiliated with the Trail Riding Alberta Conference of Western Canada, with its six rides.

The Florida Ride, as we have indicated, is part of a loose association of a total of eight 100-mile-3-day rides in the east.

Now we come to the North American Trail Ride Conference, the largest and most completely organized group of trail riders in the country today. They have many publications available covering a variety of aspects of competitive trail riding. Some time ago their Secretary advised us that they sponsored 59 rides (the number is growing all the time), with one ride hosting as many as 160 contestants and many hosting 140. There are over 1,000 members and the organization receives about 200 letters a month. This group includes the grand old ride of the West Coast, the Mount Diablo 100 3-Day Class AA ride, which is approaching its fortieth birthday.

Mount Diablo

Here we are back in California—actually in sight of the Golden Gate on a nice big mountain just across the Bay from San Francisco. It is Labor Day weekend and there is a goodly gathering of riders, some new to the game, but many veterans ready for this 3-day contest, the nearest thing we have in the West to the Green Mountain or the Virginia or the Florida Ride in the East. We must admit immediately that this Mount Diablo Ride is not as difficult as any of those eastern rides. Remember, this is a NATRC ride. Furthermore, it was members of this ride together with members of another old ride in California, which takes place nearby on Mount Tamalpais, who formed the NATRC in the first place. The rules for these rides require 13 pages. These go into amazing subtleties such as "penalty splitting" brought about by terrain, trespassing privileges, etc. They also indicate that "the horse and rider may go at their own pace on the trail unless instructed otherwise by the trailmaster or judges."

You may dismount during the contest, but you may not make forward progress on foot. Finally, between a point about two miles from the finish line and the end of the ride, you must not only be mounted, but also you cannot stop for any reason. "Horses observed zigzagging, circling, backtracking, or stopping within the final two miles will receive penalty points or be disqualified."

The trail on Mount Diablo starts out from the Riding Club area a short distance up the side of the mountain on the Concord (east) side. Having arrived in time for the pre-ride inspection, very much as in the other rides we have described, and listened to the pre-ride briefing, you prepare yourself for two long days and one short day, generally similar to the eastern rides.

The trail is well marked and weaves over all sides of this relatively small mountain, even though it is far and away the biggest thing for miles around. You cross and recross your trail at times and go right over the top, finally returning each day to the Riding Club headquarters.

For full information, we suggest you write to the NATRC.

North American Trail Ride Conference, Inc.
1995 Day Road
Gilroy, Calif. 95020

Western States Trail Ride (Tevis Cup)

We started out with a ride that ends in Auburn, California, took our magic carpet around the country and here we are again with a ride that ends in Auburn at the same fair grounds.

This contest, now coming up on its twenty-fifth birthday, is without a doubt the toughest, most grueling thing of its kind in the world today. After you have gone 98½ miles over some very rugged country, you find yourself making your way in total darkness through a nasty little brushy hole at the bottom of a waterfall, literally groping for the trail, only to emerge and have to climb without a let-up all the way to the finish line. But here we are ahead of the story.

This experience has become such a challenge that it has attracted the attention of distance runners. Now the trail hosts a small group of people who try to run the 100 miles on foot in less than 24 hours! So far only 16 people have made it in the allowed time and 12 others have finished in less than 30 hours.

About 200 horsemen start out each year on the Indian Rider's Moon, the longest moon (full moon) in late July or early August. About 100 finish. There are very few rules—actually 8 in all.

1. Riders must be at least 12 years old and until age 17 must be accompanied by an adult.
2. Contestants must comply with instructions from Veterinary Committee.
3. Horses must be serviceably sound and at least 5 years old.
4. Competition for the Tevis or Haggin Cup requires a weight of rider and tack of 165 pounds or more.

5. Contestants must follow the trail.
6. No money awards.
7. Contestants must refrain from any act that might tend to discredit the Ride.
8. Horses must be inspected after the Ride.

The Tevis Cup is awarded to the first contestant to cross the finish line in the least elapsed time and approved by the Cup Committee, and whose mount has been approved by the Veterinary Committee.

The Haggin Cup is awarded to the contestant whose horse is rated with superior performance by the Cup Committee among the first ten in elapsed time and whose mount has been found by the Veterinary Committee to be in the most superior condition to "go on."

We have mentioned earlier that it is very worthwhile to go over the trail in detail before the contest. On many occasions when we lived a few hundred miles away from Auburn we planned to take a week for this one event. We would leave our farm on a Saturday before the ride, arriving in Auburn fair grounds on Saturday night. Sunday we would ride to Michigan Bluff, going over the trail from finish line to start. This was a first day's ride of about 35 miles. We'd camp out at Michigan Bluff, then ride the second day, Monday, to Robinson Flat, a distance of about 30 miles. Again camping out, we would ride on Tuesday from Robinson Flat to Squaw Valley, about 35 miles, giving us a chance to rest on Wednesday and Thursday and be ready for the pre-ride vet check on Friday. With so many horses, the vet check takes place between 10:00 A.M. and 5:00 P.M. in several different check stations. People can check in simultaneously. Early in the evening there is the usual briefing. The facilities for horses are very limited at Squaw Valley. Many people have to leave their horses tied to the side of the trailers all night. A few may get into the limited corral facilities and some bring their own portable corrals. But watch this: It is not a very good situation. There is little to eat at Squaw Valley. Many people drive the 10 or so miles to Lake Tahoe City, where there are excellent places to eat and many accommodations. The hotels at Squaw Valley are essentially pension-type accommodations for skiers in the winter.

The ride starts at 5:00 A.M. with contestants leaving in heats of 10 at 2-minute intervals. This is a pre-dawn situation, and most

53. Bud Dardi, looking for all the world like an original Pony Express rider, gallops across the American River bridge 4 miles from the Auburn fair grounds finish line in 1968. This was the fastest time recorded in this 100-mile contest.

riders make it to the top above the ski lifts at Emigrant Pass monument just about the time the sun comes up. You proceed along the crest of the mountain range and drop down into alpine meadows where it can be very boggy in wet years; naturally you skirt residual snow in big banks along the trail. The temperature may be about 40° F. The trail is reasonably well marked, especially where it is difficult, as in the case of Cougar Rock. There are pictures of this scenic spot elsewhere in this book. The course proceeds along Jeep trails to the first 1-hour vet check at Robinson Flat.

The midday portion of this ride is spent dropping down some 3,500 feet into an American River Canyon, then back out only to go right down again and out at Michigan Bluff. At the top of the first ridge between the two canyons, there is a 30-minute vet check at a place called Devil's Thumb. What names! The location of the first drop-off is called Last Chance! The temperature may range from 85° to 110° F.

At Michigan Bluff the heat of the day has a firsthand shot at you and your horse. But it's only some 35 miles to the finish line. This is the second 1-hour vet check. Robinson Flat was a good place for your crew to be able to help, but here they may have to carry supplies for you as much as half a mile on a very steep hillside. Michigan Bluff is the bottleneck of the whole ride. Be glad when it is behind you.

Then the way leads around the corner of the "bluff" into Volcano Canyon, out of the canyon, down the main street of Foresthill, and over some rolling country into the third vet check, which varies in location depending on local conditions, but generally is between 20 and 15 miles from the finish.

Leaving this third 1-hour check, you descend to the American River and ford it for the third time, probably in the dark by now for most people, even though the winner of the Tevis Cup usually arrives at the finish just as it is getting good and dark.

Then it is up and down some little hills, which by now can seem pretty big, until you finally come to "no hands" bridge, an old railroad bridge high above the American River. It has no railings on either side and is a bit scary at first, but, strangely enough, no one has ever had any trouble here. Then up into the final series of little canyons, including the "black hole of Calcutta." But that's where we came in.

Sunday morning finds the Veterinary Committee examining al-

54. Donna Fitzgerald receiving the Tevis Cup from Mr. Will Tevis one more time! How does she do it? Well, she listens to Pat, then she rides alone and pays strict attention to her horse. If anyone comes close to her record in the balance of this century, we will be amazed.

most all of the horses, but concentrating on the "top ten" to pick the Haggin Cup winner.

The awards banquet occurs on Sunday evening, with awards of the treasured buckle bearing the Pony Express rider. These buckles are real silver and gold and are kept in the vault of the Heart Federal Savings and Loan Company until handed out. The two trophies are awarded and that's all.

As of now the West Coast of the United States has both the toughest and the easiest rides. The East Coast has that great series of 100-mile-3-day contests, which altogether are tougher by far than any competitive trail rides in the West. The Northwest has those intermediate rides of 60 miles, which are about the degree of difficulty of the 100-mile contests in the East.

The Midwest and the South are feeling their way along to develop some good contests under the sanctioning of either the AERC or the NATRC.

Canada is coming along with some good rides generally patterned on the more difficult competitive trail rides.

There should be a tough 100-mile-1-day ride in the East, perhaps in North Carolina, which has mountains to match the Western States Trail Ride or the Virginia City Ride in Nevada. Then the West Coast should present a few competitive trail rides on the order of the Rocky Mountain Association or the rides on the East Coast.

Finally we can expect, through continued efforts of the NATRC, a few competitive trail rides in the East like those in the West which offer varying degrees of difficulty but are generally in a less difficult range than the present offerings.

What It's All About

Although the award is given to the horse in many other types of equine events, including some trail rides, for the most part it is the rider who enters, not the horse. And it is the rider who wins the prize, not the horse. There is a good reason for this.

You might train one horse and have him coming along fine only to turn an ankle the week before the ride or otherwise not be able to compete. Many riders train more than one horse and take the best one ready on the occasion of the contest. This is basically why we enter riders and not horses. And it is the reason why riders win the prizes. The acceptance of a trophy by the rider on behalf

55. Nan Benzie pilots her mount skillfully on the occasion of winning her 1,000-mile buckle in the Tevis Cup Ride. She is an ideal endurance rider, taking excellent, systematic care of her horse. Year after year she rides to compete with herself and her horse's best previous performance. As she would say with that contagious little Scotch laugh, "We'll see if we can just do it again." That is very much the essence of the challenge of this sport.

of the horse seems a bit like a shallow way to dodge a point of pride. It is very interesting to observe that many of the contestants in this sport have experience in other kinds of equestrian contests, such as horse shows, and they seem to like endurance or competitive trail riding much better. We think there are many reasons for this, and furthermore that "birds of a feather do really flock together."

Almost all the trail riders we have ever known are "real people." They are not boastful, but, on the other hand, they do not feel any requirement to be superficially shy or self-effacing. Most of them take their buckle or whatever the prize and feel damn good about it without feeling they have to demur to the horse. Sure they like their horses and really do appreciate them, but they don't mind our realizing that the winning today almost certainly means they have indeed been able to pick a better than average horse, feed it right, train it, and then ride it. That is a whole lot different from simply owning one and have some trainer set the horse up for you.

There are a few sportsmen and sportswomen who are unable to ride any longer but who do still like to field contesting horses or otherwise help people by loaning them horses. But the great majority of contestants today simply decide to try this sport, read as much as they can, get the best horse they can find or afford, and "have at it." They make some mistakes, but with solid help from the people they compete with, they soon catch on. It seems to us that this sport reveals more true sportsmanship in many ways than other forms of equestrian competition.

It is awfully easy to become deadly serious about exactly how you ride or how you might bowl or use a fly rod or raise a shotgun. It is really easy for any of us to become so serious that the fun drains completely out of what we are doing. This is true for so many activities, from sailing to tennis. In endurance and competitive trail riding we see occasional trends toward such seriousness to the point that the fun begins to vanish. The veterinary examiners in many of the big rides recognize this as they watch a contestant approach with an expression of great apprehension. One veterinarian, who in our minds epitomizes a combination of pure skill and good humor, can watch that very worried person lead the horse up for examination and say, "Well, let's see which one he limps on most," in such a way that everyone around just about cracks up. It sure does take the tension out of the air.

After all, we are doing this for fun, aren't we? So let's ride, really ride. And having done the best we can by our horses, let's have a good time.

56. Nick Mansfield, one of the riders in the first group over the now famous Tevis Cup trail, accepts the 1,000-mile award for his great horse, Buffalo Bill. On this occasion the horse was led right into the banquet hall to receive his award.

57. Alex Mackay-Smith, editor of **The Chronicle of the Horse**, after this Tevis Cup Ride in 1962 became a "member" of the elite club called The Top Ten. Both he and his son, Matthew Mackay-Smith, D.V.M., have been staunch supporters of long-distance riding since the beginning.

Appendix

MAGAZINES

Chronicle of the Horse, Middleburg, Va. 22117

Trail Blazer, P.O. Box 1855, Paso Robles, Calif. 93446

Western Horseman, Box 7980, Colorado Springs, Colo. 80933

Arabian Horse World, 2650 East Bayshore Road, Palo Alto, Calif. 94303

NOTE: There are many other magazines and smaller publications that occasionally feature articles on competitive trail riding and endurance riding, but these are the ones we count on most in this sport. You can find advertisements of coming rides and other useful information in almost any issue of these publications.

ORGANIZATIONS

AERC   American Endurance Ride Conference
Julie Suhr, Secretary
2770 Weston Road
Scotts Valley, Calif. 95066

NATRC   North American Trail Ride Conference
Joan Throgmorton, Secretary
1995 Day Road
Gilroy, Calif. 95020

Rocky Mountain Competitive Trail Ride Association
Dorothy Robinson, Secretary
2122 NE Willow Creek Road
Corvallis, Mont. 59828

NOTE: There is a growing list of organizations. The best way to keep up is by reading the magazines. Of course, as soon as you begin to go to rides you will be in the main channel of information and will hear about new developments from other riders.

Probably half the other rides in this country today operate without sanction or association with any of the organizations listed here. Some of the old, established rides of this kind are listed here:

FLORIDA, Umatilla
Mrs. D. J. LeFevre
Route 1, Box 56
St. Cloud, Fla. 32769

VIRGINIA, Hot Springs
Mrs. William Hulbert
The Plains, Va. 22171

NEW JERSEY, The Wharton Tract
(Between Camden and Atlantic City)
Mrs. Paul Adams
Medford, N. J. 08055

NEW YORK, Skaneateles
Dr. Robert Nichols
Gordon Street
Skaneateles, N.Y. 13152

MAINE, Farmington
Mrs. Connie Sween
North Highlands
Wilton, Me. 04294

VERMONT, South Woodstock
Green Mountain Horse Association
South Woodstock, Vt. 05071

OHIO, Kirtland
Ohio East Branch 100-Mile Ride
Dr. Leonard Ekeggs
Blair Lane
Kirtland, O.

NORTH CAROLINA, Asheville
Mrs. William Cecil, Secretary
P.O. Box 5375
Asheville, N.C. 28800

1978 NATRC Ride Schedule

Feb. 4 Limit 50	(B)	GLENDORA (Calif.—Reg. 2) Glendora Spon.: ETI Corral No. 35; Chr.: Sue Wiley; Sec.: Gae Stock, 5395 Mount View, San Bernardino, Calif. 92407 (714-883-6139 or 213-335-1446)
Feb. 18 Limit 65	AA Open Only	BIRTHINGTON'S WASHDAY "A" (Calif.— Spon.: Arabian Riders & Breeders Soc. of San Reg. 2) San Diego Diego; Co-chr.: Richard Becker & Ken Truesdell; Sec.: Bobbi Chapman, 10278 Quail Cyn. Road, El Cajon, Calif. 92021 (714-443-7744 or 714-442-5932 or 463-8215)
Mar. 18	(B)	FIRST OF SPRING (Calif.—Reg. 1) Healdsburg Spon.: Sonoma County Riding & Driving Club; Chr.: Dale Lake; Sec.: Deanna Lake, 1155 Raplee Terrace, Fulton, Calif. 95439 (707-542-1459)
Mar. 25	(A)	PIO PICO OR GREAT EASTER EGG RIDE —PART II 7th Annual (Calif.—Reg. 2) Jamul Spon.: Lakeside Frontier Riders; Chr.: Richard Becker; Sec.: Anne Haymes, 1975 Greenfield Drive, El Cajon, Calif. 92021 (714-444-9623 or 714-442-5932)
Apr. 1 Limit 100	(B)	AUBURN LAKE TRAILS (Calif.—Reg. 1) Auburn Jim Paclik, Chr., 9521 Horseshoe Bar Road, Loomis, Calif. 95650 (916-652-5508)
Apr. 8	(A)	CAVE CREEK (Ariz.—Reg. 2) Cave Creek Spon.: Arizona State Horseman's Assoc.; Chr.: Bob Bohannan; Sec.: Margaret Bohannan, 7000 Berneil Drive, Scottsdale, Ariz. 85253 (602-948-2424)

Apr. 15   A Open   LAKE JORDAN (N.C.—Reg. 5) Tumble-
                     Only   stone Farm-Apex
                              Chr.: Ann Davis; Sec.: Faye Collins, Rt. 3,
                              Box 119, Durham, N.C. 27713 (919-544-1017
                              or 362-6503)

Apr. 15   (B)   MOUNT DIABLO SPRING RIDE (Calif.—
Limit 120   Reg. 1)
                              Spon.: Concord Mount Diablo Trail Ride As-
                              sociation; Loc.—Concord; Chr., Robert Mead,
                              D.V.M.; Sec.: Linda Mead, 4255 Morgan
                              Territory Road, Clayton, Calif. 94517 (415-
                              939-8700)

Apr. 22   (B)   2nd ANNUAL APVMA TRAIL RIDE (Ala.
                              —Reg. 5) D Bar G Ranch
                              Spon.: Auburn Pre-Vet Medical Association,
                              University of Auburn; Chr.: Laura Slappey;
                              Sec.: Caroline Montgomery, Dormitory 1,
                              Room 205, Auburn, Ala. 36830 (205-821-
                              4911)

Apr. 22   (A)   FRONTIER COUNTRY (Okla.—Reg. 4)
                              Lexington
                              Spon.: Oklahoma Equestrian Trail Riders As-
                              sociation; Chr.: Donna Wohlschlegel; Sec.:
                              Barbara Dean, Rt. 5, Box 82, Duncan, Okla.
                              73533 (405-255-1980 or 527-3632)

Apr. 29   A Open   MOUNTAIN TOP (N.C.—Reg. 5) Asheville
Limit 50   Only   Spon.: Mountain Top Trail Riders; Chr.: Karen
                              Goff, Rt. 6, Box 278, Waynesville, N.C. 28786;
                              Sec.: Mary Guenther, 26 Pinehurst Road,
                              Asheville, N.C. 28704 (704-704-7177)

May 6   (A)   DEER PARK (Colo.—Reg. 3) Debeque
Limit 60   Spon.: Western Colorado Arabian Horse Club;
                              Chr.: Cherle Mitchie, Debeque, Colo. 81630
                              (303-282-5332)

May 6   A Open   WAKE COUNTY 4-H (N.C.—Reg. 5) Ump-
Limit 25   Only   Spon.: Wake County 4-H; Chr.: Louise Bryant;
                              stead State Park—Raleigh
                              Sec.: Betty Phlegar, 3611 Ebenezer Sh. Road,
                              Raleigh, N.C. 27612 (919-782-1950 or 787-
                              0835)

May 6   (B)   SAN LUIS GANZAGA (Calif.—Reg. 1)
Limit 140   Pacheco Pass-Gilroy
                                 Spon.: San Martin Horsemen; Chr.: Mary
                                 Johnson; Sec.: Ruth Huges, 12100 Steffs Court,
                                 San Martin, Calif. 95046 (408-683-2792 or
                                 779-5008)

May 13   A Open   NAVAJO LAKE (N.M.—Reg. 3) Navajo
                  B Novice   Lake
                                 Spon: Four Corners Arabian Horse Associa-
                                 tion; Rt. 1, Box 109A, Dolores, Colo. 81323

May 13   B Open   GUNPOWDER COMPETITIVE RIDE (Md.
Limit 40   Only   —Reg. 5) Gunpowder State Park
                                 Spon.: Maryland Appaloosa Association; Chr.:
                                 Mary Ann Laslo; Sec.: Karen Spencer, Box
                                 103, Sandy Spring, Md. 21722 (301-774-4499
                                 or 635-2648)

May 20   A Open   GRAVES MOUNTAIN (Va.—Reg. 5) Syria
Open limit 40   B Novice   Spon.: Harry Lucy; Sec.: Bettye Talley, 10017
Novice limit 20   B Castille Road, Richmond, Va. 23233 (804-
                                 285-3537 or 746-5985)

May 20   A Open   PALOS VERDES PENINSULA—PVP (Calif.
                                 —Reg. 2) Palos Verdes
                                 Spon.: ETI 8; Chr.: Sandra Knox; Sec.: Jean
                                 Pieper, 2756 Colt Road, Rancho Palos Verdes,
                                 CA 90247 (213-831-1576 or 213-541-6304)

May 27   (A)   BARB'S RIDE (Colo.—Reg. 3) Del Norte
                  Open Only   Chr.: Barbara Carpenter, Four Winds Farm,
                                 Del Norte, Colo. 81132 (303-657-3640)

May 27   (A)   BARB'S RIDE (Colo.—Reg. 3) Del Norte
                                 Rosa
                                 Spon.: California State Horsemen—Reg. 1:
                                 Sec.: Judy Ellars, 1043 Yuba Drive, Santa
                                 Rosa, Calif. 95401 (707-545-4998)

May 27   (B)   BLUE RIDGE (Va.—Reg. 5) Orlean
Limit 60   Spon.: Trail Riders of Rappahannock; Chr.:
                                 Patty Alexander, Windsong, Flint Hill, Va.
                                 22627 (703-675-3307)

June 3   A Open   GRIFFITH PARK 7th ANNUAL (Calif.—
             B Novice   Reg. 2) Burbank
Spon.: ETI Corral 38; Chr.: Lorraine Smith; Sec.: Margaret Ringe, 1200 Glenoaks Boulevard, Pasadena, Calif. 91105 (213-795-3419 or 247-4100)

June 3   (A)   CAVALIER RIDING CLUB (Colo.—Reg. 3)
Open limit 55   Fort Carson
Novice limit 55   Spon.: Cavalier Riding Club; Chr.: Dick Fixott and Ike Mosgrove; Sec.: Nancy Burns, 8555 Lakeview, Colorado Springs, Colo. 80908 (303-495-2041 eve. or 495-2906 or 475-1610)

June 3   (A)   RED CARPET (Okla.—Reg. 4) Woodward
Spon.: Oklahoma Equestrian Trail Riders; Chr: Marco Bennett, Northwestern Oklahoma University, Coronado Hall 211 B, Alva, Okla. 73714 (405-327-4591)

June 10   (A)   MORMAN LAKE (Ariz.—Reg. 2) Flagstaff
Limit 110   Spon.: Sun Circle Trail Riders; Chr.: Joe Peacock, P.O. Box 260, Laveen, Ariz. 85339 Sec.: Eleanor Peacock (602-243-2167)

June 10   (B)   FEATHER FALLS (Calif.—Reg. 1) Oroville
Limit 100   Spon.: Butte Horsemen's Association; Chr.: Tommy Gardner; Sec.: Jacque Gardner, 42 Hillcrest Avenue, Oroville, CA 95965 (916-589-2244)

June 17   (A)   COLORADO WEST (Colo.—Reg. 3) Baxter
Limit 60   Pass
Spon.: Colorado West Trail Ride; Chr.: Nadja Brozina and Cherie Mitchie, 303 Alcove Drive, Grand Junction, Colo. 81501 (303-242-8224 or 283-5332)

June 24   A Open   MORAGA (Calif.—Reg. 1) Moraga
Limit 100   B Novice   Spon.: Moraga Horsemen's Association; Chr.: Lee Butler; Sec.: Joyce Butler, 1758 Donald Drive, Moraga, CA 94556 (415-376-6686)

June 24   (A)   BLACKSBURG (Va.—Reg. 5) Newport
Open limit 45   Spon.: Blacksburg Saddle Club; Chr.: Lynn
Novice limit 40   Schug; Sec.: Linda McNeil, 2817 Newton Court, Blacksburg, Va. 24060 (703-951-0642 or 552-1896)

July 1 (AA) UVAS DAM (Calif.—Reg. 1) Gilroy
Spon.: Santa Clara County NATRC members;
Chr.: Jim Jeffers; Sec.: Linda Mercer, 7790
Rosanna Street, Gilroy, Calif. 95020 (408-842-
5570 or 842-0135 or 779-4722)

July 8 (A) UGAHBOO (Colo.—Reg. 3)
Limit 60 Chr.: Louis Pavetti, D.V.M.: Sec.: Nancy
Pavetti, 2480 U.S. 6–50, Grand Junction, Colo.
81501 (303-242-2225 or 242-1222)

July 15 (A) ROCKY MOUNTAIN HIGH (Colo.—Reg. 3)
Limit 60 Chr.: Jim and Violet Peek; Sec.: July Daugh-
tery, 15240 Bronco Drive, Colorado Springs,
Colo. 80808 (303-481-2854 or 277-1272)

July 15 (B) NCCHC PACKER LAKE (Calif.—Reg. 1)
Limit 80 Sierra County
Spon.: Nevada County Cutting Horse Club;
Chr.: Ray Sherman; Sec.: Teri Personeni,
13841 Bitney Spring Road, Nevada City, Calif.
95959 (916-273-9144 or 273-9453)

July 29 (A) SOUTHERN OREGON CASCADE (Ore.—
Reg. 1) Lily Glen
Spon.: Arabian Horse Association of South
Oregon; Chr.: Jill Garvin, 530 Hodson Road,
Gold Hill, Ore. 97525; Sec.: Charlene Kim-
mons, 3832 Grant Road, Central Point, Ore.
97502 (503-664-4169 or 855-7184)

Aug. 19 (A) VAN VLEET MEMORIAL (Colo.—Reg. 3)
Colorado Springs
Wayne Van Fleet, 5235 East Princeton, Engle-
wood Colo. 80110 (303-759-9489)

Aug. 19 (A) OAKLAND (Calif.—Reg. 1) Oakland
Spon.: Metropolitan Horsemen; Tom Natuses,
14050 Skyline Boulevard, Oakland, Calif.
94619 (415-632-5946)

Aug. 26 (A) ARROWHEAD (Col.—Reg. 3) Montrose
Limit 60 Chr.: Bob Boruch; Sec.: Joyce Boruch, 129
30¾ Road, Grand Junction, Colo. 81501
(303-243-6333)

Aug. 26 A Open HEART BAR (Calif.—Reg. 2) Barton Flats
Limit 50 B Novice Char.: Ginny Hart; Sec.: Gae Stock, 5395
Mount View, San Bernardino, Calif. 92407
(714-793-4935 or 883-1307)

Sept. 2　　　　　A Open　VIRGINIA UNNAMED (Va.—Reg 5)
Open limit 40　　B Novice　Harry Lucy, 5901 Russet Lane, Mechanics-
Novice limit 20　　　　　　ville, Va. 23111 (804-746-5985)

Sept. 2　　　　　A Open　FRIENDLY PINES (Ariz.—Reg. 2) Prescott
Limit 60　　　　　B Novice　Char.: Gerry Willow; Sec.: Marian Hoagland,
　　　　　　　　　　　　　　6315 East Voltaire, Scottsdale, Ariz. 85254
　　　　　　　　　　　　　　(602-948-5612 or 971-2834)

Sept. 2　　　　　　(A)　CONCORD MOUNT DIABLO LABOR DAY
　　　　　　　　　　　　RIDE (Calif.—Reg. 1) Concord
　　　　　　　　　　　　Spon.: CMDTRA; Chr.: Robert Mead,
　　　　　　　　　　　　D.V.M.; Sec.: Linda Mead, 4255 Morgan Ter-
　　　　　　　　　　　　ritory Road, Clayton, Calif. 94517 (415-939-
　　　　　　　　　　　　7800)

AERC 1978 National Endurance Ride Schedule

Northwest . . . Washington, Oregon, and Idaho

Apr. 29　　　　Trask River N. DeRosett, Route 3, Box 267, Gaston, Ore.
　　　　　　　　97119　　　　　　　　　　　　　　　　　　　　55
May 13　　　　Sweethorne Ride, J. Wall, 789 50th Avenue, Sweethorne,
　　　　　　　　Ore. 97386　　　　　　　　　　　　　　　　　　50
May 20　　　　Prineville Ride, L. Moore, Route 1, Box 828, Prineville,
　　　　　　　　Ore. 97754　　　　　　　　　　　　　　　　　　50
May 27　　　　Fertile Valley Ride, C. Bucinski, Route 1, Box 106, Span-
　　　　　　　　gle, Wash. 99031　　　　　　　　　　　　　　50–75
June 3　　　　Hash Knife Ride, J. Eason, Box 85, Mitchell, Ore. 97750
　　　　　　　　　　　　　　　　　　　　　　　　　　　　50–75
June 10　　　　East Gaited Horse Association Ride, 8551 Liberty Road
　　　　　　　　South, Salem, Ore. 97302　　　　　　　　　　　50
June 10　　　　Boise Basin Ride, A. Morris, Skyline Drive, Boise, Ida.
　　　　　　　　97750　　　　　　　　　　　　　　　　　　　　50
June 24　　　　Oregon Elevator Ride, L. Hollander, Route 1, Box 80,
　　　　　　　　Powell Butte, Ore. 97753　　　　　　　　50–75–100
June 24　　　　IAHA Championship Ride, S. Wheeler, Route 1, Box 290,
　　　　　　　　Red Bluff, Calif. 96080 (held in conjunction with the Ore-
　　　　　　　　gon Elevator Ride)　　　　　　　　　　　　　100
July 2　　　　Raging River Ride, 20226 Bothell Highway, Bothell, Wash.
　　　　　　　　98011　　　　　　　　　　　　　　　　　　　　50
July 8　　　　Pistol River Ride, R. Walker, Box 7, Pistol River, Ore.
　　　　　　　　97444　　　　　　　　　　　　　　　　　　　　50
July 15　　　　Salem Ride, H. Ballweber, 4958 Riverdale Road, S. Salem,
　　　　　　　　Ore. 97302　　　　　　　　　　　　　　　　　　60
July 22　　　　Fossil Bowl, B. Eason, P.O. Box 85, Mitchell, Ore. 97750
　　　　　　　　　　　　　　　　　　　　　　　　　　　50–100

July 29	Flying M Ride, N. DeRossett, Route 3, Box 267, Gaston, Ore. 97119	50
Aug. 5	Targhee 50, Box 751, Ashton, Ida. 83420	
Aug. 5	Santiam-Cascade Ride, L. Wall, 789 50th Street, Sweet Home, Ore. 97386	50
Aug. 12	Mount Spokane Ride, A. Hinckley, Box 23, Valley Ford, Wash. 99036	50
Aug. 19	Washington Blue Mount Ride, G. Sanders, Route 1, 760 Patricia Place, Walla Walla, Wash. 99362	50
Aug. 26	Drinkers of the Wind, B. Bottier. P.O. Box 1186, Ketchum, Ida. 83340	50
Sept. 3	Evergreen Challenge Ride, S. Gleason, 228 Monte-Brady Road, Montesano, Wash. 98563	50
Sept. 16	So. Oregon Lung Association Ridathon, E. Wines, 2700 Bishop Creek Road, Jacksonville, Ore. 97530	50
Sept. 23	Sun River Ride, R. Peterson, Box 465, Bend, Ore. 97701	50–100
Sept. 30	Diamond Field Jack, Box 368, Twin Falls, Ida. 83301	50
Oct. 7	Gold Mount Endurance, D. Sanderfur, 5985 SE Alalla-Burley Road, Olalla, Wash. 98359	50
Oct. 14	Overland Ranch Ride, J. Butler, 4900 NE O'Neill Way, Redmond, Ore. 97756	50

West Region . . . northern California and northern Nevada

Apr. 1	Derby Ditch Ride, P.O. Box 7083, Reno, Nev. 89502	50
Apr. 8	Sonoma County 50, Dan Barnes, 348 Mount View Ave., Santa Rosa, Calif. 95401	50
Apr. 8	Four-Way Ride, Box 265, Wells, Nev. 89835	70
Apr. 22	American River Ride, Box 1593, Auburn Calif. 95603	50
May 6	San Antonio Ride, J. Pritchard, P.O. Box 454, Carmel Valley, Calif. 93924	50
May 20	Castle Rock, 3290 Todd Way, San Jose, Calif. 95125	50
May 28	Trinity Trails, F. Myers, P.O. Box 746, Hayfork, Calif. 96041	50
June 3	Nuggett 50, P.O. Box 92, N. San Juan, Calif. 95960	50
June 10	Ruby Mountains 50, M. Branscomb, P.O. Box 453, Elko, Nev. 89801	50
June 10	Mariposa 50, C. McWilliams, 5287 Darrah Rd, Mariposa, Calif. 95338	50
June 10	IAHA Championship, S. Sheeler, Route 1, Box 290, Red Bluff, Calif. 96080	50
June 18	Levi Ride and Tie, B. Johns, Levi Strauss Company, Two Embarcadero, San Francisco, Calif. 94106	32
June 24	Bonanza Ox-Trail, P.O. Box 1284, Carson City, Nev. 89701	102
June 24	Devil Mountain, F. Koerber, 2001 Franklin Canyon Rd, Martinez, Ca. 94553	50

July 4	Auburn Lakes Trail, 2691 Shirland Trail Rd, Auburn, Calif. 95603 50
July 22	Western States Trail Ride (Tevis), Box 1228, Auburn, Calif. 95603 100
Aug. 26	Mapes Cup 50, B. Cox, P.O. Box 1284, Carson City, Nev. 89701 50
Sept. 16	Virginia City 100, P.O. Box 7083, Reno, Nev. 89502 100
Sept. 16	Drakes Bay 50, P. Austin, 4164 Blank Road, Sebastopol, Calif. 95472 50
Oct. 7	Cow Mountain, C. Ranta, P.O. Box 396, Uklah, Calif. 95482 50
Oct. 21	Mount Burney, C. Evans, Box 10, Big Bend, Calif. 96011 50

Southwest Region . . . Southern California, southern Nevada, New Mexico, Arizona, and West Texas

Mar. 25	Land of the Sun, R. Lester, P.O. Box 727, Wickenburg, Ariz. 85358 50
Mar. 18	Malibu Mountains, Ride, P.O. Box 84, Agoura, Calif. 91301 50
Apr. 8	Earthquake Valley Ride, 14325 Midland Road, Poway, Calif. 92064 58
Apr. 15	Lost Dutchman Ride, W. Mahew, P.O. Box 1206, Apache Junction, Ariz. 85220 50
May	Hickory Creek Hunt, H. Hogan, Route 7, Box 447E, Fort Worth, Tex. 76028 50
May 13	Mount Whitney 50, P.O. Box 602, Lone Pine, Calif. 93545 50
May 20	Huachuca Mountain, R. Newton, P.O. Box 851, Fort Huachuca, Ariz. 85613 50
May 28	Fort Baynard Ride, J. Taylor, P.O. Box 246, Hurley, N.M. 88043 50
June 17	Tehachapi Ride, 112 West Tehachapi Boulevard, Calif. 93561 50
June 24	Tar Springs Ride, S. Dyke, P.O. Box 486, Arroyo Grande, Calif. 93420 50
Aug.	Kirtland Base 50, D. Teasdale, 2058 B Crossroads, Kirtland AFB, N.M. 87118 50
Sept. 3	Madonna 50, P.O. Box 55, Paso Robles, Calif. 93446 50
Sept. 3	Los Alamos 50, 213 Rio Bravo Drive, Los Alamos, N.M. 87544 50
Sept. 16	Faraonson 50, R. Bingham, P.O. Box 519, Norco, Calif. 91760 50
Oct.	BAHA Ride, P.O. Box 2409, Las Cruces, N.M. 88001 50
Oct. 7	Las Vegas 50, J. Curtis, Las Vegas, Nev. 89110 50

Oct. 7	Copper Country Mountaineers Ride, D. Davis, Star Te, Box 32, Winkelman, Ariz. 85292	50
Oct. 14	San Gorgornio, Redlands Express, 12798 9th Street, Yucalpa, Calif. 92399	50
Nov. 11	Skull Mesa, H. Eastlake, Box 544, Cave Creek, Ariz, 85331	50
Nov. 25	Sunland Ride, D. Wasden, 10419 McBroom Street, Sunland, Calif. 91040	50
Nov.	Sizzler 50, 2543 Via Dieguenos, Alpine, Calif. 92001	50

Mountain Region . . . Montana, Wyoming, Colorado, and Utah

April 1	Color County 50, L. Prince, Box 195, LaVerkin, Ut. 84745	50
May 7	Ken Caryl 50, P. Bremer, 1330 Leyden, Suite 105, Denver, Colo. 80220	50
May 7	Pleasant Valley, A. Christensen, 315 E. 1st North, Mount Pleasant, Ut. 84647	50
June 3	Wyoming 50, T. Van Gelder, Box 31, Grey Bull, Wyo. 82426	50
June 17	Upper Rio Grande, Four Winds Farms, Del Norte, Colo. 81132	50
July 8	Chaffee County Ride, 1009 E. St., Salida, Colo. 81201	50
July 15	Big Horn 100, T. Van Gelder, Box 72, Grey Bull, Wyo. 82426	100
July 22	Odgen Pioneer Ride, K. Grambles, P.O. Box 9003, Odgen, Ut. 84409	50
Aug. 19	Utah Valley Ride, C. Johnson, R.F.D. Box 375, Pleasant Grove, Ut. 84062	50
Aug.	Big Sky, S. Minyala, Gild Edge Rte, Lewistown, Mont. 59457	50–100

Midwest Region . . . North Dakota, South Dakota, Nebraska, Kansas, Minnesota, Iowa, Missouri, Wisconsin, Illinois, Michigan, Indiana, and Ohio

Apr. 15	Chickasaw County 1, 310 N. Church Street, Okolona, Mich. 38860	50
May 6	Northeast Kansas Ride, L. Syverson, 1634 S. W. Auburn, Topeka, Kans. 66512	50
May 6	Meriden 50, L. Reidel, 455 Moore Heights, Dubuque, Ia. 52001	50
May 6	Battle Creek Hunt Ride, 614 Main St., Middleville, Mich. 49433	50
May 20	Badger Ride, J. McDonald, Route 1, Box 250, Helenville, Wisc. 53137	50
June 3	Keystone Half Hundred, 556 Park Ave., Poland, O. 44514 44514	50

July 8	Hossier Half-Hundred, 556 Park Ave., Poland, O. 44514 50
July 15	South Dakota AHA, E. Wiesma, Armour, S.D. 57313 50
Aug.	Neillsville Ride, L. Reidel, 455 Moore Heights, Dubuque, Ia. 52001 70
Aug. 5	Southeast Minnesota Ride, G. Bonnicksen, Route 1, Spring Valley, Minn. 59975 50
Aug. 12	Minnesota Valley Ride, S. Svendsen, Route 1, Montrose, Minn. 55363 50
Sept.	North Dakota Govnr's 120, 980 North 3rd, Carrington, N.D. 58421 120
Sept. 9	Underdown Ride, W. Ringham, Box 245, Merrill, Wisc. 54452 50
Sept. 16	Illinois Palisades Ride, G. Richard, Hennepin, Ill. 61327 50
Sept. 16	Illinois Jubilee Ride, C. Essig, 60 S. Elm Street, Washington, Ill. 61571 50
Sept. 23	Pillager Cup. W. Karalak, Route 2, Box 164A Cold Springs, Minn. 56320 50
Sept. 23	Iowa AHA Ride, L. Reidel, 455 Moore Heights, Dubuque, Ia. 52001 50
Sept. 31	Kettle Moraine 100, E. Schwartz, Route 1, Oostburg, Wisc. 53070 100
Oct.	Quad City Arab Finals, L. Reidel, 455 Moore Heights, Dubuque, Ia. 52001 50
Oct. 1	Buckeye State 50, W. Briggs, 2085 Riceford Road, SW, East Sparta, O. 44626 50
Oct. 7	Heart of Illinois Ride, L. Reidel, 455 Moore Heights, Dubuque, Ia. 52001 50
Oct. 14	Wisconsin Hoofbeat Ride, B. Bennett, Hoofbeat Ride, Mazomanie, Wisc. 53560 50
Oct. 21	St. Croix 50, E. Huttner, Park Stables, Dresser, Wisc. 54009 50
Oct. 21	Chickasaw County II, 310 N. Church Street, Okolona, Mich. 38860 50
Dec. 9	Big Foot Fifty, 1003 Eastwood, Pascagoula, Mich. 39567 50

Northeast . . . Maine, New Hampshire, Vermont, Massachusetts, Connecticut, New York, Pennsylvania, New Jersey, West Virginia, and Maryland

May 13	Cockaponset 50, K. Fullerton, P.O. Box 441, Ivoryton, Conn. 06442 50
May 28	Freedom Trail Ride, T. Lancaster, P.O. Box 1796, Plainville, Mass. 02762 50
July 22	Empire 100, Dr. James Morse, Ackert Hook Rd., Staatsburg, N.Y. 12580 100

Southeast . . . Oklahoma, East Texas, Arkansas, Louisiana, Mississippi, Kentucky, Georgia, Tennessee, Alabama, Virginia, North Carolina, South Carolina, and Florida

Apr. 8	Cherokee 50, P.O. Box 671, Avondale Estate, Ga. 30003 50
April	Wood Riders, B. Ector, Wood Junior College, Mathiston, Miss. 39752 50
April 22	Go Get Um, P.O. Box 1024, Douglasville, Ga. 30133 50
May 6	Tar Heel 100 R. West, 7700 Saint Anthony Chapel Road, Louisville, Ky. 40214 100
June 17	Old Dominion 100, P. Botts, II, 118 Georgetown Pike, Great Falls, Va. 22070 100
June 24	Daniel Boone 50, J. Taylor, Route 1, Box 233, Winchester, Ky. 40391 50
Sept.	Schuyler County 4-H, J. Hammond, R.D. 2, Watkins Glen, N.Y. 14891 50
Sept. 16	Robbers Route Ride, S. Capron, Route 2, Box 2736, Choctaw, Okla. 73020 50
Sept. 30	Glassy Mountain 50, B. Mucci, Route 4, Log Shoals Road, Greenville, S.C. 50
Oct.	Cotton Land Fast Fifty, 6458 Spring Street, Douglasville, Ga. 30133 50
Oct.	Hamburg Riding Club, P. Goodwin, 704 S. Main, Hamburg, Ark. 71646 50
Oct. 21	Tennessee 50 J. Seneker, Route 1, Seymour, Tenn. 37865 50
Oct. 28	Appalachian 50, J. Reeves, P.O. Box Drawer 4, Clarkesville, Ga. 30523 50
Nov. 25	Palm Aire II, 4040 42nd Street, Sarasota, Fla. 33580 50
Dec. 8	Sandlapper 50, ESTRA, P.O. Box 67, Douglasville, Ga. 30134 50
Mar. 11	Palm Aire 1, 4040 42nd Street, Sarasota, Fla. 33580 50

Eastern Competitive Trail Ride Association
1978 Sanctioned Rides

For more information on ECTRA, contact:
> ECTRA
> Judy Voll
> 66 Dalton Division Road
> Dalton, Mass. 01226

Apr. 23	Sharon Hills, E. Dotson, Box 942, West Cornwall, Conn. 06796 25–30 miles
Apr. 23	The Doncaster Ride, J. Morgan, Box 444-A, Route 1, Indian Head, Md. 20640 35 miles

Apr. 29–30	The Chesire Ride, J. Wylie, 1301 Birmingham Road, West Chester, Pa. 19380 2 days, 50 miles
May 6	Golden Horseshoe Ride, M. Miles, R.D. 2, Voorheesville, N.Y. 12186 25 miles
May 14	Conkaponsett Ride, K. Fullerton, Comstock Avenue, Ovoryton, Conn. 06442 25 miles
May 14	Ohio Ride, A. Friche, Route 1, Spring Valley, O. 45370 30 miles
May 20	Pine Spills Ride, L. Lester, Raymond, Mass. 04071 25 miles
May 28	Bluegrass Julip Cup Ride, T. Conner, 610 Dorsey Way, Louisville, Ky. 40223 30 miles
June 3	Reading Raggedy Riders, C. Smith, Side Hill Farm, Reading, Vt. 05062 25 miles
June 3–4	Arabian Horse Association of Ohio, A. Fricke, Route 1, Spring Valley, O. 2 days, 60 miles
June 4	Dirigo Horseman's Ride, B. Lyford, R.F.D. 1, Box 63, Milo, Mass. 04463 25 miles
June 11	Bass Lake Ride, L. Nowakowski, 17872 GAR Highway, Huntsburg, O. 44046 35 miles
June 17	Down East Ride, S. Verrill, The Counting House, Searsport, Mass. 04974 25 miles
June 17	Hampshire Riding Club, C. Hill, 52 Laurel Street, Northampton, Mass. 01060 35 miles
June 17	Old Dominion Ride, V. Imgram, 12000 Thomas Avenue, Great Falls, Va. 22066 50 miles
June 17	Old Dominion Ride, V. Imgram, 12000 Thomas Avenue, Great Falls, Va. 22066 100 miles
June 25	Green Mount Horse Ride, C. Parker, Box 8, South Woodstock, Vt. 05071 25–35 miles
July 16	Smoke Rise Ride, S. Bellevance, Smoke Rise Farm, S. Woodstock, Vt. 05071 25 miles
July 19–22	The Pine Tree 100 (Maine 100), J. Brunjes, Box 66, Norway, Mass. 04268 3 days, 100 miles
Aug. 12	Windsor Co 4-H Ride, C. Smith, R.R. 1, Reading, Vt. 05062 25 miles
Aug. 19	Down East Ride, S. Verril, The Counting House, Searsport, Mass. 04974 35 miles
Aug. 30–Sept. 2	Green Mount Horse 100 (Vermont 100), C. Parker, Box 8, S. Woodstock, Vt. 05071 3 days, 100 miles
Sept. 2–4	Arabian Horse Association of Ohio, A. Fricke, Route 1, Spring Valley, O. 3 days, 100 miles
Sept. 9	Molly Ockett Ride, J. Brunjes, Box 66, Norway, Mass. 04268 35 miles
Sept. 17	Maryland Appaloosa Association, C. Hood, Pine Break, 624 Streaker Road, Sykesville, Md. 21784 35 miles
Sept. 23–24	Arabian Horse of Michigan, R. Sugzda, 11740 W. Parkway, Detroit, Mich. 48239 2 days, 60 miles

Sept. 23–24	Kedron Valley Ride, P. Kendall, Kedron Valley Inn. S. Woodstock, Vt. 05071 2 days, 50 miles
Sept. 24	Lucky Trail Riders, M. Franco, 119 Bridgham Hill Rd. Essex Junction, Vt. 05452 35 miles
Sept. 24	Silver Mills Ride, M. Howard, Silver Mills Road, Dexter, Mass. 04930 25 miles
Oct. 1	Vermont Arab Horse Ride, V. Frye, R.D. 2, Box 315-B, Bristol, Vt. 05443 25 miles
Oct. 26–29	Maryland 100, J. Morgan, Box 444-A, Route 1, Indian Head, Md. 20640 3 days, 100 miles

Upper Midwest Endurance and Competitive Trail Ride Association 1978 Sanctioned Rides

For further information on UMECRA, contact:

UMECRA
c/0 Louise Reidel
455 Moore Heights
Dubuque, Ia. 52001

May 20–21	Badger Ride, 50-mile endurance, 25-mile competitive, John MacDonald, Route 1, Box 250, Helenville, Wisc. 53137
May 27–28	N.E. Kansas Ride, 50-mile endurance, 25-mile competitive, Al Norby, Route 2, Meriden, Kans. 66512
Jun. 10–11	Palymyra 2-day competitive, John MacDonald, Route 1, Box 250, Helenville, Wisc. 53137
Jun. 17	Wolf Creek, 25-mile competitive, Jan Worthington, Route 2, Rochester, Ill. 62563
Jun. 24–25	Iowa Arabian Horse Association, 50-mile endurance, 25-mile competitive, Louise Reidel, 455 Moore Heights, Dubuque, Ia. 52001
Jul. 8–9	Hossier Half Hundred, 50-mile endurance, 25-mile competitive, Carolyn Girton, Route 14, Box 614, Brazil, Ind. 47834
Jul. 15–16	South Dakota, 50-mile endurance, 25-mile competitive, Dick Burt, Box 132, Watertown, S.D. 57201
Jul. 22–23	North Dakota/Western North Dakota Arabian Association 50-mile endurance, 25-mile competitive, Mel Webster, Star Route 1, Box 157, Bismarck, N.D. 58501
Aug. 5–6	Neillsville, 50-mile endurance, 25-mile competitive, Lindsay Taliaferro, Route 1, Box 247, Neillsville, Wisc. 54456
Aug. 12–13	Minnesota Valley, 50-mile endurance, 30-mile competitive, Skip Svendsen, Route 1, Montrose, Minn. 55363
Aug. 19–20	Int'l Arabian Championship Competitive Ride, Dr. R. A. Beecher, Box 289, Cascade, Ia. 52033 (This ride is supported by UMECRA, but points will not be given for it.)

Aug. 26–	S.E. Minnesota, 50-mile endurance, 25-mile competitive, Bill Holzer, Route 2, Box 74, Stewartville, Minn. 55976
Sept. 9–10	Undertown, 50-mile endurance, 25-mile competitive, Wayne Ringham, Box 245, Merrill, WI 54452
Sept. 16–17	Palisades, 50-mile endurance, 25-mile competitive, Louise Reidel, 455 Moore Heights, Dubuque, Ia. 52001
Sept. 23–24	Pillager Cup, 50-mile endurance, 25-mile competitive, Wendy Karulak, Box 326, Cold Spring, Minn. 56320
Sept. 30–Oct. 1	Kettle Moraine, 100-mile endurance, 50- and 25-mile competitive, Esther Schwartz, Route 1, Oostburg, Wisc. 53070
Oct. 7–8	Jubilee, 50-mile endurance, 25-mile competitive, Connie Essig, 601 South Elm, Washington, Ill. 61571
Oct. 14–15	Hoofbeats, 50-mile endurance, 25-mile competitive, Betty Bennett, Hoofbeat Ridge Ranch, Route 2, Mazomanie, Wisc. 53560
Oct. 21–22	Quad-Cities, 50-mile endurance, 25-mile competitive, Alyce Carter, Box 286, Route 3, Geneseo, Ill. 61254
Oct. 28–	Shawnee Hills Appaloosa Club, 50-mile endurance, 25-mile competitive, Carol Hartman, Route 1, Box 51D, Steeleville, Ill. 62288

Index